No Limits to Literacy

FOR PRESCHOOL ENGLISH LEARNERS

D1511833

*I dedicate this book to the many children, families,
teachers, and collaborators who participated in the classrooms,
research studies, and professional development that informed its content.*

No Limits to Literacy

FOR PRESCHOOL ENGLISH LEARNERS

Theresa A. Roberts

CORWIN
A SAGE Company

Copyright © 2009 by Corwin

All rights reserved. When forms and sample documents are included, their use is authorized only by educators, local school sites, and/or noncommercial or nonprofit entities that have purchased the book. Except for that usage, no part of this book may be reproduced or utilized in any form or by any means, electronic or mechanical, including photocopying, recording, or by any information storage and retrieval system, without permission in writing from the publisher.

For information:

Corwin
A SAGE Company
2455 Teller Road
Thousand Oaks, California 91320
(800) 233-9936
Fax: (800) 417-2466
www.corwinpress.com

SAGE India Pvt. Ltd.
B 1/I 1 Mohan Cooperative
    Industrial Area
Mathura Road, New Delhi 110 044
India

SAGE Ltd.
1 Oliver's Yard
55 City Road
London EC1Y 1SP
United Kingdom

SAGE Asia-Pacific Pte. Ltd.
33 Pekin Street #02-01
Far East Square
Singapore 048763

Printed in the United States of America.

Library of Congress Cataloging-in-Publication Data

Roberts, Theresa A.
No limits to literacy for preschool English learners/Theresa A. Roberts.
        p. cm.
Includes bibliographical references and index.
ISBN 978-1-4129-6563-7 (cloth)
ISBN 978-1-4129-6564-4 (pbk.)
    1. English language—Study and teaching (Preschool)—Foreign speakers. I. Title.

PE1128.A2R545 2009
372.65'21—dc22   2008044782

This book is printed on acid-free paper.

09   10   11   12   13   10   9   8   7   6   5   4   3   2   1

Acquisitions Editor:	Jessica Allan
Editorial Assistant:	Joanna Coelho
Production Editor:	Eric Garner
Copy Editor:	Cate Huisman
Typesetter:	C&M Digitals (P) Ltd.
Proofreader:	Theresa Kay
Indexer:	Jean Casalegno
Cover Designer:	Lisa Riley

Contents

Acknowledgments

I thank my two children, Kean Roberts-Yee and Cassidy Roberts-Yee, for teaching me so much about literacy and for inspiring me to study it.

I express special appreciation to the California Preschool Instructional Network and all its participants for their interest in much of the content of this book and the opportunities they have provided me to craft its content in my work with them.

I thank Linnea Ehri for encouraging me to continue pursuit of my research and for building my confidence in its value.

Additionally, Corwin Press would like to thank the following peer reviewers for their editorial insight and guidance:

Pamela S. Allen
Lead Teacher / Gifted Facilitator
Charlotte-Mecklenburg Schools
Ballantyne Elementary School
Charlotte, NC

Tanya Flushman
Doctoral Student
Vanderbilt University's Peabody
    College
Nashville, TN

Sharon Latimer
ESL PreK Teacher
Parker, TX

Susan B. Neuman
Professor
University of Michigan
Ann Arbor, MI

Elaine M. Schmidt
Principal
Barron Early Childhood School
Plano Independent School District
Plano, TX

About the Author

Theresa A. Roberts, PhD, earned her doctorate from the University of California, Los Angeles, and is currently a professor of child development at California State University, Sacramento. She has published studies on early literacy development, with a focus on children who are learning English as a second language, in journals such as *Reading Research Quarterly, Journal of Educational Psychology,* and *Contemporary Educational Psychology.* Her research interests include alphabet and vocabulary learning, classroom instruction experiments, and family engagement. She has collaborated with preschool and elementary teachers to develop instruction programs and teacher training on these topics. She was a member of the panel of experts that developed the State of California Prekindergarten Guidelines. She serves as a research consultant for the California Preschool Instructional Network (CPIN) and is a consultant on an Early Reading First grant. She is an elected voting member of the Society for the Scientific Study of Reading, a reviewer for the *Journal of Educational Psychology and Applied Linguistics,* and a member of the editorial board of *Reading Psychology.*

Introduction

It is an exciting time to be working with preschool English learners! The importance of the preschool years for later reading and writing is well established. There is increasing interest in and dedication to ensuring that young English learners acquire strong early literacy foundations. There is burgeoning research on best early literacy practices in general, and there are similar studies specific to English learners. Professional development is increasingly provided for preschool teachers. These circumstances establish the promise of providing high-quality literacy programs for preschool children. The goal of this book is to respond to this current positive climate by providing a resource that contributes to young children's early literacy competence, which in turn leads to later reading success.

However, the optimism engendered by these developments in the early childhood field must be tempered by the reality that many reports document large differences in the quality of preschool programs. While the emotional needs of young children are typically supported in preschool settings (e.g., La Paro, Pianta, & Stuhlman, 2004; Pianta, Hamre, & Stuhlman, 2003), preschools differ markedly in the degree to which they stimulate the academic foundations for learning in specific areas such as literacy and math (e.g., Dickinson, McCabe, & Clark-Chiarelli, 2004; Whitehurst & Massetti, 2004). In addition, children more at risk for difficulties in achieving school success are also less likely to have the benefit of high-quality preschool experiences (e.g., Helburn & Bergmann, 2002; LoCasale-Crouch et al., 2007; McGill-Franzen, Lanford, & Adams, 2002). At-risk status is most consistently defined as low family income, but it also includes minority status and speaking a primary language other than English (e.g., Llagas & Snyder, 2003; Snow et al., 1998). There is also a significant overlap between family income and speaking a primary language other than English. In 2003, 71% of Hispanic fourth-grade students qualified for free or reduced-price lunch (Wirt et al., 2004), and 22% of children under the age of six had parents who were immigrants (Capps, Fix, Ost, Reardon-Anderson, & Passel, 2004). For these reasons, creating high-quality literacy experiences for preschool English learners is an educational priority. Still, there is variability within the overall patterns. There are programs where English learners are achieving critical early literacy competencies, and there is a growing knowledge base on how to foster their literacy learning. This book has two primary goals that can contribute to narrowing the distance between actuality and possibility.

The first goal of this book is to enable the reader to reach a deep understanding of the intellectual, emotional, and social foundations of literacy for preschool English learners. To promote an understanding of these foundations, I hope to help you step inside a child's mind to appreciate how it must work to learn these essential foundations. A second way that I hope to promote deep understanding of these foundations is by helping you to internalize knowledge of the specific language and literacy domains important for preschool learners to master. These critical literacy domains include strong language skills, knowledge of the alphabet, and the ability to pay attention to and manipulate the sounds in words. Whether you are a teacher, a student, an administrator, a parent, or another interested party, this knowledge will help you promote the development of literacy skills in preschool English learners.

The second goal of this book is to contribute to the development of highly effective teachers who can translate their understanding of preschool literacy into practices that will lead children to high levels of literacy competence, engagement, and enjoyment. Potential literacy teachers include parents and other family members and family care providers as well as preschool teachers. I hope this book will help you to think like a child, to understand what is required for a child to learn about language and literacy, and to implement preschool practices that ensure this advancement occurs. Creating effective and engaging literacy experiences and environments where children eagerly apply their understandings to real literacy activities is key. My experience as a teacher, a researcher, and an advocate for English learners and their families is that there are no limits to literacy for young English learners.

I have been very fortunate to have had input from hundreds of teachers, site administrators, trainers, and regional and state literacy leadership groups. These individuals include early education and care professionals working within Head Start; state-funded organizations; and family, friend, kin, and private provider settings. They have helped shape my understanding of the important topics and issues to examine in this book. Their wisdom, thoughtful questions, and keen observation of children have been a source of great personal learning for me. These same individuals have made it clear to me that there is both a hunger and a need for early care and education professionals to have a greater knowledge of preschool literacy, English learners, and their families, communities, and cultures in order for them to deliver on the mandate to ensure the language and literacy achievement of English learners. By providing professional development I have learned that early childhood professionals are very capable of achieving and internalizing a sophisticated understanding of preschool literacy, the practices that support it, and the unique linguistic and cultural/social influences on it that English learners bring. These experiences have encouraged me to set the learning bar high for early childhood educators, knowing that as with children, it is what is inside minds that will determine what they are able to accomplish.

RESEARCH-BASED PRACTICE

A strong commitment to using research to guide practice is represented in this book. I have been studying and publishing studies on the literacy development of English learners for 15 years. Studies that I have published on English learners are discussed in several chapters. The research base on English learners and English-only preschool children presents the early childhood field with an important challenge to continue recent trends to change and improve traditional approaches to preschool literacy. This research evidence leads to four points about preschool literacy that indicate the direction for continuing change in preschool literacy teaching:

- Preschool children can achieve sophisticated early literacy competencies (e.g., Report of the National Reading Panel [National Institute of Child Health and Human Development, 2000]).
- Preschool children learn in diverse ways and are dependent on both teacher-guided and child-guided experiences (e.g., Connor, Morrison, & Slominski, 2006; Ehri & Roberts, 2006; Graue, Clements, Reynolds, & Niles, 2004).
- Preschool children who *enter* kindergarten with higher levels of literacy skills and language competencies are likely to be better readers (e.g., Adams, 1990; Duncan et al., 2007; Hammer, Lawrence, & Miccio, 2007; National Institute of Child Health and Human Development Early Child Care Research Network, 2005; Snow et al., 1998; Storch & Whitehurst, 2002).
- There is growing evidence of the teaching practices that promote what children can learn and need to learn, and some practices are more effective than others (e.g., Debaryshe & Gorecki, 2007; Fischel et al., 2007; Han, Roskos, Christie, Mandzuk, & Vukelich, 2005; Preschool Curriculum Evaluation Research Consortium, 2008).

While most of this evidence has been obtained with English primary language children, there is emerging evidence that much of it applies to English learners. The sources of evidence for these four points are cited within the book chapters and are discussed in relationship to the chapter topics.

With your help, preschool children can learn more about early literacy than what many believed they could learn, even relatively recently. This evidence calls for changing the expectations of what is considered developmentally appropriate literacy achievement in preschool—and this call is more critical for English learners and other groups of children at risk. There is growing evidence that high-quality instruction can positively influence children's literacy learning in preschool (Mashburn et al., 2008) and that teacher-guided instruction is a critical component of the quality. This research suggests the importance of a significant focus on children's language, literacy, and cognitive development in preschool (Karoly, Ghosh-Dastidar, Zellman, Perlman, & Fernyhough, 2008) and shifting the traditional balance between teacher-guided and child-guided instruction to include more teacher guidance within a well-structured and research-based curriculum.

Children's literacy competence when they enter kindergarten is substantially related to their later success in reading. What happens in preschool has a strong influence on whether children will learn to read with ease or difficulty and the ultimate level of their reading skill. These relationships hold true for both English-only and English learner children. Because English learners are more likely to enter kindergarten with lower levels of early literacy, a strong focus on preschool literacy for English learners is particularly important (e.g., U.S. Department of Health and Human Services, 2003). Early childhood professionals who embrace this responsibility to prepare children for literacy success when they enter kindergarten are responding to the research evidence of what preschool children can learn and need to learn to become strong readers.

Studies focusing on preschool English learners are limited. However, the largely universal nature of how language is learned—which is rooted in biology—suggests there will be more commonalities than differences between children from different language groups. Results of several studies with early elementary English learners are consistent with this expectation, showing significant similarity between English learners and English-only children in early reading processes (Geva, Wade-Woolley, & Shany, 1997; Geva & Zadeh, 2006). There is also evidence from school-age English learners demonstrating the effectiveness of explicitly teaching beginning reading skills. Confidence that teaching practices, parenting practices, or other practices will lead to literacy learning for English learners will be greater when research results have been found with that same group. Studies specific to preschool English learners are given prominence in this book. Research based on English-only children and older English learner children is included when it relates to aspects of literacy learning likely to be similar across language groups or when the evidence it provides is particularly strong or important. Throughout the book, I have indicated when research evidence is specific to English learners or has come from children who are English-only.

ORGANIZATION

The book is organized so that you can select chapters and sections within chapters to pursue in a sequence that accommodates your interests. Following each section within the chapters are teaching and educational principles and/or exercises to apply your knowledge. These exercises are designed to help you consolidate your understanding and see how the topics in the book come to life through children, classrooms, and communities. A number of sections are devoted to hot topics in the field that have captured attention and debate. For example, the amount of oral English proficiency that English learners need to have in order to be ready for literacy instruction is one of these hot topics. Another is the appropriateness of explicit, group, and teacher-initiated instruction for preschool English learners. A third hot topic centers on the degree to which play leads to literacy development. These and other hot topics are examined through the lens of the available research. At the end of each chapter, all of the teaching and educational principles are listed together. Reviewing them should give you an integrated view of what a comprehensive teaching/ educational approach for that topic will look like. Within each chapter, bulleted lists, graphic organizers, vignettes, research highlights, and self-reflections are abundant.

STORYTELLING

I have assumed the role of a storyteller within this book—a storyteller of literacy ideas and the connections between them and the life they can lead in preschool settings. As a storyteller, I have tried to take complex ideas and ideas that may seem mysterious and strange at first and explain them with enough fact and logic that you will feel as though you can make them happen—"Of course that makes sense—I understand that story." There is complexity in the language experiences of English learners who may also live within social and cultural organizations that are not familiar to you.

Children's particular language background, their skills, their exposure to different languages, the language environment in the home, the literacy level of parents and other family caregivers, the family's immigration status and socioeconomic level, and how language is used among family members add to this complexity.

There is complexity in the domains of literacy learning and literacy teaching as well. In language there is vocabulary, pronunciation, story retelling, and pretend reading, for example. With the alphabet there are uppercase and lowercase letters, letter names and letter sounds, children's personal names, pretend writing, and alphabet books. Knowing sounds in words brings in rhyming, sounding out, and hearing the first sound in a word. There is even more complexity in learning how to select, orchestrate, and implement different strategies to teach all of this well. I apologize in advance for instances where I have missed the mark by either telling too much of the story with unnecessary detail or rushing along too quickly and leaving you behind and confused. I hope you find that the study, thought, effort, and time that this book will ask of you to hear its story will lead to your sense of empowerment as a teacher—a teacher who believes in and can create literacy experiences that result in *No Limits to Literacy for Preschool English Learners.*

Resources English Language Learners Bring to Literacy Learning

1

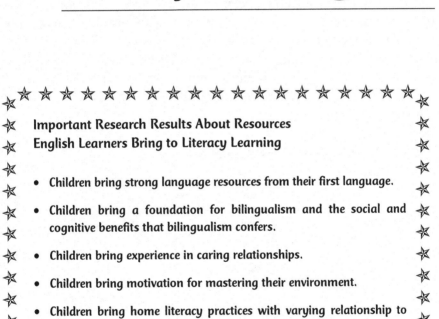

★ **Important Research Results About Resources English Learners Bring to Literacy Learning**

- Children bring strong language resources from their first language.

- Children bring a foundation for bilingualism and the social and cognitive benefits that bilingualism confers.

- Children bring experience in caring relationships.

- Children bring motivation for mastering their environment.

- Children bring home literacy practices with varying relationship to school literacy practices.

- Children bring cultural and community frameworks and practices that provide social identity and community integration.

Children who are learning English as a second language bring many resources with them to preschool settings. These resources emanate from language specific and other child characteristics and from children's families and the broader cultural and social settings they have participated in. In this chapter a *developmental systems approach* is taken to identify and to organize these multiple sources of resources that English language learners (ELLs) bring with them to preschool settings. *Subsystems* within the child such as language, motivation, and emotion are assumed to interact. This interaction means that each *subsystem* communicates with and influences the others. An example showing the interaction between the emotional and language subsystems is that enjoyable language interactions encourage the use of more expressive language. These subsystems within the child also interact with other subsystems in the external environment. For preschool English learners, these important *external subsystems* include their families, their communities, and their cultural frames of reference. A developmental systems approach to children's resources for literacy learning leads us to consider children's individual resources that are directly related to literacy, such as language and literacy experiences. A developmental systems approach also orients us to look at other subsystems within the child and the external environment that are less directly related to literacy but nevertheless communicate with and influence it. The graph in Figure 1.1 shows the child and external environment subsystems that provide preschool English learners with resources for language and literacy growth in preschool settings.

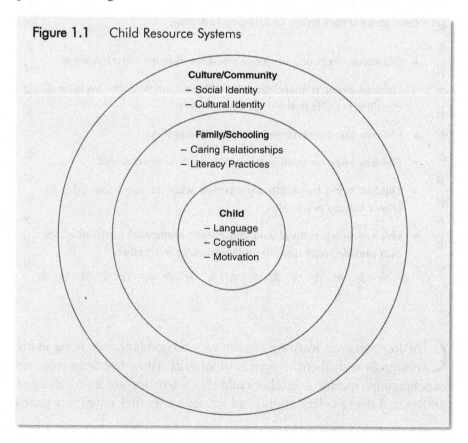

Figure 1.1   Child Resource Systems

Culture/Community
- Social Identity
- Cultural Identity

Family/Schooling
- Caring Relationships
- Literacy Practices

Child
- Language
- Cognition
- Motivation

The strengths-based orientation to children's preparedness for language and literacy learning that emerges from focusing on understanding these resources will support maintaining high expectations, valuing children's competencies, and respecting the richness of their familial and cultural experiences. A strengths-based orientation also leads to instructional practices that establish connections between children's preexisting experiences and new learning in classrooms, as their previous experiences will be seen as a wellspring to draw from rather than a limitation to fix. Yet a strengths-based orientation does not mean to ignore the challenges faced by preschool English learners as they engage in the process of acquiring a second language, meet and become embedded in what for many is a new culture, or face the very real challenges experienced by those families of English learners with limited economic resources. It means recognizing that English learner children have resources, building on and with the resources children have, and providing them with those they need.

Teachers who believe in English learners' capacity for growth reflect this belief by holding high expectations for them, teaching them well, and viewing children's families and cultures as resource-laden contributors to higher school achievement for these children (e.g., Foster, Lewis, & Onafowora, 2003; Ngo & Lee, 2007; Snow, 2008). To inspire this orientation in early education and care professionals is a primary reason for taking the strengths-based perspective represented in this chapter. The term *wellspring* was selected to highlight the varied and plentiful sources of strength that English learners bring to literacy learning. I will begin by examining the individual child's wellsprings of resources and move out—like a ripple—to those resources provided by the external environment.

THE LANGUAGE AND LITERACY WELLSPRING

Preschool English learners developing typically bring a well-formed basic communication system with them when they enter preschool settings. Of course, this language resource will most likely be in their first language, although some children will come with emerging competence in English as well. When children learn English after they have a basic primary language foundation, they are described as *sequential bilingual* children—one language follows basic acquisition of the other. When children have been learning two languages before preschool entry (typically the language of their family and culture in addition to English), they are described as *simultaneous bilingual* children. *Sequential* rather than *simultaneous* bilingualism is more common among preschool ELL children in the United States, particularly if they come from low-income families. Because of the dominance of English in most preschool settings, it is easy for educators to focus more on children's limited English proficiency than on the resource of their first language.

To understand how this occurs, create an image of a preschool child who speaks a language other than English—make the child male or female, detail the face and clothing. Now think of that child as having almost no English. What does the child need? How would you help him or her with English language and literacy? Now focus in on the child as having a primary language that she or he uses quite fluidly at home—imagine the child talking with caregivers, playing with siblings and friends, and reading storybooks with caregivers. What does the child need? How would you help him or her with English language and literacy? Hopefully this pretending has helped you appreciate that focusing on the primary language wellspring draws attention to English learner's language strength. Recognizing that English learners have language resources, albeit in a language other than English, identifies the primary language of children and their families as an important foundation for learning about English and the broader preschool curriculum. It also encourages viewing the child as capable.

The value of speaking more than one language is increasingly recognized in a global society. Because of their primary language competence, preschool English learners are in advance of English-only children in their potential for competence in more than one language. You might think of them as having half of what is needed for knowing two languages and of their families as having provided this gift, although of course their primary language development is far from complete.

Another way that primary language is a wellspring for English language and literacy is that bilingualism confers thinking advantages that are evident in preschool age children (Bialystok, 2001). Bilingual children have advantages in controlling their attention and greater flexibility in thinking than children who speak only one language. They may also have advantages in the ability to attend to the sounds of words, a skill that is a powerful predictor of reading achievement. They may also be particularly adept at acquiring a second language during the preschool years, and thus they are positioned to learn English well when in a high-quality English language development preschool (Campbell & Sais, 1995; Diaz, 1985; Gonz & Kodzopeljic, 1991; Rubin & Turner, 1989; Yelland, Pollard, & Mercuri, 1993). The language wellspring is rich and complex with several tributaries flowing toward language and literacy learning.

Educational Principle 1: Assume children have language and literacy resources, and draw on these resources in preschool practices.

THE EMOTIONAL WELLSPRING

Preschool English learners are raised in caring families by caregivers who love them. The benefit of these caring relationships is reflected in a large study of entering kindergarten children. Parents and teachers similarly reported that about 80% of English learner and English-only children typically demonstrated positive social skills (Llagas & Snyder, 2003). In fact the same data suggested that in spite of having several risk factors, English learners may have some emotional strengths that are greater than those of less at-risk children (Crosnoe, 2004). It has been suggested that the extensive social contacts and family cohesiveness emphasized by some cultures and incorporated by individual families within those cultures may serve to contribute to social-emotional well-being and resilience in the face of familial and individual stressors (e.g., Espinosa, 2006). The greater prevalence of two-parent families within the English learner population has also been suggested as a resource for emotional well-being. When children are very sure that they are cared about, it encourages them to step out into the larger world and to be open to the experiences such as language and literacy learning that it has to offer. It is like having a little security blanket that is tucked deep inside of them. The emotional wellspring encourages English learner children to flow into new settings and experiences with eagerness and focus.

> **Educational Principle 2:**
> Assume that English learners have emotional well-being that derives from caring relationships within their families, and view this as a foundation for language and literacy learning.

THE MOTIVATIONAL WELLSPRING

All humans have an inborn need to be competent (White, 1959). This need for competence is directed toward mastering and adapting to one's environment. Preschool English learners come to preschool settings with that need already humming and flowing—they are ready to master and adapt. This biologically based need for competence is directed toward mastering challenges perceived by the organism (child in our case) to result in greater adaptation, which is needed for survival. In addition to the need for competence, needs for autonomy and relatedness also motivate behavior (Reeve, Deci, & Ryan, 2004). Autonomy is not the same as independence—autonomy implies that one endorses one's own behavior. It is aligned with self-regulation. For example, if group participation is valued, a child could have a sense of autonomy when working in a group. Children could have a sense of autonomy when they strive to accomplish things that will please their family, if they agree that pleasing their family and accomplishing these things are meaningful and appropriate.

Children's own individual beliefs and values, those of their families and cultural groups, and the larger society interact and shape how this motivation for competence will be directed. Preschool settings for early education and care are social settings that can influence whether or not preschool English learners' inherent motivation for competence is tapped into and engaged by language and literacy learning. To the degree that language and literacy learning in preschool settings is seen by the child as a potential and important opportunity for increasing competence, autonomy, and relatedness, the inborn motivation that children bring to preschool settings will be activated—and they will be eager and motivated language and literacy learners. When experiences with language and literacy in preschool settings are not seen as an opportunity for increasing competence, autonomy, and relatedness, children's inherent motivation will be thwarted and suppressed. English learners' motivation is flowing—increase its velocity by ensuring that children experience competence, autonomy, and relationships with others in their preschool language and literacy learning.

> **Educational Principle 3**: Assume that English learners come motivated to learn, and use language and literacy learning practices that engage this motivation.

THE FAMILY WELLSPRING

Families provide both language and social-emotional resources to their children that then accompany the children as they enter preschool settings. Families provide children their first exposures to language. All families also provide children experiences with literacy, although the extent of these experiences, and particularly experiences that are most supportive of school literacy achievement, may vary (e.g., Purcell-Gates, 2004). Practices such as oral storytelling, paying bills, reading fliers, managing coupons and banking, filling out forms with an interpreter, assembling household tools, reading a newspaper, navigating the TV guide, cooking with recipes, and using written instructions are all practices that involve literacy. Experience with written language—whether in, for example, storybook reading, or some other form—has been suggested as providing the type of expanded and vocabulary-laden language that is most supportive of school achievement. The degree to which children are actively involved in or attend to these practices contributes to how much literacy learning they garner from them.

Similarly families have *funds of knowledge* (Moll, Amanti, Neff, & Gonzales, 1992). Work experiences, hobbies, and traditional cultural practices are some of the funds of knowledge that exist in families. When these funds of knowledge are recognized and drawn in to the preschool setting, these family resources come alive to support children's literacy learning and create positive emotional conditions that also contribute to learning in preschool settings. These family literacy experiences have not been sufficiently recognized or capitalized on in schools, but when they are, children's language and literacy learning can benefit (e.g., Bernhard et al., 2006).

Failure to draw on family literacy resources may be particularly significant, as it may lead to (1) underestimation of children's preparedness for literacy learning, (2) lost opportunities for connecting relevant family-provided literacy experiences to preschool settings, and (3) creation of barriers to engaging families in promoting children's literacy learning by not drawing on the families' literacy practices and funds of knowledge. Activities that are more directly related to school experiences, such as storybook reading, vocabulary building, conversation, and print experiences similar to those associated with school settings, are more likely to be focused on by early childhood professionals. While these efforts are appropriate and to be encouraged, there are other resources for language and literacy learning of preschool ELLs to uncover and draw upon.

Families of English learners also value education, want their children to learn English, and hope for their academic success (Ngo & Lee, 2007). Yet the ways in which families demonstrate their valuing of education may differ from what is expected by professionals in preschool settings. For example, some families of English learner children may demonstrate their valuing of education by deferring to the teacher as the authority. Consequently they may not offer to participate or ask questions about their children's participation and achievement. Other families of English learners may be uncomfortable or feel unable to show their valuing in ways expected by the school because of language challenges, their own limited experience with schooling, or a lack of understanding of the English preschool setting. And yet other families may exert a strong

Educational Principle 4: Assume that families care about their children's language and literacy success, and find ways to include family caregivers in preschool language and literacy experiences.

influence on their children's study practices at home, restrict social outings so children have time to study, and instruct children that their school performance reflects on the entire family, even though these efforts may not be visible to school staff (Ngo & Lee, 2007). The family wellspring flows deeply and broadly.

THE CULTURAL WELLSPRING

Language and culture are intimately related (Gee, 1989). English learner children very often have learned their primary language where its use is embedded in a cultural context that differs from that of the mainstream English language culture. Family beliefs, parenting practices, spirituality, political and historical experience, and practices of daily living may differ markedly from those of the mainstream culture. These cultural frameworks provide children with resources to aid them in constructing their unique sense of self and their social identity as a member of a particular cultural group. Alignment with and a strong sense of integration within a cultural framework secures children's understanding of who they are. Evidence suggests that English learners who have strong affinity with the cultural group in which their primary language is embedded perform better in school than those who do not have these strong affiliations with the cultural identity of their families and cultural community (Caplan, Chou, & Whitmore, 1991; Thao, 2003; Zhou & Bankston, 2006). In addition, because preschool ELLs participate both in the cultural context associated with their non-English primary language and in the mainstream English language culture, they have an emerging understanding of diversity. They are aware of diversity and live it more intimately than many children who speak only English.

> **Educational Principle 5:**
> Assume that children have important and positive cultural experiences, and find ways to include these experiences in preschool language and literacy experiences.

CONCLUSION

A developmental systems approach for considering the resources that preschool English learners bring to preschool settings reveals that they have language and literacy resources, emotional resources, family resources, and cultural resources. They are strong. Believe in this strength, and you are well on your way to creating high expectations for language and literacy learning, a positive orientation to children and their families, a belief that English learners are ready to engage in preschool language and literacy learning, and a trust in their desire to partner with you to advance their competence. Embracing these beliefs is the bedrock for language and literacy practices and programs that will lead to preschool English learners acquiring the necessary preschool foundations for successful literacy. Subsequent chapters in this book will build on this strengths-based belief system. There are specific chapters to help you learn how to

- Find out about and build language and literacy competence with preschool children's existing language and literacy resources.
- Promote further social-emotional well-being while fostering language and literacy development.
- Sustain and further enhance children's motivation to speak, read, and write in English.
- Engage family caregivers and their familial and cultural resources.

Summary of Educational Principles

Educational Principle 1: Assume children have language and literacy resources, and draw on these resources in preschool language and literacy practices.

Educational Principle 2: Assume that English learners have emotional well-being that derives from caring relationships within their families, and view this as a foundation for language and literacy learning.

Educational Principle 3: Assume that English learners come motivated to learn, and use language and literacy learning practices that engage this motivation.

Educational Principle 4: Assume that families care about their children's language and literacy success, and find ways to include them in preschool language and literacy experiences.

Educational Principle 5: Assume that children have important and positive cultural experiences, and find ways to include these experiences in preschool language and literacy experiences.

2 Building On and Scaffolding With Primary Language

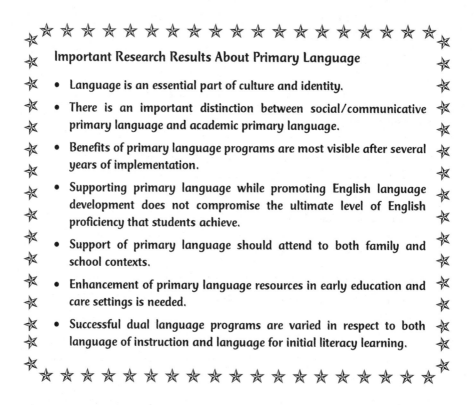

★ ★ ★ ★ ★ ★ ★ ★ ★ ★ ★ ★ ★ ★ ★ ★ ★ ★ ★

Important Research Results About Primary Language

- Language is an essential part of culture and identity.

- There is an important distinction between social/communicative primary language and academic primary language.

- Benefits of primary language programs are most visible after several years of implementation.

- Supporting primary language while promoting English language development does not compromise the ultimate level of English proficiency that students achieve.

- Support of primary language should attend to both family and school contexts.

- Enhancement of primary language resources in early education and care settings is needed.

- Successful dual language programs are varied in respect to both language of instruction and language for initial literacy learning.

★ ★ ★ ★ ★ ★ ★ ★ ★ ★ ★ ★ ★ ★ ★ ★ ★ ★ ★

English learners come to the preschool classroom with a well-developed primary language. They are able to communicate their needs and wants; to negotiate their relationships with parents, siblings, and members of their extended families; to infuse their play with language; to generate utterances that delight and astound with both their linguistic creativity and insight; and to express and increase their cognitive abilities through using language. Primary language is also the linguistic context in which first emotional relationships are formed, developed, and expressed. It is in this sense that ELLs' language is well developed. Awareness of these competencies affirms children's language strength and encourages early childhood professionals to see this strength as a foundation upon which to build. By contrast, a focus on children's limited English proficiency overlooks this strength and consequently may lead to a tendency to view ELL children as linguistically impoverished.

Children's primary language is intimately intertwined with their understanding and knowledge of the world in which they live, their earliest emotional and relationship experiences, and the sculpting and crafting of their cultural and personal identity. These close relationships between language, cognitive development, and social-emotional development are implicated by the developmental systems perspective introduced in Chapter 1, Resources English Language Learners Bring to Literacy Learning. They are well established when preschool English language learners enter preschool settings. To most fully and easily draw upon and activate the linguistic, cognitive, and social-emotional experiences, knowledge, and strengths that have been developed in the context of the child's first language and that are represented in the child's mind in that first language, teachers must use the first language when working with these children. When children's first language is used for important purposes in preschool settings, it also affords children continuity between their previous experiences and their new ones in school. In addition, it shows children that the language used by themselves, those close to them, and possibly even broadly in the community in which they reside is recognized and important. It is through the use of the primary language that true valuing of it is expressed.

The use of the primary language can also yield language and literacy benefits that will help English learners secure the highest possible levels of second language literacy. In the case of primary language, we will need to look more broadly than we will at other topics to fully portray its role in the literacy development of preschool English learners. This look will be the focus of this chapter. In this chapter, the connections among primary language, cognitive and social-emotional development, and second language subsystems will be explained. The graph in Figure 2.1 shows the important elements of cognitive and social-emotional functioning that are associated with primary language.

WHY SUPPORT CHILDREN'S PRIMARY LANGUAGE?

Communication, cognitive, social, and emotional development are interdependent in young children (Kohnert, Yim, Nett, Kan, & Duran, 2005). Children use their primary language to navigate, respond to, understand, and learn from their social and physical environments. For preschool children,

Figure 2.1   Elements of Cognitive and Social-Emotional Functioning Associated With Primary Language

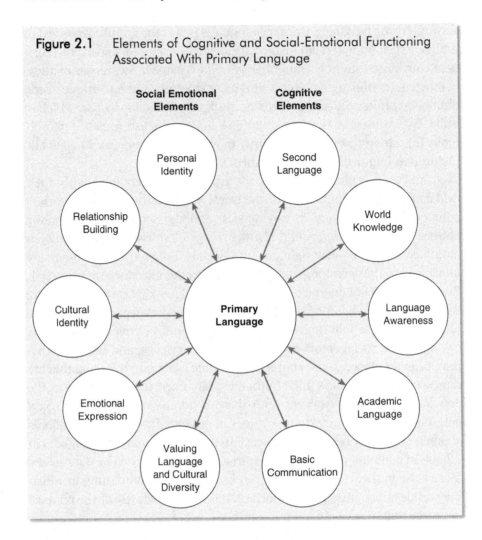

these experiences occur mostly in the context of the family. For children to continue to optimally benefit from the learning and socialization experiences that occur within the family, their competence and motivation to use the primary language must be maintained. Sharing a common language with family caregivers remains critically important for children across development, as it allows children and their family caregivers to navigate together the increasing social, emotional, and cognitive complexity accompanying children's development.

In addition to its role in familial and cultural communication, primary language is an important element of self-identity. Primary language is a foundation that enables children to communicate their unique experiences with and reactions to their world; to express their preferences, desires, needs, and perspectives; and to establish their roles as sons, daughters, brothers, or sisters. I had a good friend during college who was from the Dominican Republic. He was a university student who had strong English language competence, although Spanish was his self-described dominant language. On the weekend, he would regularly and purposefully search for opportunities to use Spanish. I asked him about this, particularly since his English was so strong. He explained it to me: "Ah, Theresa. The first time I heard 'I love you,' it was in Spanish.

Teaching Principle 1: Use primary language for both cognitive and social-emotional purposes.

All of my birthday celebrations were in Spanish. The language of my first romantic relationship was Spanish. When I speak Spanish I am most fully 'Alphonso.'" I understood the connection between language and personal identity. This same relationship between primary language and personal identity holds for preschool children.

In the discussion of the close connections among family communication and relationships, personal identity, and primary language, we have looked at factors indirectly related to promoting literacy. There is also evidence of a more direct relationship between primary language skill and literacy achievement. In general, the evidence shows that strength in the primary language contributes to both L2 (second language) language acquisition and L1 (first language) and L2 literacy achievement (August & Hakuta, 1997; August & Shanahan, 2008; Lindholm-Leary, 2001; Riches & Genesee, 2006). Explanation of this evidence will be considered more fully in the next section.

Educational Principle 1: Include maintenance and development of primary language as an explicit preschool program goal.

PRIMARY LANGUAGE AND LITERACY ACHIEVEMENT

Most English learners in the United States are learning to read in their second language. While some Spanish-speaking children may have opportunities for learning to read in their primary language, L1 reading programs for children from other language groups are very limited, at least in the public school sector. Some children may learn L1 reading in afterschool programs, Saturday school, or summer programs. In situations in which children are learning to read in their L1, L1 oral proficiency also has a robust relationship to L1 reading (Genesee, Lindholm-Leary, Saunders, & Christian, 2006). Higher oral proficiency in a language confers benefits to learning to read in that language.

But what about the relationship of primary language skills to L2 reading? Primary language maintenance and learning to read and write in primary language literacy are associated with success in acquiring English literacy with elementary-age children (August & Hakuta, 1997; Bialystok & Hakuta, 1999; Cheung & Slavin, 2005; Cummins, 1999, 2000). Stated differently, the research indicates that learning to read in the primary

Teaching Principle 2: Implement literacy experiences at home in L1 or L2 depending on home language resources.

Educational Principle 2:
Incorporate primary language and knowledge developed in primary language in preschool literacy experiences.

language does not impede or interfere with L2 reading. In fact, children can draw on their primary language vocabulary knowledge, primary language reading strategies, primary language skills in attending to and manipulating the sounds in words, and knowledge represented in their primary language to aid them in second language reading (Genesee et al., 2006; Lanauze & Snow, 1989; Langer, Barolome, & Vasquez, 1990). Most of this evidence has come from children older than preschool age, however. The degree to which L1 instruction benefits second language reading is a long-standing hot topic related to English learners and remains so in light of recent policy and legislative actions in several states that establish an English-only orientation to the education of English learners.

One study showing how first language helps second language that included young children reported that family literacy practices in first or second language and L1 literacy experiences before formal reading instruction contributed positively to children's later L2 reading achievement (Reese, Garnier, Gallimore, & Goldenberg, 2000). In a very recent study where L1 and L2 storybook reading at home was compared (Roberts, 2008), I found that preschool English learners were just as successful in acquiring English storybook vocabulary words when they read books at home in primary language as when they read the same books in English. There was also some evidence that the storybooks in primary language may have been most useful for English vocabulary growth. Rather than being in competition with each other, first and second languages are interdependent in children's language development.

Apply Your Knowledge

1. If you are a teacher, select two English learners in your class. Find out two types of knowledge they have (gardening, cooking, folk dancing, etc.). Write two ways that you could incorporate each of these two knowledge sources into classroom literacy practices. For example, have a child who knows a lot about gardening bring seed packets of items the child has planted and tell you the names of these plants in the child's primary language; you add the English label. Attention could be drawn to the print on the envelope that shows the name. A bilingual individual

such as a parent, teacher, or teaching assistant could take a story dictation from this child telling about how the child planted and cared for the
plant. A conversation could be held with this child that begins with an
open-ended prompt such as "Tell me about your garden at home."

2. If you are not a teacher, imagine a child who is raising chickens and collecting their eggs to help with a family small business. Imagine another
who is learning traditional embroidery with her mother. Plan activities
for how this knowledge could be drawn in to the preschool setting. One
idea would be to invite the mother to the preschool and have the mother
and child demonstrate how to do the traditional embroidery while the
teacher describes the steps in English.

ADDING SOME MAGIC: METACOGNITIVE BENEFITS

You have learned how L1 and L2 can team up to help each other in language
and literacy learning. There is another well-documented benefit of knowing
two languages that shows some magic. The teamwork between the two languages and the magic I am about to describe to you may help explain how it
is that even though children in bilingual programs spend less time with their
second language than do English learner children in nonbilingual programs,
they come to be just as good, if not better (more probably), with it. When children have the benefit of knowing two languages, they turn this knowledge
into thinking advantages (Bialystok, 2006). That's the magic. These thinking
advantages include greater ability to think abut things in more than one way
and greater ability in controlling attention, compared to children who know
only one language. Exposure to two languages also sharpens children's awareness of the nature of language. More concretely, bilingual children appear to
learn what a word is earlier, to understand that words and the things to
which they refer are not the same, and to comprehend that words are made
up of sounds (a critical skill for learning to read print). These language skills
are called *metalinguistic awareness*. Metalinguistic awareness can help children learn about the alphabet, understand sounds in words, and comprehend what they read.

BEYOND THE WORDS: SOCIAL-EMOTIONAL
ASPECTS OF PRIMARY LANGUAGE

One of the most important reasons for richly incorporating primary language into school programs is that it demonstrates that schools value the

child's linguistic and cultural background (Au, 1998; Cummins, 1999, 2000; Delpit, 1988). This validation can generate a sense of empowerment for both children and their families, which should serve to support academic engagement and therefore literacy achievement. Cummins (1999, 2000) recommends a *transformative pedagogy* to accomplish this empowerment. *Pedagogy* means teaching practices. The essential elements of transformative pedagogy include (a) promoting bilingualism, (b) involving families as collaborators and partners in their children's education, and (c) teaching in ways that build on personal and cultural experience to create a stance of critical literacy. Critical literacy means using literacy creatively for important personal purposes. While scholars describe a variety of ways to achieve this empowerment, the use and preservation of primary language figure prominently as key ingredients for empowerment.

As children acquire a primary language, they learn words, how to put words together, and the sounds that make words. As children acquire primary language, they also learn how to organize their cognitive and emotional experiences and how to express what they know with language (Schiefflin & Ochs, 1986). In addition, children learn the expectations and rules that tell them how, when, where, and to whom they are to use different aspects of the language. How do you speak to parents? Is that the same or different from how you speak to grandparents? Who has the right to start and end conversations? What are considered interesting and forbidden topics of discussion? How are conversations and turn-taking expected to proceed? Are stories, fables, or storybook reading a part of language use?

To illustrate these ideas, imagine the practice of "show and tell," where children bring some object from home to share with the class. This show-and-tell event is a language event. Typically, the expectation is that the child stands before the group and presents the object, telling about its nature and how it is related to the child. The teacher may ask a few questions that are object specific, and there may be an opportunity for other children to ask a question or two. Success at show and tell requires (a) an understanding of the importance of describing your object to others, (b) staying object centered, and (c) the inclination to be in front of others and speak while they listen. If you are a member of the audience, a few understandings that you need to have are that (a) one does not contribute until the end of the show-and-tell presentation and (b) one is expected to question the speaker- rather than share one's own experiences. For show-and-tell success, one needs to have skill with the language, and an understanding of how to use the language, both of which occur from cultural learning.

Sociocultural variations related to turn-taking, inclination to offer an individual opinion, answering a question that may appear to set one off from the group, and verbally performing alone in front of others have been documented (Phillips, 1972; Tharp, 1989). Children from mainstream, middle class families are more likely to have learned how to use language in the same ways that schools have traditionally rewarded, such as those practices expected during sharing. And here is an interesting "Which came first— the chicken or the egg?" question: Do schools mirror how language tends to be used in mainstream, middle class families, or do mainstream, middle class families teach their children to use language as it will be used in school? When children speak a primary language other than English or a dialect variation of English, they are likely to use language in different ways than do English-only children, and their language use is more likely to be different from typical language use in schools.

Teaching Principle 3: Incorporate ways of using language that are familiar to English learner children.

Teaching Principle 4: When using language in ways less familiar to children, explain what is expected, demonstrate the practice, and allow time for English learners to become familiar with it.

Teaching Principle 5: When using language in ways less familiar to children, select topics and activities that will motivate children to use these new ways.

Finding out about these variations can help early childhood professionals understand how children tend to use language and to then provide classroom experiences that mirror these usages. For example, Hawaiian children's language participation was increased in elementary school classrooms when teachers modified classroom language use to match the way children were likely to have learned to use language at home. Hawaiian children had learned to use overlapping talk during conversation: These children may start speaking before other speakers have completely finished speaking. When classroom talk rules were modified to permit this overlapping and teachers were helped to not view this way of using language as interrupting, children had higher rates of academically oriented behaviors (Au & Mason, 1981).

WHAT HAPPENS TO THE PRIMARY LANGUAGE WHEN CHILDREN ENTER PRESCHOOL?

A great deal of concern has been expressed about the ultimate fate of children's primary language when they enter preschool settings that present significant exposure to English. For some, the concern is focused on settings where the main language of instruction is English. Others are concerned that even bilingual programs where instruction in both L1 and L2 occurs presents a significant challenge to continued development of the primary language. The significance of what may be at stake makes it clear that these concerns about children losing their first language are very important. Children's continuing ability to communicate within their families at the ever-increasing levels of language complexity that will accompany childhood development will depend on ensuring the children's continuing primary language development in the early years. Social-emotional advantages related to strong identity formation such as self-esteem have been reported for older children who remain bilingual compared to those who are fluent in English but do not also have fluency in the primary language (Portes & Hao, 2002).

An important factor in American society that influences the fate of the primary language is how much it is used. When the primary language is not broadly used in educational and other settings in the community, it is less likely that children will continue to acquire and use it. When a primary language is associated with a lower social status than other languages, it may even be valued less by native speakers of it. This diminished valuing may lead to diminishing usage. When individuals have a well-developed first language or are exposed to a second language after the primary language is reasonably well learned, there is less risk of its loss. However, for preschool English learners, the primary language is still being acquired. Therefore a heightened concern about what happens to the primary language when preschool children encounter a second language environment is warranted, particularly when the encounter will be extensive and with the socially dominant language.

There are a few studies in preschool settings that look at what happens to L1 when children encounter a second language. A mixed picture emerges from these studies. Some studies revealed evidence of L1 loss (Leseman, 2000; Schaerlaekens, Zink, & Verheyden, 1995) in settings where L1 was the language used in the classroom. Others found no primary language loss when children participated in high-quality, Spanish-English bilingual preschool programs where both languages were systematically supported (Rodríguez, Díaz, Duran, & Espinosa, 1995; Winsler, Díaz, Espinosa, & Rodríguez, 1999). A recent study reported L1 stabilization with substantial L2 growth in an English-language preschool setting (Kan & Kohnert, 2005). In the study on primary language storybook reading that I have recently completed and that you will soon read about in detail, Spanish-speaking children who were in English language preschool classrooms continued to show significant growth in their Spanish vocabulary (Roberts, 2008). Spanish-language storybooks were read at home and provided opportunities to encounter sophisticated primary language.

Another well-known study concluded that any exposure to English in the preschool period was associated with primary language loss (Wong-Fillmore, 1991). Loss of primary language was reported when children attended English-only preschool *or* bilingual preschool. In this study, parents of children who had attended preschool reported on their beliefs about the type of preschool program their children had attended and their estimates of their children's primary language proficiency after the children completed preschool. Several publications have commented on the significant problems from a research perspective of relying on parents' memories and having no actual measure of children's language skills (e.g., Winsler et al., 1999). Other studies with better methodology have not consistently reported similar primary language loss.

Together these studies suggest that the primary language is fragile. Promoting and preserving it will depend on the implementation of carefully thought-out practices that extensively use it. I suggest that successfully preserving and promoting children's primary language will require a two-fold set of practices:

- One set of practices should use the primary language for basic communication and social-emotional purposes.
- One set of practices should draw upon primary language during literacy learning.

This second set of practices will promote the sophisticated and decontextualized primary language development needed for strong literacy learning. Kan and Kohnert (2005) observed that in a Hmong-English bilingual program, the two languages were used in different ways that loosely match the distinctions just described. Hmong, the primary language, was used for managing the flow of classroom activity and social issues. English was the language used mostly for learning. This pattern was associated with significant gains in English vocabulary but not Hmong vocabulary. The language that was used for learning showed greater development. It is critical to do more than respecting and valuing the primary language. For a language to be nourished, it must be used. And the greater the usage and the more sophisticated the usage, the better a language is learned. Children are also sensitive to how much primary language they hear. When adults and other children use primary language more, children will increase their frequency of its use as well (Chesterfield, Chesterfield, Hayes-Latimer, & Chavez, 1983; Paradis & Nicoladis, 2007).

Educational Principle 3: Explain the value of primary language use to children and their families.

The Kan and Kohnert (2005) study does not show that it was actually how the two languages were used that accounted for the differences in language growth, because there are other possible interpretations. The use of English may have grown more anyway because of its higher social status, or perhaps the teachers were more proficient in English than Hmong. A good follow-up study would be to compare several Hmong-English bilingual classrooms. Some could have teachers assigned (by chance) to provide instruction in Hmong and social support and classroom management in English; others could have teachers provide instruction in English with Hmong used for social support and classroom management. Measures of children's Hmong and English language development could then be compared between the two types of classrooms. In this case we would have a true experiment that would help us clearly see if using a language for literacy instruction influences its development. In the next section we look more carefully at using primary language for social-emotional purposes.

Apply Your Knowledge

Write a letter to a site administrator or community leader recommending that he or she establish bilingual preschool settings where possible. Base your letter on information from this chapter. Be sure to include information on the social-emotional benefits (personal and social identity, valuing diversity, family communication) and cognitive benefits (primary language benefits, second language and second literacy benefits, language awareness, academic language) of bilingual classrooms.

USING PRIMARY LANGUAGE FOR SOCIAL COMMUNICATION AND SOCIAL-EMOTIONAL PURPOSES

It certainly seems logical that using primary language would result in children understanding the practices, expectations, and routines of classrooms. The use of primary language would also logically allow children to establish social connections to other children and to express their social-emotional needs, and it would allow teachers to respond appropriately. In fact, Chang et al. (2007) found just such evidence in their study of Spanish-English bilingual preschoolers. These researchers reported that as Spanish was used more between teachers and children, there were increases in teacher perceptions of close relationships with children, child social skills, and child assertiveness. So the use of primary language appears to have social-emotional benefits regardless of whether it occurs during specific literacy experiences or in other contexts. These social-emotional benefits are likely to

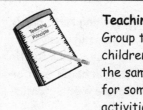

Teaching Principle 6: Group together children who speak the same language for some literacy activities.

Educational Principle 4: Incorporate primary language for promoting strong social relationships.

indirectly promote literacy achievement, as close relationships with teachers are conducive to cooperative and responsive interactions between teachers and children during literacy learning (Pianta, 2006). These positive exchanges are related to better literacy learning.

BENEFITS OF USING PRIMARY LANGUAGE FOR LITERACY LEARNING

Two desirable outcomes from using primary language for literacy learning are increased second language literacy learning and possibly the continued development of the primary language. There are a few studies that include specific first language literacy practices with preschool English learners that suggest possible benefits for second language learning of using primary language during literacy experiences (e.g., Bernhard et al., 2006; Roberts, 2008). There are also indirect sources of evidence and reasons why using primary language for literacy learning may also support continued development of the primary language. So follow along, and see if you think these ideas are compelling even though they have not yet been affirmed by systematic research.

The first idea for the potential benefit of primary language literacy experiences for promoting primary language competence is that literacy experiences provide opportunities to develop decontextualized language competence. *Decontextualized language competence* is strongly connected to early reading (Dickinson & Snow, 1987; Genesee et al., 2006; Olson, 1977; Snow, 1991). For example, decontextualized language would be used to discuss yesterday's field trip, to describe an imaginary land, or to

Teaching Principle 7: Provide primary language opportunities to talk about past and future events, fantasy, and imaginary worlds.

Teaching Principle 8: Prompt children to use primary language in sociodramatic play.

describe the life cycle of a silkworm to a child who has neither observed this cycle directly nor seen it represented in pictures. Decontextualized language refers to language that is used away from ongoing experience or supportive context. Literacy experiences are a rich source of decontextualized language. Children experience imaginary lands and new experiences in books. They can make up stories through writing. During storytelling activities they can talk about past or future experiences. The use of decontextualized language fosters children's ability to rely on language by itself as a source for learning. This ability to learn from language is at the heart of academic, school learning. Therefore, as children gain skill in their ability to learn from decontextualized primary language as they use it during literacy experiences, their primary language and a linguistic foundation for literacy achievement in L1 or L2 is strengthened. Put simply, early literacy experiences in a language expose children to more decontextualized use of that language.

Another benefit to primary language development that could come from primary language literacy instruction is vocabulary growth. Many different types of literacy experiences have the potential for helping children learn new vocabulary. Experiences such as storybook reading, story retelling, language-rich sociodramatic play, cooperative language experiences, and one-to-one conversations can provide children opportunities to learn new and sophisticated words. If these experiences occur in the primary language, then the vocabulary benefits will directly accrue to that language.

Apply Your Knowledge

Write two conversation-starter topics to inspire children's talking within each of the following five categories: past and future events, fantasy, imagination, and sociodramatic play. Here are a few examples: Past—What did you do yesterday after you got home from preschool? Future—What would you like to do for a perfect play date with a friend?

> Imagination—Let's make up the funniest looking creature we can think of! What would it look like? Sociodramatic play—Story prompt for the farm center: "It's time to get the animals into the barn—there's a big storm coming! There are three of us to do it. Let's get started!"

PRIMARY LANGUAGE RESOURCES

Thoughtful consideration of the cultural, social, emotional, personal identity, and literacy learning support that can be realized from preservation and utilization of the primary language leads to the conclusion that efforts to do so are warranted. To accomplish this goal, preschool programs need rich and varied primary language resources for use in the classroom. The most significant of these resources is likely to be teachers who are bilingual or trilingual themselves. While this assertion is likely to be uncomfortable for some, it is

> **Educational Principle 5:**
> Identify and recruit as many primary language capable resources as possible.

critical to recognize that the ability to build language is dependent on resources in the target language. An established fact of language acquisition is that the quality of the language model the child learns from is one of the most important resources for language development. This principle applies in both L1 and L2 acquisition. When teachers have more than English language resources, they should be encouraged to use them, and when teachers use a particular language, children will also elect to use it more (Chesterfield et al., 1983; Paradis & Nicoladis, 2007). In addition to teachers, there are many other primary language resources that might be recruited to develop and sustain primary language as shown in the following box:

Language Capable/Bilingual Resources

- Teachers, assistant teachers, bilingual paraprofessionals
- Parents, extended family, and other caregivers
- Siblings and classmates
- Other preschool staff and support personnel
- Primary language television, Internet, video, and educational software
- Community ethnic and faith-based organizations
- Primary language literacy materials: storybooks, children's magazines, educational games, and so forth
- Other resources identified by staff, students, and community members

Apply Your Knowledge

How can you identify these primary language resources? Who are the teachers, assistants, and other staff at your site who have dual language competencies? Who are the family caregivers that might participate as primary language resources in the classroom or setting? Examine the Scholastic Books Web site to find what materials are offered in languages other than English. Are there primary language afterschool or Saturday school classes for children in your community? Are there any community groups or libraries that have materials? Can any of the funds for your program be used to purchase primary language literacy materials? What are more ideas for locating both human and material primary language resources?

PRACTICES FOR SUPPORTING
PRIMARY LANGUAGE AT HOME

Children's homes are a rich source of primary oral language. Children's homes are not troubled by the same lack of language capable people as are many preschool settings. Family caregivers and children will most likely share the same language. What may be much more limited in children's homes will be written and other material resources in primary language such as books, software, and so forth. In fact studies show that children from low-income families, no matter what their primary language, have only a limited number of literacy-related resources (McLoyd, 1998). Two important focuses for supporting primary language in home settings then are to marshal the oral language resources that are available and to supplement existing primary language literacy materials.

One key first step for marshalling the primary oral language resources in children's homes is to communicate the reasons why using primary language is beneficial to children. In my studies, I have encountered family caregivers of preschool English learners who are so motivated for their children to learn English that they may request that their child be grouped only with English-only children, that they ask that their child receive English storybooks even after they have told us that there are no adults who read English in the home, and who will attempt to use English with their children in spite of their very low level of proficiency with it. Helping families use the language that they and their children know best is important for promoting and maintaining primary language and for fostering social-emotional development and cognitive development. An example of one approach for helping family caregivers appreciate the benefit of primary language is highlighted in the following box.

Helping Family Caregivers Appreciate the Benefit of Using Primary Language

In one preschool setting, a primary language storybook reading program was introduced to the families of children in the preschool classrooms. Some family caregivers were unsure about using primary language storybooks for reading at home. I made arrangements to attend a Spanish-speaking caregivers' group meeting and to have storybook reading practices placed on the agenda. Prior to the meeting, I arranged to have one of the English-Spanish bilingual parents who worked in the preschool classroom and her daughter provide a storybook reading demonstration at this meeting where the mother would read the storybook in English and then Spanish. When book reading occurred in English, the mother read the book verbatim, and the child was silent. When the mother switched to reading in Spanish, her own reading became more animated and went beyond the words on the page as she responded to her daughter's eager verbal participation. Mother and daughter shared much positive emotional interaction with smiling and "back and forthing" as well. The benefit of using primary language was concretely demonstrated for the participating family caregivers.

Reading storybooks, telling traditional folk tales and other stories, recounting events from the past, and making up new stories in either the first or second language are oral language practices that can promote facility with decontextualized language and expose children to new, varied, and challenging vocabulary. Providing classic storybooks in children's primary languages for at-home reading, encouraging primary language storytelling and retelling, and encouraging family caregivers to engage with language in ways that are enjoyable can provide challenging words and expose the children to important ways of using language in their familial and cultural lives.

Exposure to decontextualized and emotionally supportive language has been found to differentiate children's home environments (DeTemple, 2001) and to lead to literacy achievement as discussed previously. Establishing opportunities for family caregivers, older siblings, and others with primary language ability to use primary language in classrooms for similar decontextualized and emotionally supportive language experiences will benefit preschool English learners' language and literacy development. Even in situations in which the teacher is not dual language competent, primary language can receive a fair amount of support in preschool settings by locating and collaborating with others who have this dual language competence. I am not proficient in either Hmong or Spanish, but I have found ways to work with bilingual teaching assistants and bilingual family caregivers to write letters about program activities to other family caregivers; to write children's stories in primary languages; to help translate and clarify social-emotional issues between children; to translate children's storybooks into multiple languages; to collect real life material written in different languages from homes, churches, grocery stores, and so forth; and to provide training on storybook reading practices. Older children who speak or read various primary languages have served as language guides during art, building, and play center time and as language facilitators in sociodramatic play centers when given specific prompts to expand creativity and increase language. Older children really seem to enjoy these activities.

Practices for Marshalling Primary Language Resources at Home and in Classrooms

- Request that families use primary language with their preschool children.
- Help families take pictures of their families, communities, and activities and create oral or written descriptions of them.
- Suggest that family caregivers tell fables and family histories to their children.
- Send home regular, specific suggestions for using primary language for literacy learning.
- Encourage families to write stories their children dictate.
- Read storybooks aloud to children in primary language.

Resources Needed for Home Primary Language Use

- Storybooks in primary language
- Story pictures and small flannel boards for story retelling
- Paper and writing implements
- Models of the alphabet
- Web site addresses for sites in various languages

DIFFERENT PRIMARY LANGUAGE PROGRAMS

Cummins (1999, 2000) argues that the fundamental criterion for a program to effectively promote and preserve primary language and also build the critical English skills necessary for English learners is that the goal is for children to be bilingual. The term *bilingual* refers to children who are equally proficient in spoken and written language in both their L1 and L2.

However, even at maturity, most bilingual individuals have different levels of proficiency in their two languages. Many bilingual adults have a language that they feel more skilled in or more comfortable with or simply prefer. They may also have different degrees of balance in more specific components of their two languages. For example, they may have stronger pronunciation in one language and write better in the other.

There are many different models and approaches for bilingual education that can be used successfully. In addition to the goal of balanced bilingualism discussed above, other essential ingredients are that the program must be of sufficient duration, must have strong human and material resources in both languages, must have an articulated plan for how oral and written proficiency in the two languages will be orchestrated across the program duration, and must create the sociopolitical conditions that are affirming of children's identity, families, and cultures. It is even the case that children may learn to read first in L1 *or* L2. The box that follows shows important characteristics of these potentially effective bilingual programs.

Essential Characteristics of Effective Bilingual Programs

Goal

Bilingualism: Speaking, reading, and writing proficiency in both languages

Sufficient Duration

Four to ten years

Articulation and planning with K–6 partners

Human Resources

Bilingual teachers

Teachers with shared goal of bilingualism and affirmation of children's personal, family, and cultural identity

Family and community involvement and support

Material Resources

Teaching and learning materials for oral language development, reading, writing, spelling, and content area learning in each language

Organized into a comprehensive program that can be explained by those using it

Represent experiences and values of participating children

(Continued)

(Continued)

Plan for Orchestrating Written and Oral Language

Usually begin with minimum of 50% L1 instruction, moving to 70% to 90% L2 instruction by Grade 6

May structure language according to different days, subjects, times (does not simply translate between languages)

May teach reading initially in L1 or L2, with specific strategies to transition to reading in the alternate language

A type of program with very promising possibilities is a *two-way immersion program,* also called a *dual language program.* In two-way immersion programs, the goal for participating children is to become fully bilingual in both language and literacy. In these programs, children from both minority and majority language groups participate and are immersed in large amounts of both L1 and L2. For example, a two-way immersion program could include both English-only and Spanish-primary language children and would have an organized program for extensively using both languages. Children might do center time and storybook reading in Spanish, while art activities and alphabet learning experiences are conducted in English. Another variation would be to teach the first half of the day in Spanish and the second half of the day in English.

Most two-way immersion or dual language programs have been implemented with elementary school children. The results show at least comparable growth in English compared to English-only instructional programs, whether the student's primary language is English or the other language. Many of these studies show greater English reading performance—if you are patient—with the clearest evidence of benefits observable after about sixth grade (August & Hakuta, 1997; August & Shanahan, 2008; Cheung & Slavin, 2005; Genesee et al., 2006; Rolstad, Mahoney, & Glass, 2005). And of course in the two-way programs, there is the added benefit of higher performance in the non-majority language as well (Lindholm & Aclan, 1991).

There have been a few studies with preschool English learners and English-only children in two-way immersion programs showing similar positive results (Barnett, Yarosz, Thomas, Jung, & Blanco, 2007; Campbell & Sais, 1995; Campos, 1995). The Barnett et al. study is particularly significant, because children were assigned to either a two-way or an English-only program on a random basis. When children are assigned to programs on a random basis, we can have the greatest confidence that there are no important differences in the children in each of the programs being compared that could influence the outcomes. The study included three- and four-year-old children and lasted for one year. At the end of the year, children in both groups showed evidence of language and literacy gains. Child in the two-way immersion program performed just as well on measures in English as children who received all their instruction in English. And of course, children performed better in Spanish as a result of being in the two-way immersion program. One issue with this study though is that teachers in the two-way immersion program were more educated, and the two-way immersion program was longer each day.

The achievement data, social-emotional outcomes, and goal of valuing diversity all point to the desirability of fully bilingual education experience for English learners. There is much to be gained and no evidence of anything that is lost, including English language or English literacy achievement. The discussion also identifies the careful planning, comprehensiveness, and long-term educational support needed for these programs to be successful. A low-quality bilingual education program without sufficient commitment, resources, effective program features, qualified teachers, or duration may produce worse literacy achievement than a high-quality, nonbilingual program.

Local policies and school/student population conditions may limit early childhood professionals' ability to provide true bilingual programs. In situations where bilingual programs are not an option, it is still possible to have classroom practices that richly incorporate primary language and use primary language as tools for helping children access the English literacy curriculum. There is good evidence that English learners can learn literacy foundations in English at the preschool level (reviewed in Ehri & Roberts, 2006) and learn to read in English quite well in the early grades even in the presence of limited English proficiency (Geva & Zadeh, 2006).

A new project that I am working on that involves using the primary language for second language literacy learning is a bilingual teaching toolkit that accompanies an English literacy program used in an Early Reading First project. Early Reading First

> **Educational Principle 6:** Implement high-quality bilingual preschool literacy programs.
>
> **Educational Principle 7:** Plan very carefully how and for how long each language will be used.
>
> **Educational Principle 8:** Partner with K–6 schools to develop bilingual programs that will continue for three or four years after the students leave preschool.

projects are funded by the U.S. Department of Education. Their focus is to promote preschool language and literacy foundations for at-risk children, specifically including English learners. This toolkit is directly aligned with the thematic units in the English literacy program and includes specific activities and lessons for ELLs on the core literacy components of the program using program materials. The lessons specify when to use L1 and when to use L2. The activities are designed for small groups of three to six students. Bilingual resource teachers have been trained and coached in how to use these materials.

SPENDING "TIME ON TASK" IN ENGLISH

"Time on task" is a central argument used to either explicitly or implicitly challenge policies, programs, or practices that position primary language preservation and growth as an important educational outcome. "Time on task" refers to the idea that the more time children spend using and learning L2, the greater will be their L2 proficiency. Devoting instructional time and educational resources to L1 deprives learners of valuable time for learning L2, according to the time on task idea (Porter, 1998). While the logic of this argument may be appealing, the evidence does not support it. There are two sets of research results that show the time-on-task argument to be inaccurate (August & Hakuta, 1997; Cummins, 2000; Genesee et al., 2006; Rolstad et al., 2005).

The first set of results are those that show students do not have lower academic skills in their second language when they participate in a substantial amount of instruction in their primary language. The second set of results are those that show there is no positive relationship between student outcomes and the amount of English instruction children receive.

The major problem with the time-on-task argument is that it assumes that the processes involved in acquiring both language and literacy in two languages are not related. It assumes that each language system is separate and not communicating with and helping the other. As we have seen, though, the two languages developing in a child are members of a highly cooperative and interactive team. The team name is Language Interdependence, and the two teammates are L1 and L2. They work together to accomplish more than could either one alone. They share common spaces in the brain, with each individual language also marked separately. This organization in the brain can be thought of like a language house with separate spaces for aspects of each of the languages the house is structured from. The issue of time on task provides a good opportunity for noting the importance of always examining the research, as there are many things that may seem logical from one perspective, yet the evidence actually supports a different logic.

PATIENCE IN ACHIEVING BILINGUALISM

However, for early childhood educators there is an important challenge that needs to be recognized. It may take several years of participating in a high-quality dual language program before its full benefits are realized. Estimates, and not very precise ones, are that it takes between four and seven years before achievement in a second language will catch up to achievement in the primary language. Thus, children and teachers participating in early childhood programs supporting the goal of full bilingualism may be under particularly intense internal and external pressure, as children will not likely show equal levels of oral and literacy proficiency in their two languages for several years. But remember, there are no compelling reasons to think that if we abandon the primary language and provide English-only instruction, no matter how high the quality, students will achieve oral and literacy proficiency any better or any faster. While both languages can be working together, and effective programs will find ways to promote this communication between the two languages, there is a bigger language-learning space for aspiring bilingual preschoolers to travel, and it will take them more time (Genesee et al., 2006). So, fellow travelers, hold the course, be an excellent guide, and patience, patience, patience.

Educational Principle 9: Allow sufficient time for bilingualism to develop.

Teaching Principle 9: Measure language proficiency in both L1 and L2.

CONCLUSION

Maintaining, using, and enhancing primary language is important for familial, cultural, personal, emotional, and cognitive reasons. Primary language can be used effectively in a variety of ways when the goal of bilingualism is embraced and shared among children, families, preschool settings, and the larger community. Careful planning for bilingual programs of sufficient duration and intensity in each language, when accompanied by teachers with strong language resources in each language and high-quality literacy materials and practices in home and school, can result in bilingualism— which means being strong in both the primary language and English. In contexts where bilingual programs are not feasible and where teachers themselves may not be proficient in more than one language, there are still many ways to effectively incorporate and draw upon children's primary language resources that will serve to maintain and enhance primary language and contribute to strong English literacy. A commitment to the goal of bilingualism will lead to a discovery of resources and application of research-suggested practices that will truly scaffold and build with primary language. And remember patience, patience, patience.

Summary of Teaching Principles

Teaching Principle 1: Use primary language for both cognitive and social-emotional purposes.

Teaching Principle 2: Implement literacy experiences at home in L1 or L2 depending on home language resources.

Teaching Principle 3: Incorporate ways of using language that are familiar to English learner children.

Teaching Principle 4: When using language in ways less familiar to children, explain what is expected, demonstrate the practice, and allow time for English learners to become familiar with it.

Teaching Principle 5: When using language in ways less familiar to children, select topics and activities that will motivate children to use these new ways.

Teaching Principle 6: Group children who speak the same language together for some literacy activities.

Teaching Principle 7: Provide primary language opportunities to talk about past and future events, fantasy, and imaginary worlds.

Teaching Principle 8: Prompt children to use primary language in sociodramatic play.

Teaching Principle 9: Measure language proficiency in both L1 and L2.

Summary of Educational Principles

Educational Principle 1: Include maintenance and development of primary language as an explicit preschool program goal.

Educational Principle 2: Incorporate primary language and knowledge developed in primary language in preschool literacy experiences.

Educational Principle 3: Explain the value of primary language use to children and their families.

Educational Principle 4: Incorporate primary language for promoting strong social relationships.

Educational Principle 5: Identify and recruit as many primary language capable resources as possible.

Educational Principle 6: Implement high-quality bilingual preschool literacy programs.

Educational Principle 7: Plan very carefully how and for how long each language will be used.

Educational Principle 8: Partner with K–6 schools to develop bilingual programs that will continue for three to four years after the students leave preschool.

Educational Principle 9: Allow sufficient time for bilingualism to develop.

3 Oral Language Development in a Second Language

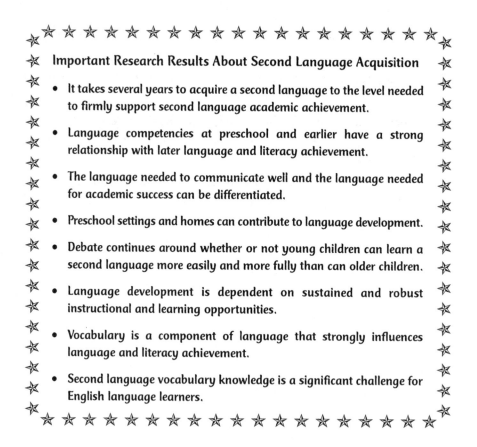

✸ **Important Research Results About Second Language Acquisition**

- It takes several years to acquire a second language to the level needed to firmly support second language academic achievement.

- Language competencies at preschool and earlier have a strong relationship with later language and literacy achievement.

- The language needed to communicate well and the language needed for academic success can be differentiated.

- Preschool settings and homes can contribute to language development.

- Debate continues around whether or not young children can learn a second language more easily and more fully than can older children.

- Language development is dependent on sustained and robust instructional and learning opportunities.

- Vocabulary is a component of language that strongly influences language and literacy achievement.

- Second language vocabulary knowledge is a significant challenge for English language learners.

Language development and literacy development, while related, are different processes. Both enable children to store in the brain what they know about the world and to further develop the knowledge they have stored. In addition, both language and literacy development are supported when they are used in the context of personal, familial, and cultural experiences (Dickinson & Tabors, 2001). Other features of language development differentiate it from literacy acquisition. Language development in the preschool period is primarily an oral competence, while reading and writing are tied to print. Children all over the world develop language even in absence of specific teaching or schooling, but learning to read and write must be taught with significant amounts of teaching effort.

While it may appear that language development occurs spontaneously through exposure to language, it requires significant language development opportunity and is a very complex learning process. Family caregivers and other adults serve as important guides and models for language learning. Differences in how caregivers and other adults guide and model language use substantially influence child language competence. Fortunately, there is a wealth of research that has yielded an understanding of how children acquire both first and second language and how variations in these acquisition opportunities lead to differences in language strength. An important insight from this research related to literacy is that there is a distinction between the *basic oral language* competence that enables children to effectively interact within their families and other social groups and the *academic language* that is necessary for high levels of literacy learning and school achievement. A related insight from the research is that the number of words that children know, their *vocabulary knowledge*, is a pivotal component of language competence for literacy acquisition and school achievement (Biemiller & Boote, 2006; Scarborough, 2001).

Providing language-learning opportunities that incorporate features maximizing language development is particularly important for English learners who are acquiring a second language. This chapter focuses on explaining how children acquire language, particularly a second language, and what classroom and home opportunities can promote it. It explains how to plan and implement classroom centers, adult-child conversation, mealtimes, classroom transitions, and sociodramatic play in ways that build second language. Specific attention is given to academic language and vocabulary learning because of the pivotal role they play in literacy learning. Language learning is complex when one language is being learned and more so when children are learning two. The complexity of language learning necessarily leads to the need for sophisticated and multifaceted classroom practices to enhance it. A teacher who understands well how children learn a first and a second language will be able to engineer and provide the myriad types of preschool language experiences essential for strong second language learning. So this chapter is a lengthy one. Feel free to take it in pieces—it is divided into many sections. The following graph shows the major topics that are covered in this chapter and the flow of the chapter. Spend a little time reviewing the graph in Figure 3.1, as it will help you get the big ideas about second language development that are covered in this complex chapter. Take the time you need to reflect, review, and digest all that is here.

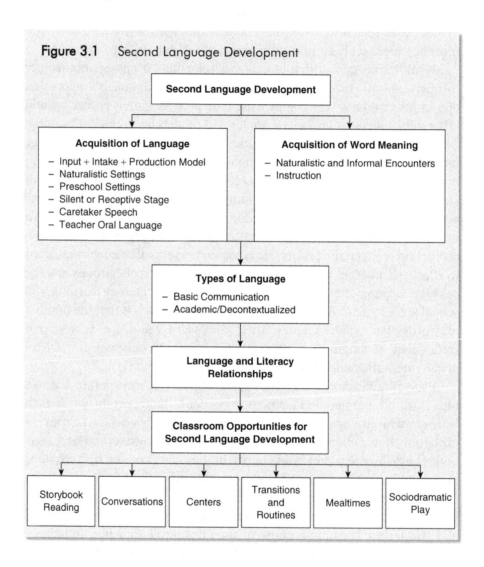

Figure 3.1 Second Language Development

SECOND LANGUAGE LEARNING IN NATURALISTIC SETTINGS

To promote language development, it is necessary to have an understanding of how languages are learned. A very brief explanation of this complex process is provided in this section. Luckily, the processes involved in learning a first language are similar to those for learning a second. Both are dependent on the language experiences children are exposed to and their engagement with those opportunities. At first blush, it appears that children learn language easily and almost automatically. Indeed, the human species appears to have a "language instinct" (Pinker, 1994). In spite of this biological foundation for language learning, a great deal of exposure and an extended period of time is needed for language development. And it is not exposure alone, because variations in the amount and quality of that exposure will also significantly impact the ultimate language competence of a child. In an extended and very detailed analysis of the vocabulary development of a small group of English-only children, Hart and Risley (1995) found that both the number of words that children had heard in their homes and the number of different words included in child-directed talk before age three were the two factors having the greatest influence on later language and school achievement. In addition to exposure or *input*, children must *intake* the language they hear. It is necessary to attend to language and to have some capacity to understand and remember what has been heard. These are *receptive language* skills. To have full language power, language use or *language production* is necessary. This is the simple model of second language development used in this chapter:

Language input (caregivers, others) +
Language intake (child) + Language production (child)
⟶ **Language Learning**

Children acquire substantial competence in four major areas—or domains—of their first language in their first five years. These domains are *semantics, phonology, syntax,* and *pragmatics* (Gass & Selinker, 2001). *Semantics* includes the meaning part of language. Children learn the meaning of words and larger chunks of language such as sentences and whole discourses or "stories." *Phonology* is concerned with the sounds used in a language to construct individual words. Children learn how to produce, overlap, and use the sounds of their language. Children learn the three individual sounds in the word "cat" (/c/ /a/ /t/) and how to combine them together. *Syntax* refers to a language's rules that govern how words are put together to make utterances. Children learn the syntax rules needed to correctly communicate the difference between "The dog bit Cassidy" and "Cassidy bit the dog." *Pragmatics* refers to the ability to use language effectively in social settings and is tied to the language values, usage, and

Teaching Principle 1: Include practices for developing all four of the domains of English: *semantics, phonology, syntax,* and *pragmatics.*

Teaching Principle 2: Plan lessons and activities that provide language *input,* promote *intake,* and ensure *production* from all children.

practices shared by speakers of a particular language. There are differences between languages, for example, in how turn-taking in conversation proceeds. Some language groups use overlapping turns, while others expect one speaker to finish before another begins. Developing proficiency in all four major areas is important.

Preschool English learners vary in how much English they have been exposed to prior to entering preschool. English learners will need to develop all four of these areas in English in order to have strong English and learn to read well in English. Yet for most preschool English learners in the United States, their strongest language will be the language that is used most extensively in their homes, which is very likely to be a non-English language. The semantics, phonology, syntax, and pragmatics of their primary language will be a filter influencing how these same four language domains are augmented with English language knowledge (Brown, 1998; Geva, Wade-Woolley, & Shany, 1997). While it is commonly believed that children will have the most difficulty with aspects of second language that are not included in their first language, this is not necessarily the case. For example, when children use sound in primary language that is similar to a new English sound, there is a tendency to ignore the subtle difference and to treat the new sound as if it were the sound from the first language. An example of this occurs in Spanish when the English /v/ is treated as the similar Spanish /b/ and the Spanish primary language child says "biolin" (violin) or "bery" (very).

Apply Your Knowledge

On a sheet of paper, make a chart labeled with the four domains of language: semantics, phonology, syntax, and pragmatics, as shown in the example below. Under each heading, list activities that address the four domains of language that you have used or could use or that are included in your language and literacy teaching materials or program. Some sample activities are included to help you get started.

Semantics (Meaning)	Phonology (Sounds in Words)	Syntax (Word Order and Grammar Rules)	Pragmatics (How to Use Language for Social Purposes)
1. Teach storybook words before reading.	1. Children practice sounds of alphabet letters.	1. Change word order of phrases using objects: "The girl ate the apple." "The apple ate the girl."	1. Model saying "please" and "thank you."
2. Teach words of objects in centers.	2. Children use mirrors to watch their mouths as they copy the teacher saying d-o-g.	2. Children correct the grammar mistakes of teacher: "I no find my book." "I have books two."	2. Model how to ask for help.
3. Children tell stories with flannel board.			

SECOND LANGUAGE LEARNING IN PRESCHOOL SETTINGS

To this point, we have focused on how children learn language in naturalistic settings. Preschool settings are a different context where the adult/child ratios, language variations among children and adults, and instructional practices introduce additional factors into language development. Children's opportunities for learning English from peers—who can serve as positive models and interaction partners when they have strong English skills—will vary depending on the mix of children in the classroom. When there are fewer English learners, there are likely to be more high-quality

English peer models available. Yet challenges with English learner children feeling emotionally comfortable may be more prevalent. When there are many English learners (which is increasingly common, particularly in schools serving children from low-income families), informal English learning opportunities from peers will be more limited, because fewer children will be proficient in English.

In both preschool settings just described, the teacher(s) will have the strongest English language skills. Yet due to the high child/adult ratio, her language resources for providing the kind of ongoing, one-to-one, or very small group interactions that characterize children's language learning in home settings and provide for rich language modeling will be stretched. A constant focus on how to distribute teacher language resources to benefit the most children is needed in preschool settings. Group learning opportunities where teachers provide high-quality language input is one means for children to receive maximal amounts of English language *input,* particularly in settings where there are many English learners. *Intake* is promoted by providing experiences where children's motivation and interest is activated or when they can connect what is being talked about to things they have some experience with. Language *production* can be encouraged in these settings by creating a desire to speak, by allowing choral responding or other forms of emotionally safe production (particularly when asking children to stretch their production capabilities), by creating a warm emotional climate, and by structuring production requests that are sensitive to the child's level of English proficiency. For example, "yes" or "no" questions may be appropriate for those children with the most limited English, for others providing a partial sentence where they only have to fill in a word or two, and for more proficient children expecting a child-constructed utterance. Language production requires the orchestration of all four domains of language: semantics, phonology, syntax, and pragmatics. English learners may take longer to construct each utterance as they search for words, puzzle out correct word order and grammar, and use their speech apparatus to make sounds they are just learning. Give them time to respond.

EXAMINING THE SILENT OR RECEPTIVE LANGUAGE STAGE IN SECOND LANGUAGE ACQUISITION

The simple model of language development that I have presented in this chapter includes language use or language production as one of the three major components for language development:

Language input (caregivers, others) +
Language intake (child) + Language production (child)
⟶ **Language Learning**

Yet you may have been taught that English learners have a *silent period* in second language acquisition (e.g., Tabors, 1997). An extension of the silent period idea is that teachers should not expect, or press for, language use until children reach the stage where they begin to use language on their own—which has been suggested as possibly taking a year to emerge. This is a very long time to wait for language production, for reasons soon to be explained. The suggestion that a silent period exists in second language acquisition has been based on what children have been observed to do spontaneously in a limited number of descriptive studies (e.g., Dulay & Burt, 1974; Saville-Troike, 1988; Tabors, 1997). This is different from what children may be invited, encouraged, and led to do in the presence of instruction or interactions with teachers and other skilled language users. And it is likely important for the child's literacy achievement that they produce oral English. The reasons why this is so are explained in the following paragraphs.

Evidence on connections between hearing, speaking, and learning exists for all of the four domains of language (semantics, phonology, syntax, and pragmatics). Language production consolidates language learning. To learn words (semantics) children must store the word's meaning *and* the word's pronunciation in memory. Speech sounds of a language (phonology) are closely tied to the movement of the lips, tongue, nose, throat, and so forth that produce them (Browman & Goldstein, 1986, 1989; Liberman, 1999; Nittrouer, Studdert-Kennedy, & McGowan, 1989). Therefore, when children produce oral language, they refine their understanding of the individual sounds of the language they are speaking. Language use also makes language sounds, words, and sentence structures (syntax) more concrete, because concrete information from the child's speech apparatus and body are

Teaching Principle 3:
Create English language use situations that are emotionally safe, such as choral responding, simple repetition activities, talking in pairs with a peer, and small groups.

Educational Principle 1: Strive for English language use (production) from all children in all domains (semantics, phonology, syntax, and pragmatics) of language.

Educational Principle 2: Be patient and helpful in getting children to speak English.

involved when language is spoken. Emerging evidence suggests that how well children, including English learners, pronounce words influences literacy acquisition (Liberman, 1999; Roberts, 2005). Learning to effectively use language for social purposes (pragmatics) is dependent upon orally using language with others. Thus, the use of language ties together the hearing and speaking processes and enables meaningful communication with others. Producing language confers many language benefits.

Early care and education professionals should be sensitive to possible variations in children's inclination to use language by showing gentleness, encouragement, and patience as they aspire to engage more reticent children in language use. Providing language use situations in which the child wants to participate, can respond with others, and has a teacher who is a supportive partner helping them along can enable children to comfortably engage in English oral language production as they are just beginning to acquire English. Several specific practices for encouraging English language production are presented in the following box.

Practices to Encourage Early Oral Language Production

- Singing
- Group recitation of repeated poems and nursery rhymes
- Choral (group) responding
- Peer partner activities
- Individual pretend reading of familiar and new books
- Finger plays
- Participation in repeated storybook reading
- Chanting along with predictable books
- Interaction with English speaking models in dyads and informal settings such as sociodramatic play and centers

> ### Apply Your Knowledge
>
> If you are a teacher, select a child from your class who uses English the least; if you're not a teacher, imagine a child who is in an English preschool setting and does not speak except when she is riding bikes with other children. You have noticed that all of her language interaction is in the primary language. Based on the three teaching principles above, write ideas for how you could entice this child into English language use. Plan something for every day of one week.

LEARNING ABOUT LANGUAGE ACQUISITION FROM CAREGIVERS

Around the world, caretakers use very similar language practices with their young children. This speech may be referred to as *motherese, caretaker speech,* or *child-directed speech* (Snow, 1977). This type of language is structured to help children to understand ongoing activity and to embed it in language *and* to challenge children to expand their language capabilities. Language related to the immediate activities and environment is most used. Caregivers will talk about food items during mealtimes and will talk about a family member working on a car as they are doing it. Caregivers also respond to meaning (semantics) over form (correctness of syntax rules or phonology). These practices are the same ones that can be used to help English learner preschoolers develop their basic English competence, described earlier in this chapter.

Yet, caregivers also present children with language structures and words that are more complex than those of the child's current language ability, which is necessary for further language learning. When children encounter linguistic input that is slightly more difficult than their current level of functioning, their language competence grows. For example, in teaching their child new vocabulary words, caregivers may initially use the new word at the end of a simple sentence and use pointing, voice changes, and other strategies to help their child acquire the meaning of that word. They may say, "Here are some grapes" as they hold up a cluster of grapes. Later on they may use the new word in a five- to seven-word sentence even though the child is only producing two-word utterances. "The grapes look like tiny balls and they taste very sweet." Caregivers craft language development by both meeting children where they are and by helping them move linguistically forward.

Teaching Principle 4: Be a good model of caretaker speech.

Teaching Principle 5: Embed language in all of the activities children engage in (block, large motor, science, routines, play, book-reading).

Teaching Principle 6: Follow children's lead by responding to and extending their language.

Early care and education professionals who use these same types of practices will promote children's second language acquisition. They will provide children ample opportunity for meaningful conversation and language use in the presence of ongoing activity. They will also offer children language that stretches their current abilities. Expansions of children's language—adding new related information, asking clarifying questions, and answering children's questions—are examples of adult talk, focused on meaning, that will promote language development (Wells, 1985). Language growth is also fostered by adult use of more sophisticated vocabulary, or what Dickinson and Tabors (2001) call "rare words."

Children who are acquiring basic English need to experience language linked to ongoing activity where the conversational partners (adults, others) are listening to and responding to each other. Small-group language activities with the teacher are an important way to maximize English language exposure. Linking language with art, mathematics, science, and play activities enhances children's language acquisition through the availability of rich context. These practices also foster concept development by helping children represent in language what they are learning in art, math, science, and play.

Yet experiences with challenging language are also important for second language development, particularly for developing the academic language important for English school achievement. Exposing English learners to language more sophisticated than what they can use, asking them questions that will call for more than one-word responses, encouraging use of their emerging abilities in oral production, teaching and using challenging vocabulary, and presenting opportunities to use more decontextualized language are some of these important language expanding possibilities.

Apply Your Knowledge

Use the following summary of the characteristics of caretaker speech to evaluate how extensively you use these second language development practices as an early care and education professional. If you are not a teacher, estimate how extensively you think you might use them (1 means a lower self-rating; 5 means a higher self-rating). What did you learn about your professional practice from this exercise?

Characteristics of Caretaker Speech					
1. Emphasize talking that goes with what children are currently doing.	1	2	3	4	5
2. Add to what children say, ask them questions, and respond to their questions.	1	2	3	4	5
3. Engage in conversation where several turns are shared.	1	2	3	4	5
4. Use vocabulary that is new and challenging.	1	2	3	4	5
5. Focus on meaning rather than "correctness" of language.	1	2	3	4	5
6. Help children express in language what they are learning in math, art, and so forth.	1	2	3	4	5
7. Present children with language expressions, forms, and words that stretch their language ability.	1	2	3	4	5

CULTURAL VARIATIONS IN CAREGIVER SPEECH AND A CHALLENGE FOR EDUCATORS

Although the basic nature of caretaker speech is similar across many cultural groups, there are notable differences. Cultural differences in language pragmatics, or how language is used for social purposes, may result in caregivers using more or less language with children at different ages. There is also cultural variation in talkativeness. Several years ago, I traveled between Finland and Italy on the same day. While riding a public bus

Educational Principle 3:
Find out how home language use is similar to or different from school language use.

Educational Principle 4: Talk with families and other professionals about how to address the differences.

in Finland, I was repeatedly struck by how quiet the passengers were. I was rather painfully self-conscious in this experience and wondered if my presence had created it. Later that day as I stepped off the plane in Florence, Italy, I immediately experienced a very noisy, even raucous airport handling crew. Life in the cultural differences in pragmatics lane!

These types of differences are associated with a very challenging issue related to language development and school achievement. Children and their families have learned to use language in different ways. There are important reasons to accept and validate these differences. Yet at the same time, there is extensive research that repeatedly documents, with both English-only and English learner children, relationships between children's academic and decontextualized language use and school achievement. In addition many studies show that home practices where there is a great deal of talking from early on and talking where children are considered conversational partners contributes to early and later literacy achievement (Dickinson & Tabors, 2001; Hart & Risley, 1995; Landry & Smith, 2006; Raikes et al., 2006; Wells, 1985). When to alter classroom language to accommodate these differences and when to press for change or augmentation of home language practices is another of those hot topics. A critical step for moving forward on this issue is to talk about it as a challenge. A second critical step is to foster respectful, broad thinking and discussion on how it can best be addressed. All stakeholders, including families and community representatives as well as early care and education professionals, should be involved in the discussion. What ideas or experiences do you have with how to respond to variations in how language is used in different primary languages?

Apply Your Knowledge

Imagine that you observe a parent who does not respond during several attempts by his or her child to get the parent to look at a fancy bike that is parked in front of the daycare home where you work. The child asks questions: "Whose bike is it?" "Where do you get a bike like that?" and makes comments: "Wow a polka dot bike" and receives no response from the adult except "Don't touch it." How do you respond? You're informed that this is fairly typical of how adults and children interact in language X. Does this change your response at all? Should the daycare try to increase the level of adult response to child language? Or should the daycare accept it and emphasize more responsive practices in the home? How sure are you of your views? What are they based on?

LANGUAGE FOR BASIC COMMUNICATION AND ACADEMIC LEARNING

When children enter preschool, they typically have a basic system of primary-language oral communication that is effective for navigating their familial and social contexts (Pinker, 1994). The school setting builds on these basic competencies. Children also experience increasing exposure to language that requires them to make meaning from language that is set apart from ongoing activity and concrete support (Snow, 1983; Wells, 1985). Children are asked to learn concepts and language from language alone. For example, typically in early development children and their adult partners talk about experiences and activities as they are occurring. They talk about the food that is being eaten, they talk about their clothes as they are dressing, and an animal is named as it is seen in the street during a walk in the stroller. In decontextualized language experiences, children might learn about food they have never eaten while hearing a story about grocery stores, they might learn about traditional clothes worn in a cultural group different from their own by a child talking about it during circle time, and they might be introduced to the names of animals they have never seen when the teacher is telling about the meaning of the words "hog" and "frog" during a rhyming game. To learn to read, children will be asked to pay attention to the sounds of words rather than their meaning, and this too is a more abstract and decontextualized use of language.

For English learners these expectations for more decontextualized and abstract language use occur in a language in which they do not as yet have basic oral competence. Thus an important distinction between fostering basic English language acquisition and extending and building on basic language must be carefully structured into English learners' classroom experiences. A very significant challenge is how to provide novice English language learners with basic English acquisition *and* at the same time ensure they have access to the kinds of decontextualized and abstract language use that extend basic competence and are so important for high-level English literacy. So an important approach for planning language development for English learners

Educational Principle 5: Make a specific teaching plan for basic language development.

Educational Principle 6: Make a specific teaching plan for decontextualized/academic language development.

in early care and education settings is to differentiate and provide experiences for building

- basic language for oral communication and
- decontextualized language use and abstract language skill needed for academic success.

Apply Your Knowledge

Imagine that you are a child who walks into a preschool setting for the very first time and the language that is being used is Ugandan. What Ugandan words or phrases would be most important for you to have so that you could fit in, feel comfortable, and go with the flow? Write down 20 English words or phrases that would most help you. A few phrases that would be very useful to me are "I want" and "I have to use the bathroom." You have just begun to identify the nature of basic language competence.

HOW CHILDREN LEARN THE MEANING OF WORDS

Now that you have been given an introduction to how children learn language in general, you will be provided information to help you understand how children learn the meaning of words and the implications of this knowledge for preschool teaching. Recall that how many words children know is a strong predictor of how well they read in any language. In addition, vocabulary limitations pose a significant challenge for the language and literacy achievement of English learners (Fitzgerald, 1995; Garcia, 1991, 2000). Words also form the backbone of language meaning. That is why words or *vocabulary* is emphasized in this chapter on second language development. How do children learn words? What words do they learn in preschool? What words should they learn in preschool? A simple answer to the first question is that learning the meaning of words, or *vocabulary learning,* is similar to brushing your teeth in several respects. By studying the box below you can learn a great deal about how children learn words and about practices that can activate their word learning processes.

Vocabulary Learning Is Like Brushing Your Teeth

- Common experience that occurs every day
- Regular, repeated effort and attention necessary
- Technique and knowledge required
- Benefits are cumulative
- Objects and tools help
- Get better at it with time
- Easy to forget about its importance

Basically, English learner children have the capacity to learn many words every day. While they may have limited knowledge of English, they have a large amount of knowledge and experience in learning words in their first language. Children learn words with similar processes across languages. Vocabulary learning may even occur particularly quickly for English learner children when they know a word in their primary language, because all that is required for English vocabulary learning is an English label for a meaning they already have. Monolingual preschool children learn an average of about three new words per day (Bloom, 2000). There are certain kinds of information and processes that children use to learn words. When preschool teachers provide the types of information that helps children learn words and activate processes that help them secure their word knowledge in memory, children's vocabulary will grow.

The simple answer to how children learn words is that they learn them by hearing lots of them and by hearing a large number of different words. The teaching implication of this is to talk a lot and use many types of words. Talk! Talk! Talk! This point is particularly important in working with English learners, because well-meaning teachers may simplify and limit their talk and even consciously use mostly familiar and simple words. Large amounts of talk with many different words embedded in it provides the *input* needed for language learning within the *input* + *intake* + *production* = *language learning* process. There is also evidence that children's word learning strategies improve with time, and that it really is the case that children with larger vocabularies learn more words from both instruction designed to teach words and from more informal exposure to words in the environment. The vocabulary rich get richer and the poor stay poor (Stanovich, 1986). This point highlights the value of getting going on second language vocabulary development early and with vigor during the preschool years.

Now for a few more concepts on word learning that are not as simple as lots of words and lots of different types of words. Young children up to about the age of five use a process called *fast-mapping* for learning words (Carey, 1978). Think about the two words *fast* and *map*. Children *quickly* make meanings for words and make a *map* of the meanings and pronunciations in their brains. To learn a word you have to understand its meaning, learn its pronunciation, and remember both. Without the meaning you are lost. If you know a meaning and can't remember the word pronunciation that goes with it, you are also lost. Saying the word's pronunciation as it is being learned engages the oral production step of the *input + intake + production = language learning* process. You may have had this experience on a fill-in-the-blanks vocabulary test where you were asked to write the word that goes with a definition. You know the meaning but you can't find or remember the word for it! But there is a catch to this gift of mapping word meanings fast. While children map words in their brains very quickly—sometimes from hearing a word only one time—their initial mappings may be a little sloppy, or imprecise, because they were made so quickly. A child may learn the meaning of "dog" and then use it to refer to cats and pigs.

If children are also experiencing many words and many different types of words in their homes, they will be *fast-mapping* primary language words, and this will be a boon to their primary language development. A large primary language vocabulary is also beneficial for English vocabulary development, because children may only need to add the English label to their existing primary language word knowledge. When children have large primary language vocabularies, it will also support them in higher-level thinking, as strong language (either L1 or L2) supports strong thinking. The teaching implication of children being fast-mappers of word meaning is that English learners, even those who are just beginning to learn English, have the word-learning tools to benefit from exposure to lots of English words.

Teaching Principle 7: Expose children to many second language words and their meanings, and help children connect the meaning and the word pronunciation.

Teaching Principle 8: Have children say the words they are learning many times.

LEARNING WORDS FROM INSTRUCTION

In spite of the importance of vocabulary knowledge for both language and literacy, very little time is devoted to it in preschool settings through either explicit instruction or more informal means such as conversation or focusing on individual words during storybook reading. Connor, Morrison, and Slominski (2006) reported that teachers observed in high-quality preschool classrooms spent less than two minutes per hour (approximately) on vocabulary instruction. This amount of time is simply not sufficient.

There is growing consensus that explicit instruction in word meanings is an important approach for helping English-only children increase their vocabulary size. While English-only children are quite good at learning a word when they are given a clear definition of it, learning second language words from language alone may be more challenging for English learners due to their limited English proficiency. English learners may need the support of demonstration, pictures, or concrete "realia" to ensure that they are able to *intake* meanings of new words. Remember that *intake* is one of the components of the *input + intake + production = language learning* process. For example, to teach the meaning of *caterpillar,* a picture of one or a real one will be helpful to English learners. I have conducted three studies with preschool English learners using these realia along with verbal explanations to explicitly teach storybook vocabulary and have found with all three that English learners are little word-learning wizards (Roberts, 2008, in preparation; Roberts & Neal, 2004).

The maximum number of words that preschool children can learn from instruction is not known. Yet for preschool English learners, there are many, many to learn. Children will know many words in their first language that they do not know in their second language, as 40% to 70% of the total words estimated as known by bilingual children are known in only one language, and they are fast-mappers (Umbel, Pearson, Fernandez, & Oller, 1992). So reach for the stars. Based on computations that I have made to build a basic vocabulary for English words, I suggest about 12 to 15 new words a week to target in explicit teaching planned activities. This word-learning goal is quite reasonable based on word-learning studies with both English-only and English learner children. Of course, the myriad other language activities in addition to explicit vocabulary teaching will result in children having exposure to far more than 15 new words a week.

But what words to target? What words to teach? This is a question that is just beginning to be examined by researchers. Most of the vocabulary instruction research has been done with words related to school texts.

Teaching Principle 9: Teach vocabulary words every day.

Teaching Principle 10: Identify and teach 12 to 15 words per week.

Teaching Principle 11: Use pictures, actions, demonstrations, and concrete realia when teaching words.

Teaching Principle 12: Carefully select words that benefit children's basic language and words related to storybooks, classroom themes, and centers.

While this is certainly one important basis for word selection, preschool children who are English learners are in the process of acquiring basic oral communication in English. Words that aid comprehension of a particular storybook are different from words to support basic language competence. Selection of words to promote basic communication, provide access to storybook meaning, and support learning related to classroom themes and centers is needed.

Apply Your Knowledge

1. Imagine that you are creating a veterinarian center in a preschool setting. Make a list of all the vocabulary words related to it that could be taught. Now go through your list and select words that will be most useful for English learners' basic English communication competence. Go through the list again, and identify those words that will be most useful in the veterinarian center (more academic language). Compare the lists. How similar were they? Choose a final list of five words that you think it would be best to teach. What did you learn from this exercise? Here are some words to get you started: *animal, symptoms, sick, pain, chart, examine, head, foot, leg, tail, eye, nose, mouth, medicine.*

2. Select a favorite children's book. Go through the book and select eight words that will most help children get the main meaning from the book. Be careful not to choose words just because they would be easy or fun to teach. How could you teach the words you have selected? What objects, demonstrations, or explanations would help?

THE RELATIONSHIP BETWEEN ORAL
LANGUAGE AND SECOND LANGUAGE LITERACY

There is a strong relationship between children's oral language competence before they reach kindergarten age and their literacy achievement when they are learning to read in their first language (National Institute of Child Health and Human Development Early Child Care Research Network, 2005; Snow, Burns, & Griffin, 1998; Storch & Whitehurst, 2002). Research specific to ELLs reveals more complex relationships between oral proficiency and literacy. The research in this area is limited, particularly so for preschool age English learners, and even more so for language groups other than Spanish-speakers.

Let's look first at the role played by the first language in second language literacy. First, while it seems somewhat obvious, there is no evidence that L1 proficiency detracts from second language literacy. In fact, English learners draw upon their experiences and knowledge coded in their first language to help them meet the demands of second language literacy (Cunningham & Graham, 2000; Ordoñez, Carlo, Snow, & McLaughlin, 2002). This is a reminder of the supportive role that continued development of first language can play in second language learning. However, all children do not automatically use their first language resources to help in second language literacy. Therefore, children need to be helped and encouraged to use their first language strength. Oral language experiences in either L1 or L2 that are tied to early literacy experiences such as storybook reading and using literacy tools such as pretend reading and writing appear to be particularly useful for literacy learning, although more research is needed (Reese, Garnier, Gallimore, & Goldenberg, 2000).

In regard to L2 oral language, the evidence suggests that some aspects of second language proficiency are especially influential in second language literacy. Which of these aspects of language do you think will be most influential: how much the second language is used, second vocabulary size, second language communication skills, second language listening comprehension, second language print knowledge, or knowledge of order of words in sentences? Well, if you chose vocabulary size and listening comprehension, you would be spot on. The significance of second language vocabulary in second language reading is the reason why in this chapter a great deal of attention is devoted to fostering preschool ELLs' second language vocabulary. The 2003 evaluation of vocabulary of Head Start children found that Spanish-speaking preschool children entered and exited Head Start preschool with significantly lower

English vocabulary skills than English-only children (Administration on Children, Youth, and Families, 2003). At the same time, Spanish-speaking children had larger vocabulary gains than did English-only children from similar socioeconomic backgrounds. This result shows that preschool English learners do gain second language vocabulary from participating in preschool programs. While this is promising, it must be tempered with the sobering understanding that Spanish-speaking children still remained significantly behind English-only children on vocabulary and below 76% of preschool children who have completed Head Start.

CLASSROOM CONTEXTS FOR LANGUAGE DEVELOPMENT

Throughout this chapter, I have emphasized the amount of time and opportunity that is necessary for language development. In the context of second language acquisition, this message is amplified, because English learners have had far less opportunity for English learning than their English-only peers. If they are to catch up to their English-only peers after having started behind, they will have to accelerate their rate of language learning. A focus on language development should permeate the entire day. Yet, on average, language and literacy activity in preschool classrooms only occurs 15% to 18% of the time (Connor, Morrison, & Slominski, 2006). There are five contexts for language development that can be capitalized on in order to maximize language-learning opportunities for preschool English learners. These five contexts are these:

- Storybook reading
- Individual conversations (narrative)
- Centers
- Classroom routines and transitions
- Meal time

How to promote language development by extensive use of each of these classroom contexts will be presented in the following sections.

THE WONDER AND LIMITS OF STORYBOOK READING

Storybook reading is a rich context for enhancing children's first language, particularly their vocabulary knowledge (Bus, van IJzendoorn, & Pellegrini, 1995; Dickinson & Smith, 1994; Elley, 1989; Pemberton &

Watkins, 1987; Robbins & Ehri, 1994; Sénéchal & Cornell, 1993; Sénéchal, Thomas, & Monker, 1995; Snow, Burns, & Griffin, 1998; Whitehurst et al., 1988, 1994). Studies also show that English learners learn vocabulary from storybook reading (Roberts, 2008; Roberts & Neal, 2004). But not all types of storybook reading are equally effective. Two types of storybook reading are particularly effective with children who are participating in storybook reading in their first language. These two types of storybook reading are

- interactive reading where children are invited to contribute their reactions and ideas and
- storybook reading where children are encouraged to reflect upon and use more sophisticated thinking.

These two types of storybook reading are better for language development than storybook reading, where children simply listen as the teacher reads or repeat back information from the story. Effective storybook readings are characterized by the presence of a great deal of child language. Repeated readings of stories have also been found to be beneficial (Brabham & Lynch-Brown, 2002; Eller, Pappas, & Brown, 1988; Elley, 1989; Leung & Pikulski, 1990; Penno, Wilkinson, & Moore, 2002; Robbins & Ehri, 1994; Sénéchal, 1997; Sénéchal & Cornell, 1993; Sénéchal et al., 1995). Repeated reading may especially benefit English learners, as they may be more dependent upon the repeated readings to gain full understanding of the story. Teaching vocabulary words with direct explanation during or before reading makes it easier for children to learn new words than practices that leave them to use context or pictures or to otherwise figure out the meanings of unknown words on their own. However, an important challenge, as discussed previously, is deciding which words to teach. Should words be selected that will most contribute to building overall English language abilities? Or should words be selected that are most critical for understanding the specific story? Teacher explanations of the meanings of key words will help children to access story meaning and will reduce the amount of mental effort that children will need to expend to gain story and word meaning (Roberts & Neal, 2004). This benefit may be even more valuable for English learners who are challenged by the sounds of the second language and the rules of how sentences are formed in it and who may have limited knowledge of the experiences portrayed in some storybooks, for example, a trip to a veterinarian office.

Story retelling is embedded in a strategy called *dialogic reading* where children are encouraged to increasingly take over the "reading" of familiar storybooks. Dialogic reading has been shown to lead to language benefits in several studies (e.g., Whitehurst et al., 1988). A limited amount of evidence has shown that dialogic reading is also effective with English learners. While some have criticized story retelling as a child's reading out of a remembered script, it actually provides a number of important linguistic and comprehension-supportive functions. As children construct their retelling, they have to retrieve from memory and order a number of story elements that mirror the entire story structure. They have to express this sequence in language, and language production requires more linguistic planning than does linguistic comprehension without retelling.

Storybook reading in primary language can be provided when possible. There are a few studies showing that this may be a particularly beneficial practice for English learners. Roberts (2008; discussed more fully on page 20) reported equal or superior English vocabulary learning from prior primary language storybook reading. In a study with Latino families of two- to six-year-old children who received books in English, Spanish, or English and Spanish (based on parent choice), and where children were tested in their preferred language, children who received books in Spanish or in Spanish and English scored 10 standard points higher on receptive language (Mendelsohn et al., 2001) than a comparison group. Primary language reading of storybooks may provide rich background knowledge that can then be used in second language reading to aid language growth and storybook comprehension. Building background knowledge that can be used to understand books in the second language is important for English learners. I have used a number of practices in my instructional studies with preschool English learners to build language and background knowledge. The bulleted list that follows presents a number of them that you might try.

Practices to Build Storybook Related Background Knowledge

- Providing storybooks in primary language for at home reading
- Showing a video of the story prior to classroom reading where the video graphics matched the illustrations in the book (available from Scholastic Books)
- Taking a silent picture walk of the book prior to reading (believed to activate primary language), where all the book pages are previewed in sequential order without talking
- Repeated reading of books
- Teaching core vocabulary prior to reading with concrete activities
- Individual and paired pretend reading of books after group reading
- Retelling activities with individual picture packets from books

However, storybook reading is not a magic bullet for assuring high levels of English language development. In their analysis of the research evidence on storybook reading, Scarborough and Dobrich (1994) concluded that variation in how much storybook reading English-only children had experienced accounted for no more than 12% to 15% of the variation in children's language competence. That means that about 85% to 88% of the children's language variation is due to other things. While storybook reading is a

Teaching Principle 13: Provide storybook reading experiences in primary language and English.

Teaching Principle 14: Reread books.

Teaching Principle 15: Interact with children about their comments and observations during readings, retellings, and paraphrases of book content.

Teaching Principle 16: Carefully select and teach vocabulary that is important to story meaning or that builds children's basic English competence.

wonderful language development experience, other types of and more language development opportunities are needed.

Apply Your Knowledge

Select and read an interesting children's book. Select words from the book that will be most helpful for understanding the story. Now go through the book again and select words that will be most useful in helping English learners communicate with others. Compare the lists. How similar were they? Choose the word from each list that you believe is the hardest to teach and write a plan for how you could teach it. What did you learn from this exercise?

CONVERSATIONS WITH CHILDREN

When a teacher and a child engage in a true conversation, there is a give and take of information where each partner is learning something from the other through language. A conversation is different from a series of questions and responses, where the teacher's primary goal is to teach the child something or to assess the child's understanding. For example, a series of exchanges in a small group, where the teacher is helping a child improve his or her understanding of specific vocabulary words, would not be a conversation. Key features of conversations that promote their effectiveness in building language include that the teacher-partner expands, elaborates on, and responds to the meaning of the language produced by the child. It therefore involves a significant degree of focused attention by the teacher. A facilitative context for conversational exchange includes face-to-face contact, typically promoted by being seated together. It means really listening and sharing back. Yet the use of conversations is limited in actual classrooms, with less than 5% of time spent in individual conversations with children. From the simple model of language development presented at the beginning of this chapter (page 43), *input + intake + production = language skill,* conversations maximize input, ensure intake due to the child's engagement, and promote production, because the child is a conversational partner.

While conversations are a rich opportunity for language development, there are a number of factors that must be taken into account in efforts to engage ELLs in them when they occur in a second language. This discussion is based primarily on logical analysis, as there are no focused studies that examine factors that lead to better conversations with English learners. English learners' limited knowledge of both the structural features of the language and their ability to use it for extended social exchanges is perhaps the most obvious factor to influence conversations.

One strategy for addressing challenges for having conversations with ELLs is to use a time-based sequence (first this, then this, etc.) structure, because children across all cultural groups know it (but see McCabe, 1995, and McCabe & Rollins, 1994). This time-based sequence is called *narrative*. A child's response to "What did you do with your family last night?" or construction of a story beginning with the prompt "Once upon a time . . ." would be examples of the use of narrative structure. Since this narrative structure is available to children from all language groups, it may be particularly appropriate for use with English learners.

Another practice is to listen very carefully, as children may produce very limited utterances, and to check out your understanding of what the child has said before proceeding with a response. Conversations most likely to be relatively easy are those engaging children about actual events they are currently participating in or have experienced where rich primary language has been involved. For example, children whose first language is Chinese could find it easier to engage in a conversation about Chinese New Year when they regularly participate in it and when it has just occurred. The value of this for an English learner is that the learner's recent familiarity with the topic will enhance her or his ability to participate. Checking your understanding would involve brief rephrases of what the child says or questions before offering back your genuine response. The "Apply Your Knowledge" exercise for this section will give you some specific practice in this.

There are opportunities in conversation to contribute to the child's capacity with decontextualized language too, although these may be limited for most English learners due to their emerging second language proficiency. When individual conversations involve talk about the past or future or imaginary events, language alone is being used more as the vehicle for communication. Recall that skill with the use of decontextualized language is strongly related to academic achievement.

While conversations provide very rich opportunities for child–adult language exchange, there are significant limitations to how much language-learning opportunity they can provide in early care and education settings for preschool English learners. If a teacher and assistant with 22 children devoted their entire three-and-a-half hours of a half-day program to conversation, how many minutes of language input, intake, and production could each child receive? Here's the math: 3.5 hours = 210 minutes × 2 (two teachers) = 420 minutes per day/21 children = 20 minutes per child per day, or 100 minutes per week. This is simply not enough language experience for rich language development.

One way of increasing opportunities for conversation would be to use small groups of three to five children and have conversations in this small group context. How would this be different? What would be some challenges with it? Another challenge is that it is easier to have those conversations with more outgoing or more English-proficient children. Teachers will need to monitor their use of conversation with practices such as targeting children to have conversations with and keeping records of who they have conversed with to make sure all children are conversed with.

A final challenge is that really being able to attend during a conversation is hard for teachers, as they have many competing classroom responsibilities. Good

Teaching Principle 17: Follow the child's lead, and respond to, expand, elaborate, and/or clarify child intent.

Teaching Principle 18: Establish face and body proximity for conversations.

Teaching Principle 19: Rephrase and/or clarify understanding of what the child has said before responding.

Educational Principle 7: Plan a way to monitor that all children are benefiting from conversation opportunities.

classroom management practices and time set aside time for conversations are needed for frequent and orderly opportunities for conversations. Conversations provide magic language-learning opportunities—so strive for them—but there will need to be much more language opportunity happening for every child for sufficient input, intake, and production.

Apply Your Knowledge

Take the following child language sample, and write a sentence for how you could check for your understanding and then respond to the child's meaning. You will have to imagine what you found out from each clarifying question to guide your response.

Child says: Teacher (points to rabbit in picture book)

Teacher: Clarify
Respond

Child says: Name Lollipop

Teacher: Clarify
Respond

Child says: Me like

Teacher: Clarify
Respond

LANGUAGE DEVELOPMENT DURING CENTER TIME

Learning centers specifically structured to promote language and vocabulary development are more effective for language development than others not so designed (Morrow & Schickedanz, 2006; Neuman & Roskos, 1997). Therefore, classroom centers should be specifically structured to promote language acquisition. Yet again, we are relying on research evidence from English-only children and applying it to English learners. However, the conditions that have been shown to promote language during center time do mirror the kind of context supported, meaningful language input known to promote second language development.

In general, centers that will most effectively promote language and vocabulary include a variety of materials and adult resources designed to actively engage children in language development activities. Materials and activities with center-related vocabulary and opportunities for language use such as conversation starters, or sentence frames (e.g., my favorite animal is a _____) for children with more limited proficiency to add to, will promote language development. The presence of adults who respond to, expand, and elaborate on children's language use at the centers is an important resource. Adults who can provide center related language input and help children initiate language use will be particularly needed with English learners. A summary box showing characteristics of effective centers with examples for a grocery center (in parentheses) follows. This center might accompany the book *Whistle for Willie* by Ezra Jack Keats.

Characteristics of Centers That Promote Language Development

Whistle for Willie Book Related Center

- Is clearly identifiable and "bounded"
- Changes frequently
- Is used with ample time for engagement
- Has integrated and thematic purpose (e.g., grocery center)
- Has specific props to support theme/book related language
  (e.g., bags, containers, cash register, flannel board figures or pictures for retelling the story)
- Motivates children to want to use language (personal, related to background knowledge, novelty, etc.)
  (e.g., little purses, wallets with play money)
- Has activities specifically designed to promote language use
  (e.g., grocery store has food labels to be created and put onto toilet paper roll "cans")
- Provides pictures of key vocabulary words with word written on them
  (e.g., *groceries, shopping list, vegetables, whistle*)
- Has adult present to model and encourage language use
  (e.g., adult makes a shopping list, showing noodle package or picture as she writes "noodles"; adult shows a picture of her own family and tells about it; adult suggests "let's play what your family does when they go to get food"; adult points out printed labels on pictures of vocabulary words; adult uses sentence frame "I want to get _____ at the grocery store" with individual children)

(Continued)

(Continued)

- Includes varied materials to represent the culture and home language of children
  (e.g., grocery store has empty containers from a variety of ethnic foods that children and their families can contribute)
- Provides theme-related books, magazines, computer software
  (e.g., pictures of different types of grocery stores, trucks delivering food, a video of making graham crackers)
- Has bilingual adults interacting with children
  (e.g., adults have children retell or make up a new story about Willie and his dog in primary language that they act out)
- Provides multimodality materials such as word cards, objects, or pictures related to selected vocabulary words
- Provides a variety of types of paper and writing implements (pencils, markers, crayons, paint, and models of alphabet letters)

Another center example follows, this time of a veterinarian center to accompany perhaps a classroom animal theme. This center plan includes the characteristics of an effective center and focuses on vocabulary development.

Veterinarian Center

Theme vocabulary: *veterinarian, doctor, prescription, symptom, chart, appointment, medicine, temperature, examine, pet, cost, feeding*

Basic vocabulary: *sick, help, examine, doctor, explain, cost, feeding, pet, give, call, hurt*

Rare words: *ill, symptom, appointment, prescription*

Props/materials:
- Animal breed charts
- Pictures of children's pets (digital camera)
- Symptom checklist
- Pictures of animals to mark with where problem is
- Prescription pad
- Small bottles of "prescriptions" and materials for labeling them
- Three-by-five cards with prompts to motivate language use written on them: "What symptoms does your pet have?" "How could we take care of _____?" "What happened to your pet?"
- Pet yellow pages, enlarged sheet of veterinarian ads from the phone book yellow pages

- Dog, cat breed pictures
- Home animal care books
- White shirt
- Thermometer, stethoscope, phone
- Stuffed animals
- Could be an art project to cut, stuff, make collar and license for, with adult present to talk about all the steps in the project as children are doing it)

Story dictation ideas:

- "Me and my pet" (real or pretend)

Sociodramatic play prompt:

- "My dog gets well"

Conversation starters for adults written on three-by-five cards:

- "Have you ever had a pet? Tell me about it."
- "Imagine that in your apartment building everyone had a pet. What would that be like?"

Apply Your Knowledge

Think carefully about a center idea related to a book, theme, or science concepts. Design a center for it that will promote language and vocabulary by using the following center planning form.

Teaching Principle 20: Design centers with specific features that lead to language development.

Try your center out in your classroom. How did it work?

Planning Form for a Language Building Center

Theme:

Classroom location (how identified):

Theme vocabulary:

Basic vocabulary:
Rare words:

(Continued)

(Continued)

Materials to support word learning:

Books and other written materials:

Props and other materials:

Story dictation ideas:

Sociodramatic play ideas/prompts:

Conversation starters for adults written on three-by-five cards:

Models of alphabet letters, varied writing tools, and paper:

Bilingual resources:

Adults who will be present:

TALKING-UP ROUTINES AND TRANSITIONS

My rationale for recommending classroom transition and routines as a focus for language development is a practical one. In a large study of preschool classrooms, teachers spent more than 15 minutes per observational hour (approximately) engaged in transition and routine activities (Connor, Morrison, & Slominski, 2006). This was about the same amount of time as they spent on average on language and literacy activities!

These classroom routines and transitions times can be used for language development. Both basic language development and more academic/decontextualized language development opportunities can occur during transitions and routines. Basic language development can occur when classroom routines and transitions are accompanied with language and related demonstration: "OK, now we will go wash our hands"; "I am putting out four [show four fingers] colors of paper: pink, green, blue, and purple. Here are scissors [hold up container] and crayons [hold up box]."

When transitions and routines are used for singing, nursery rhymes, chanting, songs, finger plays, or perhaps a choral conversation about what all was accomplished before lunch, opportunities for language use that is less contextually supported are more available. An activity such as singing "Where is Thumbkin?" while washing hands would be more contextualized than reciting "One, two, buckle my shoe." These language development

Teaching Principle 21:
Include contextualized or decontextualized language development opportunities during all classroom transitions and routines.

activities will also support good management, as children will be engaged in interesting activities as they move about the classroom or have to wait.

Apply Your Knowledge

Make a list of routines and transitions that commonly occur in your preschool setting or that typically occur in any preschool setting (washing hands, moving to carpet, small tables, snack, etc.). Write one way to include a contextualized language-building activity and one way to include a decontextualized language-building activity during each routine or transition.

MEALTIME OPPORTUNITIES FOR TALKING

During snacks and meals children are engaged in a shared activity and may be together in small groups. Children are typically happy and relaxed during these times. Like other classroom routines, they take up a substantial amount of classroom time. As such, they can be capitalized on as opportunities for group and individual conversation. Interestingly, in an extensive study of language use in children's homes, mealtime talk was found to be a context for language development that was related to children's overall language competence. Families that talked more during mealtime had children who knew more vocabulary words (Dickinson & Tabors, 2000). Building into classroom practice the use of mealtimes—which occur one to three times a day—as a time for children and teachers to talk can harness some more precious minutes for language development.

In order for these mealtimes to afford language interaction, they will need to be well organized and predictable routines with shared responsibility, so the teachers can sit down and share an enjoyable and interesting talk with children. I know of many preschools where teacher and children regularly sit together at small tables during meals to make sure that the meals are used for language development. These are not structured lessons with contrived topics and one-after–the-other required turn-taking. To most benefit language, mealtime talk will provide input, motivate intake, and foster production. Topics of interest to children can be followed along roads that children want to travel, with a skillful teacher introducing more sophisticated words and responding to what children say. But most important, getting children to want and be able to talk is what the mealtime language chef will concoct.

Here's a little poem I wrote that captures these five rich contexts for promoting language development.

English Learner Learns Words!

Teacher, teacher, what do you see? You see me at a center talking to three!

Teacher, teacher, what do you see? You see a teacher talking to me!

Teacher, teacher, what do you see? You see me hearing a story and still talking free!

Teacher, teacher, what do you see? You see me washing, walking, and chanting finger plays we!

Teacher, teacher, what do you see? Talking me, talking me, talking me!

LANGUAGE AND LITERACY ENHANCED PLAY

Research supports that children's play can provide opportunities for developing representation, language, social relations, logic, problem-solving, self-regulation, and motivation (reviewed in Fisher, 1992, and Mages, 2008). In addition, research shows that not all types of play are equally beneficial for these positive possibilities. It is imaginary or pretend play that is most associated with language development, social skills, and representational abilities (reviewed in Fisher, 1992). Riding tricycles alone in the play yard may contribute to large motor development but less so to language, representation, or social skills. However, the focus in this book is to examine the relationship and influence of play on children's literacy competencies.

What is known specifically about play and preschool language and literacy development? First, in spite of strong claims that play causes better language and literacy outcomes, high-quality evidence for this claim is limited (Mages, 2008; Morrow & Schickedanz, 2006). Second, a point that has been made several times in this book needs stating again. There is very limited research that examines play and literacy relationships for English learners. In fact I was not able to locate any studies on this important topic. Even for English-only children, there is more research that looks at how play and literacy are *related*—or correlated—than studies examining how play *causes* literacy outcomes.

The available research suggests a few characteristics of play that are related to language development. When children's play experiences are structured to encourage rich language and to promote children's participation in extended exploration of themes, plots, and story lines, there is evidence of language growth and the ability to construct connected narratives (Mages, 2008; Morrow & Schickedanz, 2006). *Narratives* embody event seque-

Teaching Principle 22: Stimulate complex sociodramatic play by expanding children's interests with plot twists, play sequels, and play materials that support story lines.

nces of one thing following another that mirror the common experiences of day-to-day life. Narrative structure is typical of most storybooks and is marked by the "first this, then this, next this" sequence. Another characteristic of play experiences showing the greatest contributions to literacy is the teacher's measured participation in the play. Teachers who help children initiate and elaborate stories and plots and who provide language that stretches the child's ability but who do not take charge of the play can contribute to language development. The presence of literacy materials, such as menus or pads for writing orders in a restaurant dramatic/pretend play center, increases the number of literacy behaviors that children engage in during play (Morrow, 1990).

TEACHER ORAL LANGUAGE: AN ELEPHANT IN THE ROOM

The evidence of how children learn language—including vocabulary—is very clear on the importance of the language provided by language teachers for children's language development. Extensive exposure to good models of the English language is important for English learner children. Hence, the quality of teacher language is clearly implicated. A recent study of kindergarten teachers in bilingual classrooms found that teacher oral language was related to both English and Spanish literacy achievement (Cirino, Pollard-Durodola, Foorman, Carlson, & Francis, 2007). In other sections of this chapter, you learned how

- the type of talk during storybook reading;
- the amount of responding to, extending, and elaborating children's language during conversations;
- the selection of vocabulary words to teach;
- the pronunciation of words;
- the provision of language input that is accessible to but challenging for the child;

- the use of rare words; and
- the number and variety of words spoken to children.

all influence the quality of a child's language. A teacher with strong oral language skills is needed.

Yet at the same time, it is a long-standing commitment in the early care and education field to have teacher diversity in order to represent the range of cultural groups of the children, to provide role models, to establish the strong teacher-child relationships that may occur when teacher and children are more similar and to provide bilingual resources, among other reasons. There are also important values related to diversity and social issues associated with power, equality, poverty, and language policy embedded in these practices as well. In many states and preschool settings, individuals can become early care and education providers with limited educational experience and training related to language. There is also cultural and individual variation in degree of talkativeness. With workforce diversity comes variability in the language skills of teachers and teaching assistants.

The elephant in the room is the question about how the early care and education field should address this variability in teacher language. The sensitivity of the issues and the multiple values and needs of children and their families that inform this question require very careful thought. Yet from the perspective of second language development of English learners, the dialog is an important one to begin. What are your views on the issue? How do your own language resources influence your thinking? Respond to the brief self-ranking below, and think about how your responses on it may influence your response to the last two questions.

Please rate yourself on the following characteristics of your own English skills (1 means a lower self-rating; 5 means a higher self-rating).					
1. English vocabulary size	1	2	3	4	5
2. English pronunciation	1	2	3	4	5
3. Amount of reading in English	1	2	3	4	5
4. Talkativeness in English	1	2	3	4	5

HOME INFLUENCES ON SECOND LANGUAGE LEARNING

Research has consistently shown the influence of the home environment on language development in many languages. The evidence also suggests

that in order to promote the high levels and types of language development most supportive of school achievement, much more high-quality
language input and interaction than can be provided during a half day or
even full day preschool program is needed. Here is a fact that I ask you to
think very hard about. Hart and Risley (1995) calculated that in order for
children from homes with the lowest-quality language opportunities to
receive language experience equivalent to that of children in average
working class families, *41 hours per week* of out-of-home experience as
"rich in words addressed to the child as that in an average professional
home" (p. 201) would be needed. And that number of words heard by the
child would be 2,153 words per hour. Think about it—2,153 words per
hour. That is a very high number of words needed to catch up to the language level of children with parents having professional occupations.

A conclusion that I have drawn from understanding the importance
of language competence prior to age three and how much language
experience is needed for strong language growth at this age is that it is
critical for early childhood professionals to get really serious about
engaging family caregivers in oral language development. No matter how
high the quality of the classroom experience, more is needed.

Hart and Risley also found that there were social-emotional and
cognitive differences in how language was used in the homes that
differentiated children who entered preschool with stronger language
skills. The following box shows the characteristics of home language use
that was associated with good language development in the Hart and
Risley study. Along with an emphasis on increasing the amount of talk
with children in the home, a family engagement program for oral
language development could target these five characteristics as a
foundation for oral language development. Chapter 7, "Engaging Family
Caregivers," provides detail on how to engage family caregivers.

Help family caregivers use the following five skills:

- Just talk (many words, and many kinds of words).
- Be nice when talking (affirm rather than prohibit or criticize).
- Tell children about things in the home and community.
- Give children choices in talking.
- Listen to what children say, and show this by responding to them.

On a realistic note, the evidence for better child outcomes from parent
intervention programs is mixed (Ramey, Yeats, & Short, 1984). Yet there
is encouragement from recent interventions that specifically included

Educational Principle 8: Create a specific family caregiver engagement program that focuses on supporting family caregivers in increasing the amount and variety of talk in the home.

Educational Principle 9: Create a specific family caregiver engagement program to support parents in implementing the five social-emotional and cognitive features of high-quality language interaction.

taking into account how adults learn and provided in-home coaching of specific language interaction practices. Notable increases in the quality of mother's language input and child language outcomes for mother-child pairs from a range of ethnic backgrounds have been achieved (Landry & Smith, 2006), and mother language was related to reading scores at age eight (Dietrich, Assel, Swank, Smith, & Landry, 2006). Of course with English learners, efforts to capitalize on the capacity of family caregivers for language development will call for the use of primary language.

CONCLUSION

This chapter has provided only an introduction to second language and vocabulary development. Can you believe that? The similarity between first and second language development was described. Adults play an important role in language-learning processes, and nuances in language-learning opportunities at home and in preschool settings influence children's language development. Children who are learning English as a second language will benefit from a program that helps them develop competence in the four key domains of language: semantics, phonology, syntax, and pragmatics. Language development should permeate the entire day. Special attention should be devoted every day to English vocabulary development. Explicit instruction and more informal experiences can promote English learners' second language development and should both be amply used for language development. Storybook reading, conversations, centers, classroom routines, mealtimes, and sociodramatic play are opportunities for English language development. Helping family caregivers promote strong primary language has the potential to benefit both English language and literacy strength. Issues around teacher language competence, child language production, and what words should be taught have been explored. These issues call for more research, dialog, and attention. And to add one more strand of ribbon to the language development gift that you have been so carefully learning to create for English learners, provide one more high-quality language development opportunity in your preschool setting.

Summary of Teaching Principles

Teaching Principle 1: Include practices for developing all four of the domains of English: *semantics, phonology, syntax,* and *pragmatics*.

Teaching Principle 2: Plan lessons and activities that provide language *input,* promote *intake,* and ensure *production* from all children.

Teaching Principle 3: Create English language use situations that are emotionally safe, such as choral responding, simple repetition activities, talking in pairs with a peer, and small groups.

Teaching Principle 4: Be a good model of caretaker speech.

Teaching Principle 5: Embed language in all of the activities children engage in (block, large motor, science, routines, play, book-reading).

Teaching Principle 6: Follow children's lead by responding to and extending their language.

Teaching Principle 7: Expose children to many second language words and their meanings, and help children connect the meaning and the word pronunciation.

Teaching Principle 8: Have children say the words they are learning many times.

Teaching Principle 9: Teach vocabulary words every day.

Teaching Principle 10: Identity and teach 12 to 15 words per week.

Teaching Principle 11: Use pictures, actions, demonstrations, and concrete "realia" when teaching words.

Teaching Principle 12: Carefully select words that benefit children's basic language and words related to storybooks, classroom themes, and centers.

Teaching Principle 13: Provide storybook reading experiences in primary language and English.

(Continued)

(Continued)

Teaching Principle 14: Reread books.

Teaching Principle 15: Interact with children about their comments and observations during readings, retellings, and paraphrases of book content.

Teaching Principle 16: Carefully select and teach vocabulary that is important to story meaning or that builds children's basic English competence.

Teaching Principle 17: Follow the child's lead, and respond to expand, elaborate, and/or clarify child intent.

Teaching Principle 18: Establish face and body proximity for conversations.

Teaching Principle 19: Rephrase and/or clarify understanding of what the child has said before responding.

Teaching Principle 20: Design centers with specific features that lead to language development.

Teaching Principle 21: Include contextualized or decontextualized language development opportunities during all classroom transitions and routines.

Teaching Principle 22: Stimulate complex sociodramatic play by expanding children's interests with plot twists, play sequels, and play materials that support story lines.

Summary of Educational Principles

Educational Principle 1: Strive for English language use (production) from all children in all domains (semantics, phonology, syntax, and pragmatics) of language.

Educational Principle 2: Be patient and helpful in getting children to speak English.

Educational Principle 3: Find out how home language use is similar to or different from school language use.

Educational Principle 4: Talk with families and other professionals about how to address the differences.

Educational Principle 5: Make a specific teaching plan for basic language development.

Educational Principle 6: Make a specific teaching plan for decontextualized/academic language development.

Educational Principle 7: Plan a way to monitor that all children are benefiting from conversation opportunities.

Educational Principle 8: Create a specific family caregiver engagement program that focuses on supporting family caregivers in increasing the amount and variety of talk in the home.

Educational Principle 9: Create a specific family caregiver engagement program to support parents in implementing the five social-emotional and cognitive features of high-quality language interaction.

4

Befriending the Alphabet

Why and How

☆ **Important Research Results About the Alphabet**

- Children who know more letters when they enter kindergarten are much more likely to be good readers at the end of first grade than are children who know fewer letters.

- When children are taught letter names, it helps them learn how to read.

- Preschool English learners can learn the names of letters of the alphabet in English.

- English-only children from middle class families know about 18 to 22 uppercase letters when they are between four-and-a-half and five-and-a-half years of age.

- There are differences between features of letters (shape, sound, ease of writing, ease of speaking) that make some letters easier to learn and others harder to learn.

- Preschool children know more letter names than letter sounds, and they know more uppercase than lowercase letters.

- Children who are four years old know more about the alphabet than those who are three years old.

Typically developing children come to preschool with strong oral language skills. Some children have this oral language strength in English, while many others are strong in a language other than English. In comparison, children know far less about printed language. If they have had rich experiences with books, had their attention drawn to the print in their communities and homes, and have had opportunities to explore and work with writing materials before they come to preschool, they will have some knowledge of how books work and that what is spoken can be written. Learning the system for how spoken words and print are related is the core knowledge that children need to learn how to read. This insight into how speech and print are systematically related is called the *alphabetic principle*. While children come to preschool with rich oral language, they know comparatively less about print—the other half of the equation. A critical job then is to help children build their knowledge about the print part of the equation:

speech + print = learning how to read

And it is here that the alphabet comes in. The letters of the alphabet are the basic building blocks of the print system (Ehri, 1998; Ehri & Roberts, 2006; Ehri & Wilce, 1985; Roberts, 2003; Share, 2004). There is much to learn, and preschool children, including English language learners, need considerable help to master all there is to know about letters.

CAN CHILDREN WITH LIMITED KNOWLEDGE OF ENGLISH LEARN THE ENGLISH ALPHABET?

When you first think about it, it seems logical that since English alphabet letters are part of the English language, it would be very difficult to learn the letters if you are just learning to speak English. It is true that on average the more English preschool children know, the more they know about English letters. This relationship between oral English competence and knowledge of the English alphabet is called a *correlation*. However, knowing that there is a relationship between these two abilities is not the same as saying that unless children have a certain level of English, they cannot learn the alphabet. This would be saying that it is *necessary* to have a certain level of English oral competence in order to learn letters of the alphabet.

There is another way to think about learning letters of the alphabet that would make it seem logical that even beginning English language learners could learn them. How does a child learn to say the name "be" when he or she is shown the visual letter *B*? Take a minute to think about this. The basic process is that the letter name/sound must be connected with the letter shape. You have to remember that the shape "B" and the name "be" go together. It's as simple as that. Knowing English might help you memorize this connection faster or more easily, because you know words that have the letter name "be" as part of their pronunciation, such as *beaver* or *beet*, but basically it does not take a great deal of language to do this connection-making. What it does take is making sure the connection between the letter name "be" and the symbol "B" is very clear and that children get enough practice to make the connection strong. It is like sewing on a button—the more times you stitch the button to the cloth, the stronger the bond between the button and the fabric. Children's brains, no matter what their primary language, are well equipped for this type of connection-making, which is called *association learning.*

So, how would we find out which of these two possibilities regarding the importance of English oral language for learning the alphabet is more accurate? We do studies where English beginners are taught alphabet letters and see what happens. A few of these studies have been done. What do you think these studies showed? If you thought that preschool beginning learners of English learn letters of the alphabet very well when they are directly taught these letters, you would be correct. For example, in one study a group of Spanish and Hmong primary language children were able to name—on average—more than 11 of the 16 letters they were taught (Roberts & Neal, 2004). This understanding that children learn letter names by making connections between shapes and their pronunciations leads to an appreciation of why explicit instruction about the alphabet is beneficial.

Educational Principle 1: Include learning about the alphabet as part of the language and literacy curriculum for preschool English language learners from all languages, even when they are just starting to learn the English language.

WHY EXPLICIT INSTRUCTION IS BENEFICIAL

Explicit instruction of the alphabet refers to teaching where there is a specific goal related to the alphabet, and the lesson strategies and activities are designed to help children meet this goal. A brief description of a sample explicit lesson is shown in the following box.

Example of a Brief Explicit Alphabet Letter Lesson

Stated purpose: To review the shapes and names of the letters *P, F, M, O,* and *A,* all of which have been taught previously.

Planned activities:

- Children have before them written models of their own names. They are instructed to look in their own names for the target letters and name and point to them if present.
- Names of other children in the class containing the target letters are in a large pocket chart. Working in groups of six, children are asked to look for the letters and name them, to come forward and use a small picture frame to frame these letters, and to name each letter out loud as they frame them. The other five children in the group repeat these letter names chorally as they are framed by one child and also tell whose personal name it is.
- Children then pair up, and each pair is given a small bag containing the review letters and a puppet. One child has the puppet, and the other has the letters. The puppet asks for one of the target letters by name and continues naming the letter out loud until the other child finds that letter and "feeds" it to the puppet. Children then switch roles.
- The teacher demonstrates on a white board how to write each letter, and the children write it with her on their own small white boards.
- The lesson ends with the teacher showing large cards of the five target letters for the lesson, reviews the names, and reminds the children that the goal of their lesson has been to make sure they remember the shapes and names of each letter.
- Children leave the group chanting the names of all the children they can remember where they found the target letters.

There are a few very important things to observe about this lesson example. One is that this explicit alphabet letter lesson utilizes personalized and meaningful print—children's names. Second, in the game with the puppet, there is a high level of active and playful learning. Self-regulation and autonomy are also involved in the puppet game as children go about having the puppet call for the letters and hopefully respond with delicious alphabet names as the puppet eats each letter. Another important characteristic of this example lesson is that there is a significant amount of practice and repetition of the associations between letter shapes and letter names that children are learning. Finally children are reminded of the purpose of the lesson.

This lesson example shows that explicit instruction where there is a great deal of practice and repetition to strengthen memories for letter shapes and letter names/sounds can be active, playful, and child-regulated. Explicit instruction does not mean boring, repetitive activity where children are silent and still and the teacher is in charge with a relatively nasty and demanding demeanor thrown in to boot. This would simply be poor teaching. I have often encountered this belief that explicit instruction and a "boot camp" teaching environment are assumed to be linked. It is important to distinguish the content of instruction from the quality of instruction. A high-quality experience for children can include an explicit focus on the alphabet with engaging, participatory, and self-regulated learning. Explicit instruction experiences are typically planned ahead of time with carefully thought-out activities based on what children have learned and what they need more help on, followed by progression to the next logical level in a developmental sequence when they are ready to move on.

Now that the nature of explicit instruction has been explained, let's move on to some more thinking about why it may be beneficial for English language learners. Think back to the previous discussion of the basic connection-making nature of learning about the shapes of letters and the names/sounds that go with them. While English language learners have the ability to make connections as part of the memory architecture of the human brain, they have not had much experience with saying these names or sounds in speech or hearing others use them when they are learning the alphabet in English. So they will have a lot to learn—typically more than does an English-only child—in mastering the shapes and their related names or sounds. These circumstances call for more, not less, help for English learners.

For a moment, try to imagine that you are in a foreign language classroom where the teacher and some of the other students are speaking in Martian. The teacher is reading from a textbook written in Martian. Martian does not use the same letters as the English alphabet—the alphabet looks something like Korean, the Russian Cyrillic alphabet, or the Arabic alphabet. The teacher pauses, looks up, and students respond with answers that go by very quickly. You are flooded with language sounds from several speakers and a stream of words, and you only know the meaning of a very few of them. She begins to point to some of the print and to say something that seems to be an even smaller segment of the language, and before you can barely remember that little bit, it has faded and she has gone on to something else. The feeling one might have would be like looking for a needle in a linguistic haystack!

What would help you understand what is going on? It is highly likely that you would want the teacher to tell you the goal of the activity, what it is exactly that you are supposed to learn, and what you are supposed to do to learn it. You would also probably want her to slow down, to help you hear and remember those little bits of language that go with the print by making them very clear, and to give you a chance to say and repeat them several times on your own. One reason that explicit instruction in the alphabet is beneficial is

Teaching Principle 1: Identify the purpose and goal(s) of alphabet lessons to children.

Teaching Principle 2: Help children focus on learning the connections between the alphabet letter shapes and their names/sounds.

Teaching Principle 3: Use strategies and activities designed to help children memorize the associations between letter shapes and their names/sounds.

Teaching Principle 4: Make lessons that are engaging and meaningful and that provide opportunities for self-regulation.

that it helps children find that needle in the haystack. It helps them to focus in on what they should pay attention to in a language that is unfamiliar to them, thereby simplifying the task to one that may be more manageable. Another aspect of these explicit lessons is that children are helped to use strategies and activities that are likely to be most effective for learning the desired content when the teacher is knowledgeable and plans lessons carefully. Some have described explicit teaching as *reductionist* where reductionist carries a negative connotation because language and print may be simplified (or reduced) from their essential wholeness where meaning-making is the purpose. Hopefully, pretending to be a non-Martian in a Martian language classroom has helped you to see that

- reducing language demands,
- focusing attention on and explaining what is to be learned, and
- activating strategies that are effective for meeting the planned lesson goal(s) will help English language learners make the speech-print connection.

Learning the associations between shapes and names/sounds relies heavily on memory, and thus teaching practices that help children memorize the connection between letter names and letter shapes will be very beneficial. Repetition and practice where children use their eyes, voices, and muscle systems will help establish strong memories for connections between letter shapes and letter names or letter sounds. See the connections, speak the connections, and feel the connections. And again, there are a few studies that include English language learners from two different language backgrounds who were very successful in learning to name letters of the alphabet from high-quality, explicit instruction delivered in small groups of 10 to 12 children. High-quality, explicit instruction is just a special case of scaffolding.

Apply Your Knowledge

Using the explicit instruction lesson plan below, plan an explicit alphabet lesson. As you learn more, more elements will be added to this sample lesson plan.

Explicit Alphabet Lesson Plan

1. Specific alphabet-related goal of the lesson _____

2. Focus children's attention on the letter and letter name/sound

   _____

   _____

3. Specific activities that will help children remember the connection between the letter shape and the letter name or sound

   a. How will you include practice and repetition?

   _____

   _____

   b. How will you make the lesson engaging and meaningful?

   _____

   _____

4. How will you promote children's self-regulation?

   _____

   _____

GOING DEEPER INTO THE ALPHABET

You have been helped to see that English language learners are ready to learn about the alphabet and that small-group, explicit instruction will help them learn the speech-print connection, or the alphabetic principle. Now, we will consider in more depth the nature of the alphabet and the implications of these characteristics of the alphabet for learning and teaching.

Characteristics of the Alphabet That Influence Learning It

- There are about 40 different shapes to learn the names/sounds of.
- Some letter shapes are similar and thus confusable.
- Some letter names are similar and thus confusable.
- Some letter sounds are similar and thus confusable.
- Some letter names and sounds are difficult for preschool children to pronounce.

Here's a little alphabet math:

Alphabet Letter Shape Math

   26 uppercase letters
+ 26 lowercase letters =
   52 letter shapes
− 12 where uppers and lowers are almost the same =
   40 distinct letter shapes to learn

There are 26 uppercase and 26 lowercase letters and their association with letter names and letter sounds that children need to know to master the full system of the English alphabet. These individual speech sounds associated with letters are called *phonemes.* There are 12 letters for which the uppercase and lowercase letters are nearly the same (*Cc, Ff, Kk, Mm, Nn, Oo, Pp, Ss, Vv, Ww, Xx,* and *Yy*). So we have 26 uppercase letters + 26 lowercase letters = 52 letter shapes – 12 shapes where the uppercase and lowercase letters are almost the same. That leaves 40 different shapes for which children must learn the names/sounds. This is no small task in and of itself. In addition, many of the letter shapes are similar and thus confusable (*b* and *d; p, q,* and *g; i* and *j*). In all three of the preceding sets of confusable letters, two of them occur very close together in alphabet order and in the case of *p* and *q* and *i* and *j* right after each other. More of the lowercase than uppercase letters are confusable with other letters, which is probably one reason that children know more uppercase than lowercase letters (Worden & Boettcher, 1990). You can see this difference between uppercase and lowercase letters by examining the alphabet shown below:

A B C D E F G H I J K L M N O P Q R S T U V W X Y Z
a b c d e f g h i j k l m n o p q r s t u v w x y z

Many of the letter sounds represented by different letters are also quite similar, differing in small ways in how they are spoken (/b/, /d/, /p/; /t/, /d/, /f/, /v/).[1] Place your hand on your vocal chords on your throat and say the phoneme /v/ (like in the word *velvet*) and compare it to what you feel in your vocal chords when you say /f/ (like in the word *fabric*). You should feel vibration in your vocal chords when you say /v/, but not when you say /f/. /v/ and /f/ differ in *voicing*. As we go through the rest of the rather detailed information in this section, it will help a lot if you say out loud the letter name, letter sound, and words that are used to illustrate important characteristics of the alphabet. So talk along as you read, please.

Some letter names or letter sounds are difficult for three- to four-year-old children to pronounce. Many three- to four-year-old children will not have mastered the pronunciation of /k/ (saying "tangaroo" for "kangaroo") and /r/ (saying "wabbit" for "rabbit"). English language learners may also have carryover, or *transfer*, from the speech sounds of the first language to English, rendering the pronunciation of some English letter names/sounds problematic. An example of this would be the substitution of /b/ for the English /v/ that frequently occurs with children who have Spanish as their first language. Another example is substitution of the English phoneme /r/ with an /l/ that may occur with children (and even adults) who speak Chinese as a first language. In addition children learn to write some letters earlier than others. Children learn to print uppercase *G, K, R,* and *S* later than they learn to print uppercase *A, O, T,* and *X.* At the very least, it is safe to say that there are many things that should be considered in deciding in what order to teach the letters of the alphabet. Teaching letters in strict A-B-C order does not appear to be the best choice for alphabet learning, as such a choice would clearly introduce letters close together that would be confusable due to shape, letter name, or letter sound.[2] And for a pair like *b* and *d,* where the letter shapes are confusable and the letter sounds (buh, duh) are similar, it would be double trouble.

A final characteristic of letters that is useful to know about is that most letter names contain clues to at least one speech sound (phoneme) the letter represents. Say the letter *B* and separate it into two sounds (phonemes)— "buh e." Do the same for the letter *J*—"juh a." The speech sound that letters *B* and *J* stand for are (buh, juh) and are heard at the beginning of the letter name. Do the same for the letter *M*—"eh mmm." Do the same for the letter *S*—"eh sss." The speech sound that letters *M* and *S* stand for are heard at the end of the letter name. Go through the rest of the alphabet, say each letter name slowly, and divide it into two parts, as we did with the examples. Which letters have the letter sound at the beginning? Which have the letter sound at the end? You might want to do this exercise watching your mouth in a mirror, as it will help you "see" whether the sound occurs at the beginning or the end of the letter name. You can check your understanding by looking at Table 4.1. So when children learn letter names, they are also learning the speech sounds (phonemes) that will be taught as the letter sounds. These speech sounds are the ones that they will use to decode words in text as they begin real reading in kindergarten and especially first grade. To decode the spoken word "bus," children will need to separate the word into "buh" "uh" "s" and then put the letters together to arrive at the pronunciation "bus." Thus when children learn letter names, they are also learning about the letter sounds.

Many studies have shown that preschool children use this information about the speech sounds (phonemes) embedded in letter names in learning printed words and in their efforts to write words (e.g., Treiman & Rodriquez, 1999; Treiman, Tincoff, & Richmond-Welty, 1996; Treiman, Weatherston, & Berch, 1994). Children will spell the word *ball* as *BL* or even *chicken* as *HKN*. How does this spelling for

Teaching Principle 5: Teach letters in a sequence that minimizes the confusability among letter shapes.

Teaching Principle 6: Teach letter names in a sequence that minimizes letters whose *names* are similar being taught too close together.

Teaching Principle 7: Teach letter sounds in a sequence that minimizes letters whose letter *sounds* are similar being taught close together.

Teaching Principle 8: Teach letters that have the letter sound embedded in the *beginning* of the letter name before letters that have the sound embedded at the *end* of the letter name.

Teaching Principle 9: Consider leaving letters associated with letter sounds (phonemes) that are challenging for children to pronounce until later in the learning sequence.

Table 4.1 Characteristics of Letters of the Alphabet

Letter	Confusable Letter Shape	Confusable Letter Sound	Letter Sound at Beginning of Letter Name	Letter Sound at End of Letter Name	Letter Sound Not in Letter Name	Letter Name in Long Vowel
A[3]						X
B	d, p, q, g	d, p, t	X			
C		s	X			
D	b, p, q, g	b, p, t	X			
E						X
F		v		X		
G		j	X			
H					X	
I						X
J		g	X			
K		t	X			
L				X		
M		n		X		
N		m		X		
O						X
P	b, d, q, g	b, d	X			
Q	b, d, q, g				X	
R				X		
S		c		X		
T		p, d	X			
U						X
V		b, f	X			
W					X	
X				X		
Y		i			X	
Z			X			

chicken make sense? Say "chicken." What is the first sound you hear? It is /ch/. Now say the letter name of *H* slowly. Hear the /ch/ at the end of the pronunciation of "a ch"? As it turns out, letter names for letters such as *B* and *J* where a speech sound represented by the letter occurs at the beginning of the letter name are learned more easily than those whose embedded phoneme occurs at the end of the word such as letters *M* and *S* (Treiman, Tincoff, Rodriguez, Mouzaki, & Francis, 1998). The *Characteristics of Letters of the Alphabet* table (Table 4.1) shows the alphabet and all these characteristics that contribute to how easy or hard each letter is to learn.

You may have started wondering during all this discussion of the details about the alphabet whether children should learn connections between (a) letter shapes and letter names or (b) letter shapes and the speech sounds (phonemes) they typically represent. Or maybe they should learn the letter shapes, letter names, and letter sounds all at the same time? Discussion of these questions will be the focus of the next section.

Apply Your Knowledge

1. Using Table 4.1, come up with what you think would be a good sequence for teaching the letters of the alphabet that takes into account characteristics of the alphabet that make certain letters easier or harder to learn (confusable letter shapes, letter names, and letter sounds; letter sound at the beginning or end of the letter name). There is no perfect answer here!

2. Using your knowledge of how children use letter names to spell words, explain what word the child has written in these examples: WRS, RYS. Hint: Say the names of the letters out loud.

3. Examine a curriculum that you know or your own alphabet letter lessons to see what order the letters are taught in. What are the strengths and weaknesses of the sequence related to possible confusions, place of letter sound, and pronunciation difficulty?

SHOULD LETTER NAMES OR
LETTER SOUNDS BE TAUGHT FIRST?

Whether letter names or letter sounds should be taught first is a question that many teachers and others interested in preschool literacy are avidly discussing. This question has not been clearly answered by research in relationship to English-only preschool children, let alone English language learners. A clear answer would require experiments where one group of children was initially taught letter names while another comparable group was taught letter sounds, with the same sequence, pacing, and amount of instruction being used for both groups. After instruction, the groups would be compared to determine if the group taught letter names or the group taught letter sounds learned more of what they were taught. It would also be important to see which group did better on preschool, kindergarten, and first-grade literacy tasks that depend on alphabet knowledge. Word reading, spelling, and the ability to work with individual phonemes in words are examples of these kinds of tasks. Preschool children show the ability to attend to individual sounds in words by, for example, identifying the first sound in a word. Kindergarten and first-grade tasks would include reading and spelling words where each sound in the word's pronunciation would be shown with a letter in the word's spelling. Real words such as *dog* and *jump* or pretend words such as *dop* and *tump* are examples of words where every letter represents a single phoneme.

There are studies that shed some light on whether letter names or letter sounds may be most useful for preschool children. Several studies have shown that children bring their letter knowledge to the task of learning letter sounds (Ehri, 1987; Share, 2004; Treiman & Broderick, 1998). Letter name and letter sound knowledge are related, because letter names contain clues to the letter sounds. Preschool children who know the names of letters use letter name knowledge to access letter sounds as they attempt to spell words. A child's spelling of *dress* as *WRS* shows this influence quite vividly. The child hears the "duh" at the beginning of the word *dress* and looks for a letter name that matches this sound. She or he hits the letter *W* and hears the "duh" in the letter name "duh bull u," and bingo, *W* becomes the letter chosen to represent the "duh" sound in "d-ress." Without knowledge of how children use letter names in their early efforts to match speech and print, this spelling would seem pretty strange. But teachers with knowledge about how children learn and use alphabet letter names can tell this child is showing a systematic and advancing understanding of how speech and print work together.

Other studies also suggest that knowing letter names might be more advantageous than knowing letter sounds. These studies have shown that children learn words such as *ape* and *acorn* better than they learn words such as *apple* and *avocado* (Treiman et al., 1996). Can you tell anything different about how the letter *A* functions in the first two compared to the second two words? The important difference to notice is that in *ape* and *acorn* the letter *name* is at the beginning of the word's pronunciation while in *apple* and *avocado* the letter *sound* is at the beginning of the word. Another reason why letter names might be a better way to begin than letter sounds is the observation that preschool children typically know as much as two to three times more letter names than letter sounds. This might simply reflect that even preschool children have had more exposure and instruction related to letter names than letter sounds, though. A final point to consider is there is good evidence that preschool English language learners can learn letter names in English (Roberts & Neal, 2004), while there is no such evidence that I am aware of for preschool English language learners learning letter sounds.

There is another possibility for the advantage of learning letter names that is directly related to English language learners. This potential advantage for letter names is based on a difference in the thinking processes that are involved in learning letter names compared to letter sounds. Recall that learning the letter name of a letter shape is a connection-making process called *association learning*. The beneficial role of repetition, practice, and explicit teaching for learning these connections was noted. Learning letter sounds draws more heavily on language competencies than does learning letter names. Because the letter sounds are little bits of speech, while letter names are whole words, children's ability to segment speech sounds from words—their *phonological awareness* ability—is influential in learning letter sounds. The connection-making process for learning letter sounds is more dependent on language skill. Logically this would imply that learning letter sounds in English would be more difficult than learning letter names for English language learners because of their just-emerging English language skills.

Whether you teach letter names or letter sounds first, the fleeting nature of letter sounds and the newness of letter names is an important reason for teaching strategies that make the names and sounds of the alphabet concrete and "stand still" (Castiglioni-Spalten & Ehri, 2003; Ehri & Roberts, 2006). Letter sounds are less distinctive and harder to hear than letter names even for English-only children (Treiman & Kessler, 2003). This difference may be even more influential for ELLs who are just learning English and may be another reason for favoring teaching of letter names over letter sounds. The suggestion for making the alphabet concrete and to stand still applies more to the situation in which English

Teaching Principle 10: Teach letter names before or with letter sounds.

Teaching Principle 11: Make letters concrete by (a) teaching children how they are pronounced, (b) having all children actively pronounce the letter name/sound many times, and (c) providing children individual markers they can use to represent and count letter names/sounds.

Teaching Principle 12: Select words that include both the letter name (*acorn*) and/or letter sound (*apple*) at the beginning of the word to help children see how letters are used in meaningful print.

language learners are taught letter sounds, but it can also be beneficial for learning letter names. Helping children to notice and feel how they pronounce letter names and sounds, to speak the letter names/sounds many times to lay down the physical motor patterns that produce the names/sounds, and to represent names/sounds with small tiles that can be pushed forward one at a time as they name or give the sound of letters are ways to help make letter names/sounds concrete and to stand still. A number of materials and practices from one of my studies with English language learner and English-only kindergarten children to make letter sounds stand still are shown in the following box.

Materials and Practices for Making Letter Sounds "Stand Still"

Children were provided with a small bag that included a nonbreakable mirror, a set of small tiles (blank ones and ones with letters written on them), and a small "telephone" made of jointed PVC pipe for pronunciation amplification. These materials were used during alphabet instruction to

- explore how sounds were made (mirrors),
- represent each sound that children heard in words (tiles), and
- amplify the sounds of target sounds as children listened to themselves (small PVC telephone).

Children were also taught the meaning of the words *throat, lips, tongue, teeth,* and *sound* in both primary language and English and were given explanations of how to pronounce letters that were being taught.

So why not just teach the letter names and the letter sounds at the same time? Recall that with letter names alone there are 40 discrete uppercase and lowercase shapes and names that must be stitched together. If we add in the same number of letter sounds (even though some letters stand for more than one sound, like *C* in the word *cake* compared to *cereal*), this would mean there is double the learning to be done. A lot more teaching and attention to letters would be required. And since the letter names give clues to most of the letter sounds, children will get more "pluck for their buck" when they learn letter names. The expression "pluck for their buck" means that children will acquire both letters names and letter sounds when they learn letters. And to add a finishing touch to these points, research has not shown that learning letter sounds gives children clues to letter names (Treiman et al., 1998). Taking into account the available research and the logical analysis offered in this section, teaching letter names before letter sounds seems like the best course of action at this time. Stay tuned for important updates as the research on teaching letter names and letter sounds evolves.

Apply Your Knowledge

1. Think of three to four strategies that you could regularly use to help children make letter names/sounds concrete.

2. Divide a piece of paper into two columns. Label one column "letter name at beginning of word" and label the other "letter sound at beginning of word." For the letters *A, B, D, E,* and *P,* think of words that begin with the letter *names* (*acorn*) and words that begin with letter *sounds* (*apple*). For each of these five letters, write the words in the appropriate column as you think of them. Save this list to help you plan lessons on these letters in the future.

3. Look at the sample page from the following alphabet book. Which words would be best for teaching the letter name "A"? Which words would be best for the letter sound /a/? What is the problem with the word *artichoke* as an example for either the name or the sound of the letter *A*?

(Continued)

(Continued)

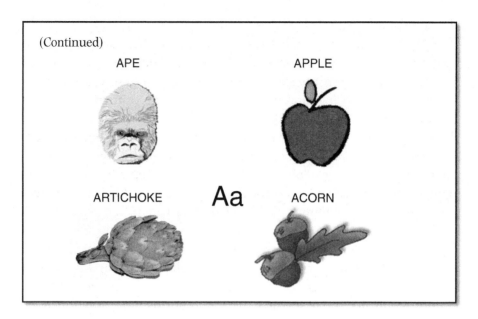

APE

APPLE

ARTICHOKE   Aa   ACORN

HOW SHOULD THE UPPERCASE AND LOWERCASE LETTERS BE TAUGHT?

There is probably no topic related to the alphabet that I have spent more time thinking and talking about with practitioners than whether the uppercase letters or lowercase letters should be taught first. And like the question of letter names or letter sounds, there is no clear research on the best way to teach the uppercase and the lowercase letters. Both English-only and English learner children typically do know more uppercase than lowercase letters. Revisiting Table 4.1 shows that the major source of letter shape confusion is with the lowercase letters. Look at the uppercase and lowercase letters shown below:

A B C D E F G H I J K L M N O P Q R S T U V W X Y Z
a b c d e f g h i j k l m n o p q r s t u v w x y z

You can also see that smaller curved lines are more characteristic of the lowercase letters. These curves are also more difficult for children to write than straight lines. These two facts would suggest that teaching the uppercase letters first might be easier for children. On the other hand, most of the print that children see in books is in lowercase letters, although there is a lot of print in the environment that uses uppercase letters—including food labels, billboards, movie marquees, toy packaging, magazines, the Internet, and computer software. Let's also not forget that many kindergarten teachers prefer children to enter kindergarten writing their names with the first letter in uppercase and the rest in lower case.

So why not just teach the uppercase and the lowercase at the same time? This takes us back to consideration of the heavy increases in learning that children must accomplish to learn both the uppercase and lowercase at the same time. Because of the significantly increased learning that would be involved if children are taught the uppercase and lowercase letters together, their progress through the alphabet will be slowed, and consequently their ability to have use of the full alphabet system will emerge later. More instructional time will also be necessary. These increased learning demands are especially important to consider for English learners. If both the uppercase and lowercase are to be taught at the same time, a good compromise might be to introduce the letter name and uppercase letter together for, say, the first three days the letter is taught, although this has not been tested in research. On day four, the lowercase letter could be introduced and thereby would be added to an already well-established pair. Another option would be to teach all children the uppercase letters and as children know these letters very well, add the lowercase letters.

Teaching Principle 13: Plan for instruction, practice, and review that takes into account the amount of learning that children are required to do as they learn letters:

uppercase + lowercase = more learning required

Teaching Principle 14: If uppercase or lowercase letters alone are used, carefully select sources of print that will show the uppercase or lowercase letters you are teaching.

Educational Principle 2: Carefully decide whether you will teach uppercase letters first, lowercase letters first, or both at the same time.

Transitioning From Uppercase to Lowercase Letters in Personal Name Writing

One idea for addressing the dilemma of whether to use all uppercase letters or just the first letter in uppercase for personal name writing is to begin with

(Continued)

(Continued)

uppercase letters and transition to lowercase as the child is ready. Children could transition from writing their personal name in uppercase to lowercase letters as their knowledge of the alphabet grows. Initially teach children to recognize, name the letters in, and write their personal names in uppercase letters. When children are solid in this ability, begin to introduce lowercase letters in their name. You might explain, "Anna, since you have learned to write your name so well, I'm going to show you another way to write the *N* in your name. You can now start to write your name with the lower case *n.*"

Apply Your Knowledge

1. Make a list of all the sources of print that you can think of that show uppercase letters. Do the same for lowercase letters. Make a collection of these different types of print.

2. Plan ways that you could obtain print representing the different primary languages spoken by children in your classroom. Determine how this print can be used to help with alphabet teaching. If it does not represent the alphabet that is being taught to your children, for what other purposes might it be used?

LEARNING PERSONAL NAMES

Children have strong connections to their own personal names. It is often the first word that they learn to recognize in print. Most take delight at their earliest success in name-writing even if it only includes a letter or two. This initial interest in personal names affects how children learn the alphabet (Bloodgood, 1999). English-only children learn letters in their personal names, especially the first letter, earlier than other letters (Treiman, Cohen, Mulqueeny, Kessler, & Schechtman, 2007). However, parallel, high-quality studies examining the role that personal names play in early literacy development of preschool English language learners have not yet been reported. One study provided limited evidence that children's knowledge of their native Hawaiian name as reported by parents had some limited connection to reading achievement. Across cultures it is likely that a child's personal name will be important to him or her because of the name's connection to personal identity, and it is therefore likely that English language learners will also have strong interest in their personal name.

This early learning of personal names by English-only children is probably partially due to the interest and meaningfulness of personal names. Personal names are also likely to be seen in print more frequently than other words and thus are learned or remembered because of this print exposure. Children see their name written on their cubbies, and they may have a name "necklace" that they wear for the first days of the preschool year. They may also have been encouraged to write their name or see their name on books, cards, artwork, and personal belongings at home. A final reason children may learn their personal names first is that in preschool settings, teaching children to write their personal name is a more universal practice than teaching all the letters of the alphabet.

Personalization and meaningfulness can contribute to positive motivation, which contributes to attention, effort, and learning. The positive motivational possibilities of attending to letters in personal names can be capitalized on by using personal names as a context for teaching alphabet letters. Personal names can be included in explicit lessons. For example, if the children are participating in a lesson on the letter *M*, all the children's names that begin with that letter can be grouped together in a pocket chart, and all the names with the letter *M* in a location other than at the beginning can be grouped together, and names without letter *M* can be placed in a third group. Children and the teacher can say the child's name together and then identify where the letter *M* is.

A small cardboard frame can be used to mask the letter *M* in order to help children attend to its unique features. The frame can be removed to see how the letter functions in a whole word. The letter is moved in and out of a meaningful context in this manner. Seeing alphabet letters in and out of context achieves two things. First, when a letter is out of context— just a bare letter—the child can focus on the attributes of that letter with the goal of learning the connection between the letter shape and its letter name/sound. Putting the letter back into context—embedded in the child's name or other word—highlights how letters work as part of meaningful print.

There are a few limitations of using personal names that should be considered. Children's personal names have varying numbers of letters, making success in writing or recognizing them much more challenging for some than for others in a way that does not align with individual differences in competence. Many Hmong names, such as "Mai," "Sua," and "Bao," are only three letters long, while some East Indian, Lao, and

Teaching Principle 15: Use personal names as a context for helping children learn about individual letters.

Teaching Principle 16: Assess children's knowledge of their personal names (writing, recognizing, or naming) in a way that clearly shows what children know about the individual letter shapes in their names.

Spanish first names, such as "Gnanathusharan," "Sihhpaseuth," and "Yessenia," may be eight to fourteen letters long. Another challenge with personal names from English and other languages is that they may obscure or not match associations between English letter names and English phonemes in speech. Consider the child whose name is "Cassidy" or "Jose." Since the names of English language learners come from many different cultures, take the time to check that the names are spelled correctly, especially those for which there is a close English equivalent, such as "Ana." Another point is that the use of personal names does not ensure that children are given opportunity to learn all the letters.

It is important not to overestimate a child's alphabet knowledge on the basis of the child's ability to write his or her personal name. Children can learn to write the letters in their name without learning the connection—here we go again—between the shape they have written and the letter name. A good idea would be to have children name each letter out loud as they write their names. This practice will enhance letter learning and is a handy way to assess how many letters a child clearly knows. Another thing to think about is that just as children may write the letters without knowing their letter names, they can know the letter names without knowing their shapes. A child may correctly spell her or his name by reciting all the individual letters, in correct order, without being able to point to each letter while spelling or to name the letters of his or her name when the letters are rearranged. Yet it is that one-to-one mapping between the letter shape and the letter name that is necessary to know a letter well enough to enable learning the speech-print connection crucial for skilled reading. Having children arrange individual letters from their name into the correct order while naming them would leave no doubt that they had learned each of those letters. The following box lists several ideas for using personal names to learn alphabet letters.

Ideas for Using Children's Personal Names to Learn Alphabet Letters

- Have children sign in and out of class or centers using a class roster with large font.
- Have children post name cards at centers while they use them.
- Place names on personal mailboxes to encourage children to write and deliver letters to others, or have one child serve as the postperson that places other children's artwork and papers in the correct mailboxes.
- Have children find their own name necklaces, or have more knowledgeable children distribute those of others.
- Place the names of children on their special days (birthdays, moving dates, got a pet, going to Mexico date) on the class calendar. Discuss the name and event on the appropriate day.
- Dismiss and call small groups of children according to which letter their names start with.
- Provide each child with a small personal name card to keep with her or him during the day as a model for how to write his or her name whenever she or he needs or wants to.
- Provide models of names as children read alphabet books, so they can match the letters in their own or another's name to the appropriate page in the alphabet book.
- Write each letter of each child's name, about two inches high, on a card; laminate the cards for durability. Place a card for each letter in each child's name into a baggie for each child. Encourage children to correctly order and name the letters each day.

Apply Your Knowledge

Plan a task where the goal is to determine if children know the individual letters in their personal names. Be careful to design your task so that ability to write or recognize their name is not assumed to be the same as knowing each of the letters that make up their name. Try your assessment task with a few children. What did you learn?

MAKING THE CONNECTION BETWEEN LETTERS AND MEANINGFUL PRINTED WORDS

The ultimate purpose of having children learn the connection between speech and the letters that represent the individual phonemes (sounds) in speech is for children to gain meaning from print—to read with comprehension. A significant part of reading comprehension is to access the meaning of each printed word, which is of course composed of individual letters. Therefore it is very important to help English learners appreciate that the individual letters they learn are used in meaningful print.

While the print that appears in books is of course a critical context for children to see that letters are used in making meaning, there are also other important sources of print that illustrate this point. Children's personal names are a motivating, attention-garnering, and meaningful context in which to gain understanding that letters represent pronunciations of meaningful words. There is also other print in the classroom and in children's homes and communities. Another context in which letters come to vibrant life is when children use them to write or when others write for them their own personal labels, comments, sentences, and stories. All of these contexts can help English learners appreciate the importance of letters for authentic and meaningful written expression.

Do you think alphabet books or other story (*narrative*) or informational (*expository*) books would be more effective for helping children see the use of letters in print? A clue to help you with this question is to compare what children do when they participate in "reading" alphabet books with what they do when they participate in reading other types of books. Children's natural orientation to language from the time they first begin to acquire it is to make meaning with it—to express themselves, to understand others, and to establish interaction with others. They bring this orientation to meaning with them when they engage in book-reading. The following vignette shows this orientation to meaning in a preschool English learner with very limited book-reading experiences.

Jasmine Shows the Meaning Orientation to Storybook Reading

One of the first storybook reading experiences for Jasmine, a preschool girl whose primary language was Spanish, was of the book *Rosie's Walk*. Jasmine entered preschool as the firstborn child, and her parents stated in the home language inventory that they spoke only Spanish with her and that Jasmine used only Spanish in her home communication. As we paused during reading and talked about Rosie being a hen, Jasmine spontaneously scooted across the floor and took the storybook *Ping* from the book rack, pointed to Ping and Rosie and exclaimed, "chicken"! She was clearly attending to the "birdness" similarity between Rosie the hen and Ping the duck and using the word she knew in English, *chicken*, to verbally express that similarity.

If I had attempted to draw Jasmine's attention to the letters in the words *hen* or *duck,* it would have required Jasmine to shift from a meaning orientation to a focus on print, which she is naturally less inclined to do. And indeed studies have shown that children and those that read with them do not pay much attention to alphabet letters while reading storybooks (Yaden, Smolkin, & Conlon, 1989). While children may learn that print carries meaning and that print represents oral language from storybook reading, they do not appear to learn much about specific letters. In contrast, when children read alphabet books, individual letters dominate the pages that go with them, and the print is limited to words that relate to those letters, orienting children more to the letters themselves (Bus & van IJzendoorn, 1988; Yaden, Smolkin, & MacGillivray, 1993).

WRITING HELPS CHILDREN LEARN THE ALPHABET

When children write and have progressed to the point that they have begun to discover relationships between letters and speech, they will begin to represent these emerging ideas in their writing. Children's writing progresses from scribbles to letterlike forms to random use of letters to using letters where the letter name and/or sound matches what they hear in spoken words. When children write, they learn how to write individual letters, how letter shapes and speech are connected, and how alphabet letters are used to express meaning.

The following example is an order taken by a four-year-old server in a restaurant dramatic play center. What can you observe about this child's knowledge of the alphabet? There are at least four letters represented—*Y, P, O,* and *R*—and the child is beginning to show that letters are arrayed in a horizontal line. To find out more, I asked this child what his customer had ordered and he told me "rice." Can you see any way this child was using alphabet letter knowledge in this writing sample? Hint: Think about the letter *R;* think about the letter *Y* and the pronunciation of the word "rice" (remember to say "Y" and "rice" out loud). Providing writing materials, prompts, and opportunities to use letters in centers is another rich context for helping English language learners understand the relationship between letters and meaningful print. The order pad from the restaurant center is an example of how using writing in a dramatic play center helps children experience the relationship between letters and personally meaningful print (see Figure 4.1).

Figure 4.1   Order Pad

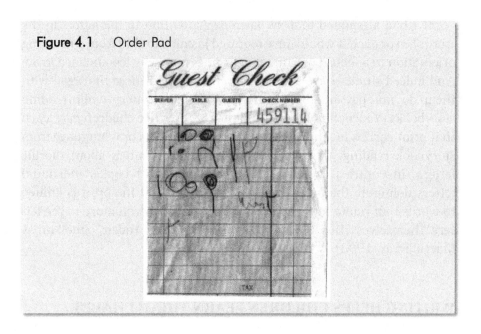

Teaching Principle 17: Use alphabet books to help children learn about letters in print.

Teaching Principle 18: Use print from children's homes and communities to connect letters and print.

Teaching Principle 19: Provide writing opportunities where children are encouraged to apply their emerging alphabet knowledge.

Teaching Principle 20: Provide rich sources of classroom print and activities to encourage children to use print in center and play activities.

Teaching Principle 21: Help children learn to write letters with an efficient and consistent process.

Writing letters is difficult and laborious for young children. Helping children learn how to write letters makes the task less challenging. One of the biggest advantages children have when they have been taught how to print letters correctly is that it motivates them to write and to be able to write more easily. By correctly I mean being taught to use a specific sequence of strokes and starting point to write the letter every time. Some commercial programs have songs, cartoons, and other engaging media to help children learn to "correctly" write letters. I am fond of using individual ten-by-twelve-inch white boards so that children can practice writing letters in every alphabet lesson. More-skilled children can be encouraged to write letters smaller and smaller, while less-skilled children can write the letter big without having to worry about lines or tearing a piece of paper. An old sock is an excellent eraser.

Apply Your Knowledge

We have considered teaching letter names versus letter sounds and upper-case versus lowercase letters. We have added the concepts of personal names, alphabet books, writing, print in the environment, and using print in centers and play to learning about the alphabet. Modify and elaborate your first lesson plan based on these new ideas. The lesson plan form below includes these additions that begin with Number 5.

Explicit Alphabet Lesson Plan

1. Specific alphabet-related goal of the lesson _____

2. Focus children's attention on the letter and letter name/sound

   _____

   _____

3. Specific activities that will help children remember the connection between the letter shape and the letter name or sound

   a. How will you include practice and repetition?

      _____

      _____

   b. How will you make the lesson engaging and meaningful?

      _____

      _____

4. How will you promote children's self-regulation?

   _____

   _____

5. How will you include children's personal names?

   _____

   _____

6. How will you encourage children to say the letter names and/or sounds?

   _____

   _____

7. How will you use alphabet books?

   _____

   _____

(Continued)

(Continued)

8. How will you include writing?

_____

_____

9. What other types of print in the environment will you include?

_____

_____

10. How will you incorporate meaningful opportunities to write letters in centers and during dramatic play?

_____

_____

TEACHING THE ALPHABET IN A LANGUAGE OTHER THAN ENGLISH

English learners can learn to read in many different ways. They can learn to read in the language they speak at home using the written system that is used to represent that language. Children can learn to read in a second language like English. They can also learn to read in two languages at the same time. Decisions on which of these approaches is optimal cannot be made on the basis of available research for children. However, I will suggest several factors that should be considered.

How the alphabet or other system for representing speech in print is taught should follow from decisions based on careful thought. Since the purpose of learning the alphabet is to prepare children to read with understanding, foremost among these considerations should be which language children will learn to read first. If preschool children whose primary language is Spanish will enter an elementary bilingual program where they will initially learn to read in Spanish, then teaching the Spanish alphabet in preschool would provide a strong foundation for their reading. If, on the other hand, children whose primary language is Spanish are to enter a kindergarten program where they will learn to read in English, then teaching the English alphabet will serve them better.

The language the child will learn to read in, the opportunity for seeing and having access to materials printed in a language, the availability of teachers who are fluent in a language, the desires and values of children's families related to language practices, and the preschool classroom composition in respect to the number of primary languages spoken by children and the number of children within a particular language group are important factors to consider in determining which alphabet to teach. Frequently a significant part of the rationale for desiring to teach the alphabet in children's primary language is to demonstrate cultural and linguistic respect, to draw on children's linguistic prior knowledge, and to forestall introduction of English in the expectation that to do so will preserve primary language. Cultural and linguistic valuing and the preservation of primary language are certainly important aspects of educational practice for English language learners. From the perspective of literacy, critical considerations of which written language system to introduce children to are also those related to reading instruction and acquisition, since the primary role of the alphabet is to foster reading ability.

The largest percentage of English language learners in the United States have Spanish as their primary language. Because of these large numbers, Spanish speakers are more likely to form a critical mass within a preschool program. There are also more Spanish bilingual preschool teachers and Spanish bilingual paraprofessionals than for other languages. Children's books and literacy curriculums are also readily available in Spanish. Most of the elementary school bilingual programs are also Spanish-English. When there are sufficient numbers of preschool children, proficient Spanish bilingual teachers, many Spanish language literacy materials, and children enter a Spanish bilingual program in kindergarten with Spanish language reading instruction, then instruction in the Spanish alphabet would be optimal.

Not all languages use the same alphabet as English and Spanish. For example, while Arabic and Russian print uses symbols to stand for sounds in speech just as English does, the symbols that are used are different and represent many speech sounds (phonemes) that are different from those used in English. A language like Spanish or French uses a similar set of alphabet symbols, and some sounds overlap with those of English, although there are also language differences in phonemes. Languages such as Korean and Chinese are not based on an alphabet where symbols represent individual sounds. Hmong uses the same alphabet as English but has taken some letters to represent tones that are added to the ends of spoken words. These high, medium, and low tones are represented by the letters *a, b, j, g, o, m, s, u,* and *w* added to the ends of words.

HOW MUCH LETTER INSTRUCTION IS NEEDED?

The amount of instruction on the alphabet that is optimal is an important emerging issue, as expectations for preschool alphabetic learning are increasing, and more and more preschools are adopting comprehensive

Teaching Principle 22: Include about 10 to 12 minutes of alphabet instruction daily.

literacy curriculums. One of these curriculums that I have examined includes one-and-a-half hours of group literacy experience daily, with about 30 to 40 minutes of alphabet instruction. In our studies, 16 weeks of instruction that covered one letter a week for three lessons of no more than 15 minutes on the alphabet was adequate for relatively high levels of alphabet letter learning. The average number of uppercase letters learned by children who participated in alphabet instruction was 11.16 letters of 16 letters taught, or 68% correct on letter naming. A total of 12 hours of explicit alphabet letter instruction, or no more than about 45 minutes per week, was adequate for significant alphabet learning. This translates to about 10 minutes per day on the alphabet.

CONCLUSION

Teaching English learners the alphabet requires a deep understanding of the alphabet. Hopefully, you have been helped to see that effective instruction needs to be carefully planned, regular, and explicit. Effective instruction in the alphabet for English learners should be engaging, participatory, and multisensory, and it should provide for self-regulation. Looking, speaking, and writing are all important in learning the alphabet. There is research that helps identify how to effectively teach the alphabet, but the evidence specific to English language learners is much more limited. You have participated in activities to apply all of the principles for effective alphabet instruction that are summarized below. These principles can be used to plan and evaluate how you teach the alphabet. They can also be used to identify strengths and weaknesses of the alphabet component of any curriculum. These analyses could be used to select a curriculum or to identify ways in which the one you are currently using may need to be modified. You are ready.

Summary of Teaching Principles

Teaching Principle 1: Identify the purpose and goal(s) of alphabet lessons to children.

Teaching Principle 2: Help children focus on learning the connections between the alphabet letter shapes and their names/sounds.

Teaching Principle 3: Use strategies and activities designed to help children memorize the associations between letter shapes and their names/sounds.

Teaching Principle 4: Make lessons that are engaging and meaningful and that provide opportunities for self-regulation.

Teaching Principle 5: Teach letters in a sequence that minimizes the confusability among letter shapes.

Teaching Principle 6: Teach letter names in a sequence that minimizes letters whose *names* are similar being taught too close together.

Teaching Principle 7: Teach letter sounds in a sequence that minimizes letters whose *sounds* are similar being taught too close together.

Teaching Principle 8: Teach letters that have the letter sound embedded in the *beginning* of the letter name before letters that have the sound embedded at the *end* of the letter name.

Teaching Principle 9: Consider leaving letters associated with letter sounds (phonemes) that are challenging for children to produce until later in the learning sequence.

Teaching Principle 10: Teach letter names before or with letter sounds.

Teaching Principle 11: Make letters concrete by (a) teaching children how they are pronounced, (b) having all children pronounce the letter name/sound many times, and (c) providing children individual markers they can use to represent and count letter names/sounds.

Teaching Principle 12: Select words that include both the letter name (*acorn*) and letter sound (*apple*) to help children see how letters are used in meaningful words/print.

Teaching Principle 13: Plan for instruction, practice, and review that takes into account the amount of learning that children are required to do as they learn letters:

uppercase + lowercase = more learning required.

Teaching Principle 14: If uppercase or lowercase letters alone are used, carefully select sources of print that will show the uppercase or lowercase letters you are teaching.

Teaching Principle 15: Use personal names as a context for helping children learn about individual letters.

(Continued)

(Continued)

Teaching Principle 16: Assess children's knowledge of their personal names (writing, recognizing, or naming) in a way that clearly shows what children know about the individual letter shapes in their names.

Teaching Principle 17: Use alphabet books to help children learn about letters in print.

Teaching Principle 18: Use print from children's homes and communities to connect letters and meaningful print.

Teaching Principle 19: Provide writing opportunities where children are encouraged to apply their emerging alphabet knowledge.

Teaching Principle 20: Provide rich sources of classroom print and activities to encourage children to use print in center and play activities.

Teaching Principle 21: Help children learn to write letters with an efficient and consistent process.

Teaching Principle 22: Include about 10 to 12 minutes of alphabet instruction daily.

Summary of Educational Principles

Educational Principle 1: Include learning about the alphabet as part of the language and literacy curriculum for English language learners from all languages, even when they are just starting to learn about the English language.

Educational Principle 2: Carefully decide whether you will teach uppercase letters first, lowercase letters first, or both at the same time.

NOTES

1. When a letter is shown between slashes, it represents the letter sound.

2. There are other reasons why knowing the letters of the alphabet is important, such as putting things in alphabetical order, making outlines, finding entries in an alphabetized list, and so forth.

3. Letters *A, E, I, O,* and *U* have the letter names when they are long vowels in words such as *play, sneeze, mice, hose,* and *huge.*

Sounds in Words   5

Phonological Awareness

★ ★

Important Research Results About Sounds in Words

- Ability to attend to sounds in words is one of the two best predictors of later reading skill.

- Ability to attend to sounds in words is difficult to learn, because it requires separation of speech sounds that are connected during talking.

- Ability with sounds in words in first language is related to both first language and second language reading.

- Teaching sounds in words leads to better reading.

- Attending to larger chunks of sounds in words is easier than attending to individual sounds.

- Accuracy in speaking the sounds in words is related to ability to attend to sounds in words.

- Preschool English learners can learn about sounds in words in their first and second languages.

- Rhyming is very difficult for preschool English learners.

- There is a known sequence of difficulty in tasks that require children to attend to sounds in words.

★ ★

In the chapter "Befriending the Alphabet" I explained that learning the system for how spoken words and print are related is the essential knowledge that children need to learn how to read. That chapter focused on the print component of the learning to read equation:

speech + print = learning how to read

The focus of this chapter will be on the speech part of the equation. Preschool children come to school with a well-developed system of spoken language. They understand what is spoken to them and how to use this language system to express their experiences, wants, and desires. Yet in order to learn to read well, they must develop a new skill with spoken language that is very different from the communication focus that most of their previous use of oral language has centered on. This new oral language skill is the ability to deconstruct whole words into little bits of sounds. This essential oral language skill, "the general ability to attend to the sounds of language as distinct from its meaning" (Snow, Burns, & Griffin, 1998, p. 52), is called *phonological awareness,* although some may call it *phonological sensitivity.* Children show this skill at a beginning level when they can, for example, clap and say the three syllables in butterfly as "but" - "ter" - "fly" with one clap for each syllable, or chunk of sound. Skill at the level of sophistication that will fully enable children to make the speech-print connection will require, for example, the ability to clap three times as they say each of the individual sounds in "cat," /c/ /a/ /t/,[1] and in reverse to be given the individual sounds /c/ /a/ /t/, put them together, and say the word "cat." And as with the alphabet, there is much for children to learn to achieve this ability.

Children's learning of phonological awareness (PA) is made more difficult because they will need to work with words in a way that is very different from how they have approached them in the past as unified wholes where all the sound parts are woven together and overlap. This overlapping phenomenon is called *coarticulation.* For preschool children who will be developing phonological awareness in a second language, the challenge will be even greater, as the words they have previously used for language communication are different and may not even be formed of the same sounds that they will be asked to pay attention to in the second language. To successfully acquire the highest possible level of phonological awareness—whether in their first or second language—preschool English learners will benefit from significant amounts of scaffolding from their teachers.

WHAT IS PHONOLOGICAL AWARENESS?

Phonological awareness means that children are able to attend to the sounds of words rather than their meanings. There are two strands of phonological awareness that influence which tasks are easier or harder. The first strand that influences difficulty is the number of sounds that the child can distinguish. The ability to attend to larger chunks of sounds such as syllables is easier and emerges earlier than the ability to attend to individual sounds. When phonological awareness is just emerging, children detect differences and similarities in how *whole words* and *chunks* of spoken words sound. Examples of this ability are shown in lines one and two of Figure 5.1. A higher level of phonological awareness comes from being able to attend to *individual sounds* in a word. These individual sounds are called *phonemes*. Budding ability to pay attention to individual sounds is usually shown when children notice the first sounds in words. Separating a word into the first sound and the remaining chunk is the *onset-rime* level of phonological awareness. Line three in Figure 5.1 shows the onset-rime level of difficulty. Sounds at the end of words are more difficult than the first sounds but are easier than the sounds in the middle of words. *Phonemic awareness* is demonstrated when children can name and manipulate all of the individual sounds in words as shown in the fourth line of Figure 5.1.

The second strand that influences difficulty of phonological awareness tasks is the nature of the thinking the child has to do with either larger or smaller chunks. The more steps the child has to do in his or her mind, the more difficult the task is. These levels of phonological awareness and examples of them are shown in Table 5.1.

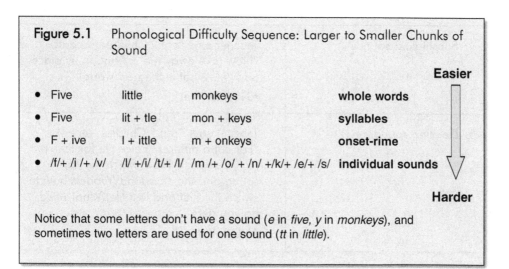

Figure 5.1 Phonological Difficulty Sequence: Larger to Smaller Chunks of Sound

Easier

- Five   little   monkeys   **whole words**
- Five   lit + tle   mon + keys   **syllables**
- F + ive   l + ittle   m + onkeys   **onset-rime**
- /f/+ /i /+ /v/   /l/ +/i/ /t/+ /l/   /m /+ /o/ + /n/ +/k/+ /e/+ /s/   **individual sounds**

Harder

Notice that some letters don't have a sound (*e* in *five*, *y* in *monkeys*), and sometimes two letters are used for one sound (*tt* in *little*).

Table 5.1 Levels of Phonological Awareness Tasks

Task	Example Activity
1. Judging whether words/sounds are the same or different	1. Teacher says, "I will say two words." Children repeat. "Would you please tell me if the words are the same or if they are different?" Word pairs: dog, dog; dog, cookie; hat, dog; cat, cat; cookie, hat; cookie, cookie
2. Combining parts of words	2. Teacher says /c/ /a/ /t/, then models how to put the sounds together. "I will say some tiny parts of words, and I want you to put the parts together and guess what the word is." Words: /d/ /o/ /g/; /tum/ /my/; /h/ /a/ /t/; /cook/ /ie/
3. Separating parts of words	Teacher says "cat." Children repeat. "Tap once with your finger for each sound you hear as you s l o w l y say cat." Teacher models how to tap each word, and the children tap along. Teacher says "crib." Children repeat. "Now take away the /c/. What is left?" ANSWER: "rib" Words: dog, toe, me, hop
4. Substituting sounds	Teacher says "cat." Children repeat. "Now take away the /c/ and in its place add /r/. What is the new world?" ANSWER: "rat"
5. Deleting sounds	Teacher says "pat." Children repeat. "Put out a different color tile for the /p/ /a/ /t/ sounds. Now switch the /p/ sound and the /t/ sound (models how to switch the first and last tile). What word do you get?" ANSWER: "tap"

English learners might even indicate "yes" or "no" with a headshake on Task 1, the "same/different" task. Of course, you will have to demonstrate or model with several pairs of words, making sure you clearly nod "yes" if the two words are the same and "no" if the two words are different. Alternatively you might have a bilingual resource person teach English learners children about "same" and "different" in primary language and the related English words "same" and "different" prior to beginning instruction. When children put together sounds or chunks of sound as shown in Task 2, more thinking steps are required than for detecting similarities and differences between whole words, and Task 2 is therefore more difficult.

On Task 3, the child has to remember the word *and* strip off the /c/ *and* tap *and* then take the /at/ *and* strip off /a/ and tap again. She or he will have to remember where she or he is in the word to tap once again for that last sound /t/. *Crib* is a more difficult word than *cat,* because to be successful the child must separate the /cr/ (called a *blend*) into /c/ and /r/, where the two sounds are very closely woven together.

While Tasks 3 and 4 are difficult, Task 5 is the most difficult, because children have to do more steps, or *cognitive operations,* to be successful. They have to strip off the /p/ and hold this sound in memory while they strip off the /t/, hold both in memory, remember to switch them, remember the middle /a/ sound, and then combine together the new sequence of /t/ /a/ /p/ to arrive at the word *tap.* Whew, that's a lot of work!

The high level of phonological awareness shown by Tasks 3, 4, and 5 requires attending to and manipulating individual sounds and demonstrates phonemic awareness. Phonemic awareness is not likely to be achieved by most four-year-olds, although some will, and more rarely by three-year-olds. True phonemic awareness emerges across the kindergarten and first-grade year for most children who are receiving instruction in learning how to read words and how print maps speech. This systematic teaching of how letters and letter groups represents specific sound in spoken words is called *phonics instruction.* Learning to read with ease and enjoyment is dependent upon the ability to make the systematic connection between sounds in speech and alphabet letters. Helping

Teaching Principle 1: Begin teaching activities with the easier phonological awareness tasks: use whole words and syllables before onset-rimes and individual sounds.

Teaching Principle 2: Help children to attend to sounds at the beginning of words before sounds at the end of words.

children achieve phonological awareness in preschool prepares them with developmentally appropriate skills to be further developed in phonics instruction.

WORDS: THE FOUNDATION OF PHONOLOGICAL AWARENESS

Words are the basic units that are used in acquiring phonological awareness. Let's look at how learning words is related to phonological awareness. In the human species, many areas of the brain are involved in learning words. One critical piece of this word-learning architecture of the brain is the ability to perceive the individual speech sounds, or phonemes, words are made of.

Babies Have Skill in Perceiving Speech Sounds

By two months of age infants have the ability to *perceive* (notice differences between) speech sounds. Infants from all cultures are able to perceive the different speech sounds that come from many different languages by two months of age (Best, 1994). This means they hear the sounds and notice differences between the sounds that are used to make up words in many languages. For example, when an infant hears the words *baby*, *mommy*, and *bottle*, he or she is able to distinguish between the four sounds in *baby*, the four phonemes in *mommy* (don't get tricked by the spelling), and the four phonemes in *bottle* (don't get tricked by the spelling again). The infant also detects sounds that are similar—but not exactly the same—in different words. Say *bug* and *tub* out loud. The /b/ is not spoken exactly the same as the /b/ in *tub*. Could you notice a difference? The neighboring sounds are different in the two words, and the position of /b/ in the words is different (beginning versus end). These factors influence the pronunciation of the /b/ sound. Yet, infants are organizing creatures and will form basic categories in their brains for the /b/ sound that are flexible such that, like you, they will hear the /b/ in the two words as belonging to the same sound category.

One tricky part of phonological awareness learning is that the speech sounds in words are always connected together when children hear and use words; they are like watercolors that bleed into each other. In speech I say the word *cat* as one integrated whole. Say the sentence "I have ten cats" one sound at a time: /I/ /h / /a/ /v/ /t/ /e/ /n/ /c/ /a/ /t/ /s/. Was it like regular speech? After exploring the nature of phonological awareness, you can appreciate that there is a lot for children to learn, and there is a lot that the teacher needs to know about the developmental progression in phonological awareness learning to ensure that her or his efforts help children learn it and about why instruction is needed. It is to these issues that we now turn.

UNNATURAL ASPECTS OF PHONOLOGICAL AWARENESS

When children use words, their primary goal is to communicate meaning. They use words to tell what they see, they use words to ask for help, they use words to get their caregivers to respond to them, they use words to share roles and play out sequences of interactions with peers during sociodramatic and pretend play, and they may even use words to make up their own poem or to control their behavior by telling themselves "wait, wait" when they are trying to wait their turn. The natural function of words in language is to receive, express, and create meaning. Typically developing preschool children have primarily used words for making meaning prior to entering preschool. They bring this experience with them to the preschool setting, although the language in which they have used words will be their first language.

Phonological awareness is reflected in what children can do with the structure rather than the meaning of oral language. Children learn the sounds of their native language by noticing differences in sounds in words and by establishing categories in their minds for the specific sounds that are used in their language. Just as children will categorize colors that are slightly different as being "red" (light red, burgundy, red-orange), they will categorize slight variations on a sound into the same category. While the sound of the /a/ in the spoken words "apple," "alligator," and "animal" is slightly different and might be pronounced differently by speakers from different geographical areas, the child will still categorize the /a/ into the same speech-sound category. These categories exist like a series of filing boxes in the child's mind and are called *phoneme representations*. The categories that are used for each sound become more accurate as children hear more language.

Preschool children hear these individual sounds and use them in speech in their everyday and natural environments so that they pet the *cat* and go to sleep on the *mat* rather than the other way around—(pet the mat and go to sleep on the cat). Their understanding of sounds in words is deeply embedded in their use of language—where they direct their attention to meaning. Yet to achieve phonological awareness skill, they must suppress their practiced and natural orientation to meaning and attend to the sound structure of words. If we were to ask the same preschool child that correctly performed the *cat* and *mat* activities to tell me what the first sound in the word *cat* was or to take the /m/ off of *mat* and to add /c/ instead (to make the word *cat*), the child would likely have difficulty. Learning experiences that assist preschool children in this somewhat unnatural orientation to words are needed to help them acquire phonological awareness. Comparing how words are used for meaning with how they are used for acquiring phonological awareness helps explain research suggesting that storybook reading is not as effective for fostering phonological awareness as is reading alphabet books with letter-sound information in them (Murray, Stahl, & Ivey, 1996). I have a series of questions to help you discover an important reason (if you have not already done so) for this result that draws on information you have learned in this section.

Why Don't Children Pay Much Attention to Letters and Word Sounds During Storybook Reading?

Question 1: What is the natural focus that children bring to words?
> ANSWER: meaning

Question 2: What is the focus of storybook reading?
> ANSWER: meaning

Question 3: What is most likely to be children's focus while participating in storybook reading?
> ANSWER: meaning

Question 4: What will children need to do to attend to sounds in words during storybook reading?
> ANSWER: shift focus from meaning

Question 5: Would it be easier for children to focus on sounds in words when there was less competition for focusing on meaning?
> ANSWER: probably

Question 6: What do you think would be the effect of using nursery rhymes to teach rhyming compared to using single rhyming words to teach rhyming?

Learning phonological awareness is unnatural in another sense as well. Recall that when words are spoken in natural speech, the sounds are all tied together—overlapping and influencing each other. I described this as being like a watercolor painting where the colors bleed together. The result of the intermingling of the watercolors is determined by

Teaching Principle 3: Help children stay focused on the sounds in words rather than their meanings.

nuances of the colors flowing into each other, color intensity, how much intermingling occurs, and so forth. The same is true with speech sounds in words. Yet when children participate in phonological awareness learning activities, they are asked to separate these sounds one from the other in a way in which the sounds do not occur in natural speech.

PRESCHOOL PHONOLOGICAL AWARENESS AND LATER READING

The reason that children need to develop phonological awareness is because it will help them learn to read and spell. It will help them learn letter names and letter sounds. Phonological awareness will also help them combine individual sounds into whole words (blending) and will help them separate whole words into the sounds that the words are made of (segmenting). Blending and segmenting skills are critical *phonics skills* for children to have in order to read words. I will illustrate this with a word designed for you, a skilled reader. Stop here. Close your eyes, count to three, and then open your eyes and look at the word on the next line.

Ubiquitous

What did you have to do to read this word that is far less familiar than my old favorite example word *cat?* Unless you are very familiar with this written word, you probably had to go through the word breaking it into little parts or syllables in order to pronounce it.

The relationship between preschool phonological awareness and later reading and spelling is clearly documented. In many studies, strong relationships between preschool children's ability on a variety of phonological awareness tasks—can you name a few?—and later reading have been found (e.g., Burgess, 2002; Wood & Terrell, 1998). Not surprisingly, the strongest relationships are found between phonological awareness and word-reading skills. I say "not surprisingly" because phonological awareness involves skill in managing the chunks of sound and the individual sounds in words, and words are the basic building blocks of reading comprehension. The strongest relationships are found between tasks that measure skill with individual phonemes and later reading (taking the sounds apart in *cat;* putting sounds /c/ /a/ /t/ together). The higher or more challenging the level on the phonological awareness continuum that children can reach, the more prepared they will be for learning to read.

CAN PRESCHOOL CHILDREN LEARN PHONOLOGICAL AWARENESS?

Yes, preschool children can learn phonological awareness from instruction. Existing studies show that typically developing children, children with various kinds of speech and language challenges and from families of a range of socioeconomic statuses, are successful when provided phonological awareness instruction (Bus & van IJzendoorn, 1999; Byrne & Fielding-Barnsley, 1991, 1993, 1995; Fox & Routh, 1976; National Institute of Child Health and Human Development, 2000; Treiman & Baron, 1983). In addition, slightly older children at risk for difficulty in learning how to read are likely to benefit from explicit instruction in phonological awareness more than other children (Castle, Riach, & Nicholson, 1994; Iversen & Tunmer, 1993; Mather, 1992; Pressley & Rankin, 1994; Raz & Bryant, 1990). Given that many children who come to school speaking a language other than English are more likely to have difficulty with reading suggests the potential importance of explicit instruction for English learners as well.

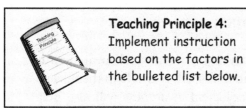

Teaching Principle 4:
Implement instruction based on the factors in the bulleted list below.

These teaching studies have used carefully designed teaching practices. They have identified a number of factors in the teaching programs that influence how well children learn phonological awareness from instruction. These factors include the following:

- Focusing explicitly on a limited number of phonological skills to be learned before others are introduced
- Providing small-group rather than large-group or individual instruction
- Including attention to how mouth movements are made
- Implementing games, active learning, and other practices to involve children

- Providing opportunity for practice and sensitive correction
- Implementing frequent assessment to determine when learning has been accomplished or needs extra support

In short, instructional procedures are planned very carefully.

CONNECTIONS BETWEEN L1 AND L2 PHONOLOGICAL AWARENESS

Studies examining speakers of a variety of languages have led to the conclusion that the ability to attend to sounds of language rather than meaning is learned once and can be applied to all languages an individual speaks. These results have been found in a few studies with preschool English learners (e.g., López & Greenfield, 2004). Phonological awareness becomes a way of thinking that can be applied to other languages. An analogy to math might help here. Once you have the concepts of quantity and order, you could count in

Teaching Principle 5: Teach phonological awareness in either first or second language.

any language—if you knew the words. Phonological awareness in one language can be shared with another language (Durgunoglu, Nagy, & Hancin-Bhatt, 1993). The ability to analyze sounds in words is the thinking skill that must be learned. Among Spanish-speaking children, one study found a relationship between Spanish phonological awareness and Spanish alphabet knowledge and print awareness (Anthony et al., 2006). This is the same relationship that has been found with English-speaking preschool children. If a child has adequate oral proficiency in any language, the foundation for phonological awareness in that language has been laid. Once the child has attained the ability to attend to phoneme segments in any language, this ability can be applied to other languages. Thus L1 to L2 *and* L2 to L1 transfer of phonological awareness would be expected.

LEARNING PHONOLOGICAL AWARENESS IN A SECOND LANGUAGE

As you have learned, the acquisition of phonological awareness is dependent upon the ability to perceive speech sounds that are embedded in spoken words. When children acquire a second language, they quite quickly show sensitivity to second language speech sounds. Interestingly, they may also develop a special awareness of speech sounds in languages by the very nature of having the opportunity to notice the differences in speech sounds that comes with acquiring a second language (Davine, Tucker, & Lambert, 1971). Children acquiring a second language are capable of perceiving phonemes in both a first and second language.

More than *perceiving* the sounds is needed though. At the heart of phonological awareness is the ability to *pay attention* to sounds in words. Bilingualism has been shown to heighten children's ability to focus attention on the sounds in words (Campbell & Sais, 1995; Gonz & Kodzopeljic, 1991; Rubin & Turner, 1989; Verhoeven, 1990). Two of these studies included minority group children who were learning a majority language in their studies, and thus these studies mirror the social circumstances under which many preschool English learners are learning a second language. Of particular relevance to preschool English learners, there is some evidence that children may even have enhanced understandings of the nature of words very early on in second language learning (Diaz, 1985; Mattingly, 1984; Yelland, Pollard, & Mercuri, 1993). Yelland et al. (1993) found as little as one hour a week of second language instruction at the beginning of second language acquisition conferred an advantage in being aware of what a word is. More recent research has extended these findings by showing that English learner children participating in early reading programs that include phonological awareness instruction compare very favorably to English-only children in L2 phonological awareness achievement and that L2 phonological awareness is associated with L2 reading skill (Geva, Wade-Woolley, & Shany, 1997).

Even though preschool English learners may have a heightened awareness of sounds in language in general, there are special challenges that English learners are likely to face with specific sounds in English words when trying to learn phonological awareness in a second language. The phonemes and chunks that they encounter in their second language may not be the same as the phonemes in their home language. Even in the case of Spanish, which is quite similar to English, 7 of the 41 consonants that appear in English do not appear in Spanish. Another challenge is that sounds from the second language that are very similar to sounds in the first language but are not used to change word meanings may be categorized into the first language sound category children have formed in their minds. For example, the initial sounds /v/ and /b/ are produced differently. In English, *very* and *berry* are different words. However, in Spanish /v/ is not a phoneme that is used to change word meanings. So a Spanish-speaking child may not distinguish /b/ and /v/ or may just think they are slightly different ways of saying the same sound. A real world example of this confusion is shared in the next text box.

A Real World Influence From First to Second Language

One of the English learners in a classroom I have worked in was a little girl whose written name on the class list was "Banessa." I called her "Banessa" as did the preschool teachers. As we attempted to follow her into kindergarten, we could find no "Banessa" registered. When we followed up on this discrepancy, we discovered that the preschool teachers, upon hearing her mother repeatedly refer to her as "Banessa" and the child herself saying her name was "Banessa," had corrected their written preschool registration form for the spelling of her name from "Vanessa" to "Banessa." But when the mother again wrote her name at kindergarten registration, she again spelled it "Vanessa." Our written "Vanessa" and spoken "Banessa" were a result of the missing spoken /v/ in Spanish!

When the first and second language sound systems conflict, the first language will override the second as happened with Vanessa. A similar process can occur with /1/ and /r/ for Chinese speakers, but not Korean spea-

Teaching Principle 6: Avoid using words that create confusions between sounds in the first and second language.

kers. While this possibility may seem like a small matter to a teacher, it could lead to substantial confusion on the part of a preschool English learner whose ability to attend to sounds instead of meaning is fragile and unstable.

THE JOINED HANDS OF VOCABULARY AND THE ALPHABET

At this point you have learned that preschool phonological awareness is an important foundation for learning how to read and that it is a challenging task for many preschool children, but one that they can make progress in with good teaching. Vocabulary knowledge and alphabet letter knowledge are helping hands for learning phonological awareness. How do vocabulary and letter knowledge help children acquire phonological awareness?

Teaching Principle 7: Include rich vocabulary development activities in the literacy program.

Teaching Principle 8: Select words that are familiar to children and are short (have fewer letters), and/or teach children the meaning of words prior to having them perform phonological awareness activities on them.

Teaching Principle 9: Teach alphabet letters, and encourage children to use them to represent related sounds as their letter mastery grows.

Children with larger vocabularies tend to do better on phonological awareness tasks (Metsala & Walley, 1998; Storch & Whitehurst, 2002). Conversely, children with smaller vocabularies do more poorly on phonological awareness tasks. To illustrate this, consider the following example. Imagine a child whose spoken vocabulary includes the words *mommy* and *cat*. Say the words out loud. The words differ on many sounds, how long they "hang in the air" when spoken, and the melody of how the sounds are connected together. You can just hear that these words are very different in their overall spoken form. Imagine next that the child adds the word *happy* to the vocabulary. Close your eyes and say "mom-my" and "hap-py" out loud, and pay attention to the end of the words. Do you hear the /e/ sound at the end of each word? The spoken words "mom-my" and "hap-py" are not completely different in how they sound—the sound at the end of the word is the same. In order to accurately understand and use these words, the child must note the difference in the beginning chunk of the two words. Noting a difference in chunks of words is one skill in phonological awareness. For English learners whose English vocabulary is small, the helping hand of vocabulary is also small.

Similarly, children who know more letters tend to do better on phonological awareness tasks a year later (Burgess & Lonigan, 1998). Since phonological awareness was dependent on how many letters were known a year earlier, it seems that knowledge of letters can set the stage for growth in phonological awareness. It is also the case that children who are better on phonological awareness tasks also tend to learn more letters (Share, 2004). The alphabet knowledge hand and the phonological awareness hand are a true team, each helping the other.

Apply Your Knowledge

Divide a sheet of paper into 2 columns as shown in the example.

Syllables	*Beginning Sounds*
Butterfly **1**	Up **S**

1. From the following list of words (see number 3 below), write those with more than one syllable in the "Syllables" column and those that have only one syllable in the "Beginning Sounds" column. (I have done two words for you.)

2. In the "Syllables" column, mark those that are made up of two words (easier) with a *1* and those that simply have multiple syllables (harder) with a *2*. For the words in the "Beginning Sounds" column, mark those that use one of the eight key consonant sounds (/p/, /b/, /j/, /d/, /w/, /m/, /n/, /h/) with a *C*, those that are shorter with an *S*, and those that are more familiar with an *F*. Some one syllable words may have more than one marking.

3. **Words:** up, old, nap, wash, coat, butterfly, hotdog, hamburger, caterpillar, chocolate, rainbow, happy, marshmallow, finger, doorknob, window, grasshopper, mommy, daddy, grandmother, grandfather, sister, brother, jacket, jump, wash, nap, tickle, snake, frog

4. Which words would be best to use for instruction based on what you discovered?

DOES SECOND LANGUAGE PRONUNCIATION MATTER?

An important source of information that children use to categorize speech sounds into the phoneme representation categories in their minds is how their mouths, lips, throats, vocal chords, and other parts of the speech apparatus produce the sounds. When children perceive, categorize, and produce sounds in words, they are guided by this knowledge of how sounds are made with the speech apparatus. They use their concrete knowledge of speech to help them learn it. When children say words, they select the sound categories for the word they want to say, combine this with their knowledge of how to actually get their speech apparatus to make the sounds, connect the sounds together into the appropriate watercolor image (word), and say it. Thus, both hearing sounds in words and using sounds in words when talking are related to how the mouth, lips, throat, vocal chords, and other parts of the speech apparatus make the sounds. So it might be the case that how accurately children say the sounds in words would affect how well they will do on phonological awareness tasks.

This is another of those hot topics in early childhood education with particular relevance to preschool English learners. Historically, educators have been instructed to not be concerned with English learners' pronunciation for two primary reasons. First, errors in oral pronunciation have been viewed as a "surface feature" of language that will not interfere with communicating meaning. It has been believed that as long as pronunciation does not seriously impede communication, there is no need to worry about it. Furthermore, since first and second language development are similar processes, one could expect that many of the pronunciation errors will self-correct just as they do in first language—thus there is no need to correct them (e.g., Terrell & Krashen, 1983). Moreover some believe that correcting children's efforts at second language production might inhibit their willingness to talk and/or interfere with communicative effectiveness, thereby reducing their motivation to use the second language. However, research highlighted in the box that follows suggests that it does matter.

Research Highlight

I conducted a study with kindergarten English learners from two language groups—Hmong & Spanish—to explore whether English pronunciation influenced beginning reading. I measured the accuracy of children's pronunciation of key English sounds by using a test with carefully selected words. I then related their pronunciations to their phonological awareness (rhyming, blending, and segmenting ability in kindergarten). One year later—at the end of first grade—I measured how their word pronunciation was related to word reading. I found that children who made more errors in English pronunciation had lower phonological awareness in kindergarten and lower word reading in first grade. In addition, pronunciation accuracy was just as important for phonological awareness and word reading as was letter sounds. There are many, many studies showing that letter sound knowledge has a very big impact on reading.

—Roberts (2005)

While the study I just described has the advantage of looking at English learners and traces accuracy of pronouncing sounds in words to reading, it began when children were in kindergarten. There are additional studies with preschool children who are English-only that have also shown that pronunciation matters for phonological awareness. An interesting detail from one of these studies, consistent with other studies, is that how accurately children said the sounds of the eight consonants in words that most English-only four-year-olds say correctly was particularly important (Mann & Foy, 2007). I hope that you are wondering what those eight consonant sounds are. They are /p/, /b/, /j/, /d/, /w/, /m/, /n/, and /h/. Other studies have also included /k/, /g/, and /t/ in the group known earlier by four-year-olds.

Teaching Principle 10: Choose words that contain the eight core consonants (/p/, /b/, /j/, /d/, /w/, /m/, /n/, /h/) at the beginning (easier) or end (harder) of the word.

Teaching Principle 11: Provide pictures that show how sounds are made with lips, tongue, teeth, throat, and so forth, and provide small acrylic mirrors to enable children to examine what the speech apparatus is doing during phonological awareness learning activities.

Teaching Principle 12: Provide many opportunities during lessons for all children to accurately pronounce words and sounds that are being used in phonological awareness activities.

Teaching Principle 13: Minimize the number of words that children have to remember while they do phonological awareness learning activities.

Some words have more complete information about all the sounds in them, making them good choices for teaching phonological awareness. Children are likely to know more of the sounds of words that

- are learned earlier,
- occur more frequently in spoken language,
- are familiar, and
- have fewer sounds.

The use of these types of words during phonological awareness activities should make it easier for English learner children to accurately pronounce the sounds in them (e.g., Storkel & Rogers, 2000). The benefit of these words to English learners is that they are more likely to draw on sounds that the child knows and avoid more of those they are unfamiliar with due to limited English vocabulary. It will also be easier for children to remember these same words. English learners are also more likely to do better if they only have to remember two words rather than three or four words during phonological awareness activities. For example, a rhyme activity where the teacher asks, "Do *hat* and *fat* sound alike? or Do *hat* and *book* sound alike?" will require children to use less memory than if they were asked, "Which word rhymes with *hat*—*dog, fat, bed?*"

HOW MUCH PHONOLOGICAL AWARENESS DO PRESCHOOL ENGLISH LEARNERS NEED?

An important finding from the National Reading Panel (NRP; National Institute of Child Health and Human Development, 2000) was that preschool children gained more from phonological awareness (PA) instruction than did K–2 students. The benefit of PA instruction for a preschooler was almost twice that of older children. The studies that led to this conclusion met high scientific standards; however, there were only seven of them. Studies where children actually received instruction provide clear evidence to guide teaching practices and teaching policies more than do those that simply look at what preschool children typically know about phonological awareness. Unfortunately, the NRP studies only included English-only children.

A very interesting characteristic of these seven studies was that they all targeted a high level of phonological awareness. Specifically, to be included in the NRP report, instruction had to teach children to focus on individual phonemes! Skill with attending to and manipulating individual phonemes is the phonological awareness skill that most powerfully contributes to skilled reading. Studies that included counting words in sentences, combining and separating syllables, and rhyme activities were not even included. Let's look at one of those studies in detail (Byrne & Fielding-Barnsley, 1991) to see what children were taught.

Research Highlight—Sound Foundations Program

Teaching Goal: To identify words that began and ended with the same sounds: phoneme identity

Teaching Practices:
- Children were taught individual phonemes.
  - Information on how the mouth makes the sound was included.

- Pictures of objects: Children were shown charts of pictured objects, and they selected pictures of objects with the sound they were learning (e.g., /s/ in *seal, sea, sailor, sand*).
- The letter for the sound was included.
- Games were used:
  - ○ Snap: Target picture (seal) and stack of other pictures with and without target sound /s/. Child goes through stack and "snaps" each time a picture with the target sound is seen.
  - ○ Dominoes: Two pictures on a card. Children join cards with pictures sharing beginning sounds.
- Children learned stories and jingles with many words with the target sound at the beginning or end of the word.
- One sound was taught each day; sounds from previous days were reviewed.
- Children were taught in small groups of four to six.
- The program lasted for 12 sessions.

Test Activities:

- Identifying words with sounds that were taught at beginning or end of each word
- Identifying words with sounds that were not taught
- Identifying written words that matched spoken words (show written word *sat*; does this word say "sat" or "mat"?)

—Byrne and Fielding-Barnsley (1991)

Preschool children (four-year-olds) given this instruction benefited from it. They scored significantly higher on the tests than did children who used the same pictures but with activities that focused on making meaning. They showed high levels of learning, with an average of about 22 correct out of 24 possible on the final tests. There were still benefits from the program on reading three years later.

Well, what do you think? I think the study shows that four-year-old preschool children can learn to attend to single phonemes in words with a high level of success when they have received high-quality instruction. Other studies with a variety of types of instruction explicitly designed to teach phoneme sensitivity have found the same evidence of sophisticated phonological awareness learning (Fox & Routh, 1976; Haddock, 1976; Solity, 1996; Treiman & Baron, 1983). So aim for the stars! While there were no English learners in these phonological awareness instructional studies, the biological basis of language processing, the phonological awareness learning success of English learners in kindergarten, and similarities in phonological awareness across languages is suggestive that the same practices will be effective with English learners.

Evidence suggests that English learners in kindergarten can be quite successful with phonemic awareness learning in English. I examined the level of phonemic awareness of kindergarten children on simple blending, segmenting, and rhyme-making tasks both before and after they had participated in a reading program that provided daily and explicit teaching. The year began with rhyming instruction followed by instruction in sounds at the beginning of the word. In the second half of the year, simple blending and segmenting were taught. Children were also taught all the letter names and letter sounds. Children began the year with very low PA ability and showed about 80% mastery at the end of the year. Their performance was compared to that of highly similar kindergarten children. Blending, segmenting, and rhyming scores were far better among the English learners who had participated in the program. In another study, we explicitly taught children rhyme-making, segmenting, and blending skills daily for seven weeks. This instruction produced advances but not at the same level as the full year program (Roberts & Corbett, 1997).

WHAT'S UP WITH RHYMING?

Rhyming is usually considered a relatively easy phonological awareness task. Yet I have some questions about whether this is true for ELLs based on data from three samples of children. You can read a description of the troubles with rhyming I have experienced with preschool ELLs in the next text box.

Troubles With Rhyming

In a pilot study with preschool English learners, we taught rhyming, believing it to be the easiest PA task. After three months of instruction twice a week for about 10 minutes each time, the mixed group of Hmong- and Spanish-speaking English learners had made virtually no progress. We began instruction by asking children to notice whether or not pairs of words presented in isolation rhymed. We then tried to embed the words in jingles and to use nursery rhymes to see if contextualization helped. Things got no better—maybe worse. We tried jungles with actions to include the whole body: "I mop, I hop, I plop." Things got no better. After trying these variations in instruction, we decided that it might be the intensity. So we increased the intensity of instruction to about 12 to 15 minutes a lesson three times weekly and continued the project for four months. It still didn't look good and indeed our assessment at the end of the project revealed an average score of less than 1 of 10 on the rhyming test.

—Roberts and Neal (2004)

In another study with kindergarten ELLs and English-only children, we found that over the course of seven weeks ELLs made significant progress in rhyming, blending, and segmenting and yet still remained significantly lower than the English-only children on rhyming but not segmenting or blending. Other researchers have also reported English learners had extreme difficulties with choosing a picture that rhymed with a target, yet they were able to complete a task where they made a judgment whether a spoken word had a correct or incorrect initial sound (Barnett, Yarosz, Thomas, Jung, & Blanco, 2007).

So I have been wondering—"What's up with rhyming?" My wonderings have led me to conclude that rhyming may be more sensitive to vocabulary knowledge than other tasks, such as saying /m/ when asked what the first sound is in "Miguel" or "metal." To determine if two words rhyme or to give a rhyming word for *dog* requires dealing with the complete word. Correct rhyming is based on what happens at the end of a word. In many rhyming tasks, children have to manage three or more words. They may be asked to pick the "odd" one from among three words: *cat, fat,* and *pig,* for example. In another common activity they may be shown a picture of a cat and then asked to choose from three choices the one that does not rhyme. Even when supported by pictures that are named by the teachers, knowledge of the words is likely to still be a factor in performance for English learners with limited English vocabulary. On a task where children are asked to come up with a word that rhymes, it seems evident that to say a word that rhymes with *dog* will be greatly aided when a child knows many related words such as *hog, fog,* and *bog.* In short, saying the first sounds in words where children can be successful by managing just the beginning of one word, do not have to process several words, and do not have to come up with their own word is likely to be a better task for ELLs. And performance on this type of *alliteration* task is also recognized as an early phonological awareness task related to later reading in studies that describe the development of phonological awareness.

Other studies on rhyme for English-only children or children from other language groups who are learning to rhyme in their first language have raised questions about the degree to which rhyming requires phonological awareness and how much it relates to later reading (e.g., Martin & Byrne, 2002; Muter, Hulme, Snowling, & Stevenson, 2004; Walton, 1995). Another study showed that while both rhyming and hearing the first sounds in words were related to reading, hearing sounds at the beginning of words was related more strongly, with about a 50% stronger relationship than rhyming (Bryant, MacLean, Bradley, & Crossland, 1990). The fact that rhyming is considered to be an early level of English PA increases the likelihood that it will be selected as the target level of phonological awareness instruction for ELLs. There are other reasonable choices.

My recommendation at this time is that beginning sounds may be a better choice than rhyming for teaching phonological awareness with English learners. This recommendation is based on six considerations:

1. Emerging evidence that rhyming is very difficult for ELLs

2. Likelihood that isolating and matching beginning sound tasks may accommodate the limited vocabulary of preschool ELLs and appears to be more related to later reading

3. The absence of any clear developmental progression placing rhyming as a necessary gateway skill

4. Questions about what the ability to rhyme really indicates

5. Questions about the relationship of rhyming to later reading

6. Evidence that training in fewer (one or two) phonological awareness skills is better than training in several

Teaching Principle 14:
Teach beginning sounds in words before rhyming.

Teaching Principle 15:
Teach the meaning of words to be used in phonological awareness instruction.

In addition, learning to identify beginning sounds may help children to secure their understanding of what a word is. This understanding is called *concept of word*. Identifying initial sounds in words is one of the features that help children determine where one word begins and another ends in both print and speech (Morris, Bloodgood, & Perney, 2003).

Apply Your Knowledge

Select two children, if possible one that you believe is very advanced and one you believe is just beginning in terms of literacy skills. Sit down with them individually with a simple picture book they have read several times before and will enjoy, and read a few pages of the book, clearly pointing to each word as you go. Now ask the child to read the book "just like I did." (If you are working with an English learner, it will take some creativity to get the child to understand what you would like him or her to do.) How well did the child point to each individual word? Next say the sentence "My name is_____," clapping as you say each word. Have the child repeat the sentence using his or her own name. What did you observe? These two activities will tell you about children's concept of word.

MAKING SOUNDS STAND STILL AND BE CONCRETE

Teaching phonological awareness calls for the best of what you can create to help make those sounds concrete. The sounds in words are spoken very quickly. They flow one into the other. They are like little wisps of smoke that hang in the air for just a moment and then are gone. Helping children make those sounds slow down, stand still, and become concrete will make it easier for them to attend to the sounds and manage them.

I have designed a little "Make It Concrete Kit" composed of items from commonly available materials and sources. Everything is stored in a small plastic storage bag. Each child has her or his own kit and brings it with her or him to phonological awareness lessons. These kits have been used by teachers in kindergarten classrooms in two large school districts. The children find them engaging and useful, but you have to establish a routine for how they are to be used and managed or they can simply become a distraction.

Teaching Principle 16: Provide a "Make It Concrete Kit" for children to use during lessons.

Teaching Principle 17: Teach the meaning of vocabulary words that will be used to describe how sounds are made (*jaw, mouth, tongue, teeth, throat, lips, air*).

Teaching Principle 18: Provide a great deal of oral repetition, and have children explore with mirrors what the speech apparatus is doing as sounds are produced.

What do you think is the purpose of the PVC telephone? You may have to have concrete experience with one to find out. Make one and see! As children learn letter names, they can add letters to their little plastic tiles with stickers, or for permanency, the teacher can do it with permanent ink markers. Evidence shows that using letters with sounds results in better learning. Using these materials and practices for making sounds concrete and to stand still are likely to be particularly useful to English learners who have limited knowledge of the phonemes in English and the words in which they are embedded.

Individual Make It Concrete Kite

Phone:

> 3-inch length of 1¼-inch diameter PVC pipe
>
> Two 1 ½-inch, 90-degree PVC elbows from a home supply store

Mirror:

> 4-inch by 4-inch acrylic mirror
> (school supply store)

Color Tiles:

> Six 1-inch plastic color tiles
> (school supply store)

Large Rubber Band

Interlocking Cubes:

> Four ¾-inch unifix cubes of different colors
> (school supply store)

Following is a brief teaching sequence that shows some of the types of activities and materials that can be used to help the sounds become concrete and to stand still. Even though it captures only a brief sequence, please notice the detail that has gone into planning the lesson. Also notice the active and concrete learning provided for children. It will help you learn if you actually perform the steps as you go through the lesson.

Phonological Awareness Lesson

Materials

Letter tub of objects that begin with the sound /b/

Lip sync card for /b/. This card shows how the sound is made.

"Make It Concrete Kit" for each student containing square tiles, unifix cubes, small unbreakable mirror, "hear myself" phone, white board

Tiles and Mirrors
Teacher:

What is the first sound in *bat?* /b/ is the first sound in *bat.* You say /b/ /b/.

What is the first sound in *bat?* Everybody say it.

Push one of your tiles forward each time you say it. Yes, that's correct; the first sound in *bat* is /b/.

Look at your mouth with your mirror while you say /b/.

Feel your throat while you say /b/. Do it lots of times!

Letter Tubs With Small Objects Whose First Sound Is /b/
Teacher:

Now I am going to show you some objects whose name has the sound /b/ at the beginning. What sound?

Say /b/ three times [teacher holds up one finger each time the children say the /b/ sound]: /b/, /b/, /b/.

[Teacher takes out the letter B tub that has a few miniature objects whose spoken name begins with the /b/ sound. Teacher shows the class three to four objects, one at a time (e.g., bat, bell, boat).]

[Teacher says the name of the object, says /b/, and then says the name again] bat, /b/, bat.

[Teacher begins slowly and then speeds up, checking that each child is saying the word, then the sound, then the word.]

"Hear Myself" Phones
Teacher:

Time to call yourself! Everybody pick up your telephone and say /b/.

Tell yourself all the words you know that have the /b/ sound at the beginning.

[Teacher shows the objects again.]

Say the words slowly to yourself in your telephone. [Teacher models with the children, /b/ /a/ /t/, and so forth.]

[Teacher watches and assesses who has learned the sound and who needs to add to his or her learning.]

(Continued)

(Continued)

Unifix Cubes
Teacher:

Now take out three cubes and hook them together. [Teacher demonstrates.] *Bat* has three sounds so I need three cubes.

[Teacher connects the three cubes together saying /b/ /a/ /t/ as each cube is added; teacher says "bat" and shows connected cubes.]

I am going to take off the first sound. The first sound is /b/. [Teacher snaps off the first cube.]

You do it and say the /b/ sound.

[Teacher repeats this process three more times, demonstrating each time.]

Follow-Up Activities

Make the tub available at a center and explain to children that they can play with the /b/ sound more there. Have alphabet books with the *B* page held open, letter models of *B*, pictures of children from the class that have the /b/ sound in their names with their name written on the photograph, and art media so children can draw pictures of objects that begin with the /b/ sound.

Individualizing Instruction

Have the teaching assistant take a smaller group of children who were not participating or were having trouble immediately afterward to play with the items in the tub where children get many turns naming items. They can make piles—the assistant hides the tub behind her back, and children ask for an object from the tub to put in their pile. Children use their mirrors and alternately practice saying the sound softly and more loudly many times.

Apply Your Knowledge

Carefully go through the lesson excerpt given above and make a list of all the elements of the lesson that will help make the sounds concrete and to stand still.

THE LANGUAGE USED IN PHONOLOGICAL AWARENESS INSTRUCTION

There are several words that are used repeatedly for phonological awareness instruction. I refer to this as the *language of instruction*. Success with phonological awareness instruction is dependent on children understanding what they are expected to do. Words used in phonological awareness instruction are listed in the box below.

Words Used in Phonological Awareness Instruction

word, sound, mouth, listen, say, sound, tongue, lips, throat, teeth, first, last, beginning, end, same, different, hear

---

Can you think of other language of instruction words? English learners face more than one challenge in managing the language of instruction. First there is the nature of the words themselves. While some of these words refer to concrete things (*lip, tongue,* etc.), others do not (*word, say, same, different*). They are more abstract and more difficult to learn. The difference between these words can be appreciated by thinking about how you could teach what they mean. How could you teach *lips?* How could you teach *same?* Yet to clearly understand what they are supposed to do and to be aided through language in learning how to do it, English learners need to know these words. They will need to be taught these words. To clearly learn the words, children will need instruction on the meanings more than once and to have the words and meanings reviewed regularly. I have taught the words for the speech apparatus to English learners with a big chart showing a face in profile with the throat, teeth, and so forth shown in the drawing. Children touch and explore their own speech apparatus with their mirrors (from their Make It Concrete Kits). At the beginning of each phonological awareness lesson, these words were quickly reviewed.

A second challenge with the language of instruction is that the nature of phonological awareness itself requires children to focus on specific parts of words *and* they are hearing many other words telling them how to perform this complex activity. Sometimes there is so much language in use during teaching that it can make it more difficult to focus on the words and sounds that are most important. It may seem a little strange for early childhood professionals to think this way—sometimes too much language can get in the way! Modeling or showing children what you want them to do should be emphasized in the presence of language and can sometimes effectively replace it.

Teaching Principle 19: Teach children the vocabulary that they will need to understand phonological awareness instruction.

Teaching Principle 20: Model all phonological awareness tasks in each lesson so children understand what they are to do.

A final aspect of language of instruction, different from the first, is the nature of the words that children will actually apply their phonological awareness skills to. Many ELLs will not know what are common words for English-only children. From the sample lesson, the words *bug* and *book* and may be even *bike* and *boy* will not be known by many English learners, particularly at the beginning of the year, if they are younger or have less exposure to English before preschool and in their homes. When a phonological awareness task asks children to manage three to four words that they do not know the meaning or pronunciation of—words they have not yet learned—it will be much more difficult for them to attend to chunks of sounds or individual sounds within the words or to compare several words, even if pictures are provided. Pictures may even interfere with their performance when the pictures represent a word they know in their first language but not English. This challenge is greatly reduced when children can learn phonological awareness in their primary language.

Educational Principle 1: Seriously consider the feasibility of teaching phonological awareness in the primary language.

Apply Your Knowledge

1. Select three to four words that you believe are the hardest to teach from the "Words Used in Phonological Awareness Instruction" box. Plan how you would teach these words. If you are a teacher, try your plan out in your classroom.

2. Go back through the lesson on pages 134–136 and put an asterisk (*) by all the examples of modeling—where the teacher demonstrates what to do. Go through the lesson one more time and put an x where the language of instruction may be particularly challenging for a child who is just learning English.

3. The following instructions are similar to those used on phonological awareness tests. Rewrite these task instructions with an eye to simplifying the language so that English learners could better understand what to do.

Instructions

1. I'll put some sounds together to make a word. Listen: /m/ [pause] /a/ [pause] /n/ [pause]. Let's practice: What word would you have if you put these sounds together?

2. I can say a word and tell you how many sounds I hear. Listen: "off." Say: /o/ [pause) /f/ [pause]. There are two sounds.

CONCLUSION

Phonological awareness is an essential part of the equation for learning to link speech and print—which is a pivotal competence for learning how to read. It is challenging for children and particularly English learners, because they must learn to separate sounds that do not naturally separate in speech and (for English learners) in a language they are just learning. The core requirement is a way of thinking where the child attends to the structure of words rather than their meaning. Learning this way of thinking will be easier when children can practice it with the speech sounds they know best and in a language where their vocabulary is largest. Thus, primary language phonological awareness is likely to be easiest to learn. Evidence showing that phonological awareness in one language carries over to a second suggests that as children's English grows, they could apply the ability to analyze the structure of words in primary language to English, their second language.

You have learned the importance of carefully selecting the words for instruction in specific ways that will take into account the emerging and incomplete knowledge of English sounds and English vocabulary characteristic of English learners. There is research that provides guidance in how to effectively teach phonological awareness, although few of these studies have been specific to preschool English learners. The nature of phonological awareness and instruction studies with slightly older students suggest that it is possible for preschool English learners to learn phonological awareness in a second language. With careful instruction tailored to take into account their English learner status, you and the children you work with can be successful.

Summary of Teaching Principles

Teaching Principle 1: Begin teaching the easier phonological awareness tasks: Use whole words and syllables before onset-rimes and individual sounds.

Teaching Principle 2: Help children to attend to sounds at the beginning of words before sounds at the end of words.

Teaching Principle 3: Help children stay focused on the sounds of words rather than their meanings.

Teaching Principle 4: Implement instruction based on the factors in the bulleted list on [pages 120–121.]

Teaching Principle 5: Teach phonological awareness in either first or second language.

Teaching Principle 6: Avoid using words that create confusions between sounds in the first and second language.

Teaching Principle 7: Include rich vocabulary development activities in the literacy program.

Teaching Principle 8: Select words that are familiar to children and are short (have fewer letters), and/or teach children the meaning of words prior to having them perform phonological awareness activities on them.

Teaching Principle 9: Teach alphabet letters, and encourage children to use them to represent related sounds as their letter mastery grows.

Teaching Principle 10: Choose words that contain the eight core consonants (/p/, /b/, /j/, /d/, /w/, /m/, /n/, /h/) at the beginning (easier) and end (harder) of the word.

Teaching Principle 11: Provide pictures that show how sounds are made with lips, tongue, teeth, throat, and so forth, and provide small acrylic mirrors to enable children to examine what the speech apparatus is doing during phonological awareness learning activities.

Teaching Principle 12: Provide many opportunities during lessons for all children to accurately pronounce words and sounds that are being used in phonological awareness activities.

Teaching Principle 13: Minimize the number of words that children have to remember while they do phonological awareness learning activities.

Teaching Principle 14: Teach beginning sounds in words before rhyming.

Teaching Principle 15: Teach the meaning of words to be used in phonological awareness instruction.

Teaching Principle 16: Provide a "Make It Concrete Kit" for children to use during lessons.

Teaching Principle 17: Teach the meaning of vocabulary words that will be used to describe how sounds are made (*jaw, mouth, tongue, teeth, throat, lips, air*).

Teaching Principle 18: Provide a great deal of oral repetition, and have children explore with mirrors what the speech apparatus is doing as sounds are produced.

Teaching Principle 19: Teach children the vocabulary that they will need to understand phonological awareness instruction.

Teaching Principle 20: Model all phonological awareness tasks in each lesson so children understand what they are to do.

Summary of Educational Principles

Educational Principle 1: Seriously consider the feasibility of teaching phonological awareness in the primary language.

NOTE

1. When a letter is shown between slashes it represents a sound.

6 Curriculum, Instruction, and Literacy Activity

★ ★

Important Research Results About
Curriculum, Instruction, and Literacy Activity

- Alphabet knowledge, phonological awareness, oral language, and vocabulary development are critical domains of literacy to be included in preschool curriculums.

- Organized, specific, and sustained teaching and learning opportunities in major domains of early literacy are needed.

- Literacy learning is optimized when literacy goals are linked to teaching practices, strategies, and activities most effective for achieving those goals.

- Literacy instruction, curriculum, and activity should attend to promoting literacy, building relationships, and supporting motivation.

- A balance of formal and informal and teacher-guided and child-initiated learning opportunities will maximize literacy learning.

- The classroom environment and activity throughout the day provide important opportunities for literacy learning.

- Quality of instruction and literacy activity matter.

★ ★

Preschool English learners will develop strong foundations for literacy achievement in the presence of a comprehensive curriculum that includes carefully planned literacy experiences implemented by skilled literacy teachers. In this chapter, the goal is to help you understand and think about the broad principles related to the literacy program as an organized whole. This organized and comprehensive program for building literacy competencies is called a *curriculum*. Many of the teaching principles from Chapters 2 through 6 will be incorporated into the discussion.

In this chapter, the very important topic of establishing positive relationships during literacy learning and how they too are an essential ingredient for promoting English learners' access to the literacy curriculum will be covered. Another new topic to be covered in this chapter is diagnosis and assessment of children's literacy competence and how this knowledge about the progress of individual children is related to curricular modification. Emerging evidence related to the outcomes associated with specific literacy programs that many of you may be using or may be in the process of adopting will be presented. Preschool English learners will develop strong foundations for literacy achievement in the presence of comprehensive curriculums and carefully planned literacy experiences implemented by skilled literacy teachers.

Literacy achievement for English learners will be enriched by a curriculum that includes participation of individuals from the community and includes community materials. When preschool programs establish continuity for children between home and school by utilizing primary language (Au, 1998) and culturally familiar materials (Rogoff & Waddell, 1982) and by providing a variety of ways of using language that are compatible with home experience (Heath, 1993; Phillips, 1972), children's language and literacy learning and engagement will benefit (Tharp, 1989). Providing an opportunity for informal and personal interaction between parents and teachers (such as potluck meals, family storybook reading events, and personal communication during classroom sign-in and sign-out), establishing a community discussion council, providing meaningful ways for caregivers to help in classrooms, providing regular literacy materials for home use, and drawing in home materials for classroom use are examples of some of these practices.

Empowerment and the educational conditions that support it should be a formalized educational goal within the curriculum to ensure that children and their families are rewarded by and maintain engagement with school (e.g., Au, 1998; Cummins, 1999; Delpit, 1988; Ogbu, 1992). Depth and quality of these family and culturally responsive practices are a part of the preschool curriculum that often needs bolstering. For children who speak English as their primary language and who come from families with significant degrees of mainstream experience and similarity, curriculum, teaching practices, and activities are much more likely to provide a match between the experiences of children in their home community and those offered through the curriculum, instruction, and activity in the preschool classroom.

Instruction and activity related to attending to the sounds of words, alphabet knowledge, vocabulary, concepts of print, storybook reading, writing, and comprehension are important to include in the curriculum. Children's experiences with these literacy components should be orchestrated in ways that reflect what is known about the developmental progression of each. For example, opportunities to learn about phonemic awareness should be guided by understanding that attending to syllables is easier than attending to individual sounds.

A range of instructional approaches and opportunities to learn is needed within a curriculum to ensure high levels of literacy competence. Child-initiated and teacher-initiated experiences; large-group, small-group, and individual instruction; language and literacy rich sociodramatic play; collaborative interaction with other children; storybook reading; writing dictation; individual child-teacher discussion; authentic literacy activity; and skill focused practice should all be widely used. Instruction and experience in all these components of literacy can proceed in tandem with English oral language development (Roberts, 2008; Roberts & Neal, 2004). Within this comprehensive and carefully planned sequence of literacy activity, ensuring that teaching, interactions, and child learning experiences are of high quality is critical.

Early childhood professionals can feel encouraged and indeed urged to implement a comprehensive literacy curriculum for preschool English learners, as there is growing evidence that preschool children make the most progress when there are high expectations embedded within a carefully planned (intentional), comprehensive, and high-quality literacy program. Evidence for this statement will be presented throughout the chapter.

ESSENTIAL ELEMENTS OF AN EFFECTIVE CURRICULUM

An effective literacy curriculum for preschool English language learners is multifaceted and complex. It will include attention to specific domains of early literacy. These major specific domains that are critical for a comprehensive literacy curriculum are

- alphabet knowledge,
- phonological awareness, and
- oral language development, with specific attention to vocabulary development.

The specific goals for each of the lessons or activities in each of the domains should be identified, so that teachers and children can have a shared direction in learning. These goals could be as narrow as to learn to quickly identify the letter name of a specific letter shape or as broad as creating a new story with the flannel board figures that go with the *Little Red Hen* storybook.

To be effective, a curriculum needs much more than to simply include regular attention of sufficient duration to these core elements. The quality of instructional practices that will be used to teach, foster, and promote children's understanding of these core elements is crucial and particularly so for English language learners who are learning the core competencies in a second language. These high-quality teaching practices will effectively

- link the goals of specific lessons with instructional strategies that are most effective for teaching them,
- systematically attend to promoting positive relationships between teachers and children, and
- promote the motivation that will sustain children's interest, effort, attention, and self-regulation in literacy learning.

For English learners, culturally relevant and culturally responsive materials and meaningful use of the primary language should be embedded within the curriculum. The box below organizes these ideas into a framework for determining the potential effectiveness of a literacy curriculum for English learners.

> **Educational Principle 1:** Select, develop, and implement a literacy curriculum that includes alphabet, phonological awareness, and oral language with special attention to vocabulary development core content.

Curriculum Evaluation Framework

1. Core Content

Is the core content for literacy included?

Alphabet

(Continued)

(Continued)

Sounds in words (phonological awareness)

Oral language

Vocabulary

2. Goals

Are goals for each lesson/activity identified?

3. Quality of Teaching

Does the curriculum link each goal with the best teaching strategies for reaching it?

Does the curriculum consistently and specifically implement teaching practices that are effective with English learners?

Does the curriculum include practices that build relationships, promote motivation, and provide children opportunities to self-regulate?

4. Materials

Are the materials needed identified and provided?

Are these materials culturally representative and culturally responsive?

5. Primary Language

Are there specific practices for using primary language?

Does the program support preserving primary language?

Apply Your Knowledge

Apply the Curriculum Evaluation Framework to the literacy curriculum that you use in your program if you are a teacher. If you do not have a formal literacy curriculum, apply the framework to the practices you use to teach literacy. If you are not a teacher, look online at Houghton Mifflin Education Place (http://www.eduplace.com; click on Pre-K, choose a state, and then click on any theme) or SRA–Open Court (SRAonline.com; click on Reading, choose Pre-K from the dropdown Browse menu, choose a product family, and then click on Sample Lessons and choose a lesson), and apply the evaluation framework to what you could find there. What did you discover about it? What questions did you come up with about the lesson?

AN ARTICULATED CURRICULUM

It is also important that the curriculum be *articulated.* When a curriculum is articulated, it can be described in terms of its purposes and goals, its content, and its teaching practices specific to promoting the learning of English language learners. An articulated curriculum means that teachers, bilingual support personnel, and site leadership must know it and be able to describe it. When the family caregivers of the children know at a minimum that a comprehensive language and literacy curriculum exists and the core components that are emphasized within in, conditions for robust family engagement are increased. Having an articulated curriculum, though, does not imply that there is only one program that may be used for literacy development or that the curriculum must be a boxed or commercially produced one. A dedicated site or teacher could create an articulated literacy curriculum by combining one program designed to teach phonological awareness with another for the alphabet with a third dual language storybook reading program created by the teachers and community. Alternatively, a site might purchase an integrated literacy, math, science, and art program that was aligned with the K–6 reading program used in the schools where the children would enter kindergarten. Many states are currently identifying standards for preschool literacy. A site or region could create a literacy curriculum that aligns with these preschool foundations.

> **Educational Principle 2:** Ensure that all teachers, site leadership, and family caregivers can describe this curriculum at the level appropriate for their involvement with it.

Examples of Articulated Curriculums

- **Comprehensive commercial program**
- **Combining different curriculums for oral language, alphabet, and phonological awareness**
- **Creating a program from known materials that aligns with state preschool standards or foundation**

Apply Your Knowledge

Brainstorm a list of ideas for how you could make sure that a literacy curriculum was articulated (explained, made visible) to family caregivers

(Continued)

(Continued)

and site administrators. For example, a family meeting could be dedicated to explaining the core literacy elements of oral language, the alphabet, and phonological awareness. Another meeting might provide family caregivers opportunities to examine curriculum materials.

MATCHING GOALS WITH TEACHING STRATEGIES/ACTIVITIES

Effective learning occurs when teaching goals and teaching practices are matched (Karoly, Ghosh-Dastidar, Zellman, Perlman, & Fernyhough, RAND, 2008). Learning the names of letters of the alphabet (Chapter 4) requires a different type of learning than that required to count the number of the sounds in words (Chapter 5). Learning to count the number of sounds in words is also different from learning the meaning of the word *wonderful,* for example (Chapters 2 and 3). Learning the meaning of the word *wonderful* is different yet again from being able to retell the story "The Wonderful Egg" with flannel board objects. Different strategies are used for different kinds of learning. The Rand report cited above estimated that less than half of three- and four-year-olds in California are in programs with a named curriculum based on the research evidence. Examples of matching teaching goals and strategies based on some of what you learned in Chapter 4 ("Befriending the Alphabet") and Chapter 3 ("Oral Language Development") are provided in the following text box.

Matching Lesson Goals With Teaching Strategies

Learning the names of letter shapes is essentially a memory task where a bond between the name and shape is formed (remember this?). Memorizing a connection is benefited by repetition of the connection. Yet this same memory function is not enough if your teaching goal is for the child to learn the meaning of the word *wonderful.* The child has to first learn the concept of "wonderful" being something extremely good. One strategy would be to tell the child directly that "*Wonderful* means really good." The child has to remember the pronunciation of the word *wonderful* as well, so practice saying the word is beneficial. And you will probably feel most sure that a child understands wonderful if he or she says to you, "See my wonderful picture." So strategies helping children to use vocabulary words on their own would be helpful when the goal of teaching is for the child to learn word meaning. An idea might be that you write the word *wonderful* on a white board in the classroom, and each time during the day any child uses *wonderful,* a check mark is placed beside it. (Important—this is not a reward system of any sort.)

One critical issue regarding matching instructional goals with learning activities is determining when learning may benefit from teaching things in context and when learning may benefit by teaching them out of context. For example, drawing attention to letters during storybook reading would be "in context." Showing and naming letters on large alphabet cards would be "out of context." In early childhood, the importance of learning in context has traditionally been emphasized. In fact, this importance has been so strong that many believe teaching anything out of context is not developmentally appropriate. In this book, I have made several recommendations for where actually removing things from context may be helpful. For example, in initial learning of the connection of letter shapes and letter names, I suggested that teaching just focusing on the individual letter and shapes—separate from meaningful text—would benefit children's initial learning. That was an example of matching the learning goal with the teaching practice. However, when the learning goal becomes to personally appreciate the use of letter names for reading, children are helped to use letters in context, such as in their names and in alphabet books. The "Research Highlight" box summarizes a study where children learned to read individual words much better when they learned them with flashcards than when they learned the same words in texts.

Research Highlight

One group of children practiced learning to read eight words on flashcards. In the other comparison group, children learned to read the same words when the words were written in text.

Children in the flashcard group learned, on average, seven of the eight words in seven minutes' teaching time. Children in the text reading condition learned, on average, three words in a total of thirteen minutes teaching.

—Stuart, Masterson, and Dixon (2000)

Similarly, in the discussion in Chapter 2 of language development (both primary and second), the benefit of using language when it is removed from a specific context (decontextualized language) to academic learning was explained. Therefore, an ideal literacy curriculum will include lessons with the goal of decontextualized language use. Retelling stories (without the pictures) is one good strategy for this, but it needs to follow several turns at telling the story with the flannel board figures. For initial learning of the story, context could be enriched with the flannel board figures. When my goal became decontextualized language, my lesson would move away from the context of the story pictures and flannel board figures. Yet to

> **Educational Principle 3:** Plan lessons and teach with a mix of in and out of context teaching practices based on teaching goals and on whether children are at the point of initial learning, refinement, or personal use.

teach new vocabulary words, the value of realia and other means of creating as rich a context as possible for securing an understanding of word meaning was emphasized. So the dance of shifting between in and out of context is one of the importance rhythmic patterns in literacy teaching and learning.

THE LANGUAGE OF INSTRUCTION

In several chapters the point has been made that for children to be able to learn, they must be able to understand what teachers want them to do. For example, when children do not know the meaning of the word *sound*, they will not be able to respond to a direction such as "listen for the first sound in your name." Similarly, after hearing a storybook, children who are novice English learners will be challenged if they are given instructions to "Put the pictures from the story in order so that they tell what happened in the book." For English learners to have the best opportunity to learn the sounds in words skills or to learn the story-retelling competence that is the goal of instruction in these two examples, they will need to understand what they are to do.

Ideas for making the language of instruction comprehensible for English learners for teaching the word *sound* might include the following:

1. Bilingual resource people teach the word *sound* in primary language and establish the connection between the primary language word and the English word *sound.*

2. The teacher makes several sounds (book shutting, foot stomping, barking, mooing, saying several children's names) and says only the word *sound* after she demonstrates each one.

3. The teacher signals children by placing her hand behind her ear, says "listen," and repeats several letter sounds (/b/, /t/, /p/, /s/); then she repeats each sound again, after each one saying simply "sound."

To make the language of instruction for the storytelling activity comprehensible, the teacher might show a copy of the first picture in a book, place it on a square background with room for several other pictures, and show how it matches the first page in the book. Then the teacher could place a copy of the picture that shows what came next to the right of the first picture on the square and flip slowly and sequentially through the pages of the book until she comes to that picture in the book; this will show how she is placing pictures in "book order." She would then have the children practice with her. A variation (that children love), is to put a picture out of order, say "Oh no, help me," and allow the children to correct the order. Can you think of even better ways to make sure that English learner children understand the language of instruction in these two examples? Helping children access learning by making sure they understand the language of instruction adds another element to teaching practice that is important for English learners.

Teaching Principle 1: Make a list of important words children will need to have to meet the goals (access the curriculum) of literacy lessons and activity.

Teaching Principle 2: Use primary language resources in teaching words of instruction.

Educational Principle 4: Create a comprehensive plan for when and how to teach instructional words that includes a plan for frequent review of them.

Apply Your Knowledge

Go to the sample lesson plan for teaching alphabet letters found on page 83. Go through this lesson and make a list of words that are most important for children to know in order to meet the goal of the lesson (access the curriculum). Beside each word, write one idea for how you could make sure children understand it.

BUILDING RELATIONSHIPS WHILE FOSTERING LITERACY

Literacy learning is affected by the quality of relationships adults and children have experienced (Erickson, Stroufe, & Egeland, 1985; Stroufe, 1996). Experiencing positive relationships with adults from infancy through preschool provides children with a number of competencies that will support their literacy learning. When preschool children have learned in their very early interactions that adults are responsive and reliable resources that offer effective help, literacy leaning will benefit. Similarly, when children experience the give and take that occurs in effective interactions with adults, they will view adults as a source of positive emotions. These mutual interactions also help children regulate their attention and their emotions (Baumeister & Vohs, 2004; Pianta, 2006).

Benefits of Strong Early Relationships

Children will

- **Attend to adult input.**
- **Approach learning positively.**
- **Control attention.**
- **Control and regulate emotions.**

Children who have experienced these responsive, emotionally rewarding, and mutual relationships will be eager for literacy learning. They will be willing and able to attend to the adult input that occurs during learning experiences, will approach literacy learning with an expectation of good things to come, and will be more able than other children to direct attention and control and express emotions in ways that support rather than interfere with literacy learning (Bus, Belsky, van IJzendoorn, & Crnic, 1997; Chang & Burns, 2005). Bus et al. (1997) found that children who had a secure attachment to their primary caregivers showed better attention, more positive emotions, and more language use during storybook reading than children without such secure attachment. Strong relationships with teachers can mirror the strong relationships with family caregivers that children establish in the first year and thereby lay the foundation for positive orientations to literacy learning.

Positive emotional relationships between children and teachers also promote literacy achievement through cognitive mechanisms. Secure emotional attachment to a primary caregiver results in the child having a basic trust in the world. This basic trust frees the child to explore, attend to, and respond to opportunities for learning presented by the environment. Exploration and engagement with opportunities for literacy learning will lead to increased literacy competence.

Positive relationships thus contribute to emotional and cognitive conditions that promote literacy achievement. Yet, the familiar refrain must be played again here: The majority of this evidence comes from English-only children. There is, however, a

Teaching Principle 3:
Infuse all literacy lessons and activities with warm emotion and responses to children's requests, language, and emotional needs.

wealth of cross-cultural evidence showing that the presence of a secure emotional attachment to a caregiver is invaluable to children, although the way attachment is demonstrated and organized may be influenced by cultural experiences.

TEACHERS' SUPPORT AND INSTRUCTIONAL ROLES

In early childhood literacy learning, teachers have two primary functions (Pianta, 2006). One function is instructional. Their instructional purpose leads them to help children learn the early literacy competencies that lay a crucial foundation for being successful in learning to read. At the

Teaching Principle 4:
Use teaching practices that maintain the instructional purpose of literacy learning while promoting positive relationships with children.

same time, teachers are also oriented to providing support for children in the form of encouraging them, responding to their interests, and engaging in friendly and emotionally warm interactions.

When teachers devote more attention to their instructional function, which is most likely to occur during group formal teaching lessons, their ability to maintain the support function may be challenged, because the instruction function takes the forefront. For example, during an alphabet lesson on the letter *F,* the teacher might write the name "Fong" (the name of one of the children in the classroom) on the board. A child may say "Fong is my friend." The teacher's support role may lead her to engage with this child about what the two children do together, who the child's other friends are, and so forth. Yet the instructional function calls her to make sure that children achieve the instructional goal of the lesson, which is to learn the link between the letter shape and its name. A talented teacher is able to balance her instructional and support functions. How could this be accomplished in the example with the child above?

Apply Your Knowledge

Rate Yourself on the Support and Instructional Functions

Assign a score of 1 through 5 (1 = low, 5 = high) to reflect your response to each of the questions below. What did you learn about yourself? How might this affect children's literacy learning?

1. How important is the support function to me? _____

2. How important is the instructional function to me? _____

3. How much do I focus on the support function during literacy instruction/activity? _____

4. How much do I focus on the instructional function during literacy instruction/activity? _____

5. How frequently do I feel a conflict between these two? _____

THE VALUE OF SMALL GROUPS AND ONE-ON-ONE TEACHING

There is evidence of the benefits of small-group over large-group learning for English learners. The term *small groups* refers to a group size of less than 10. English learners participate more orally in small-group settings. Small-group and one-on-one opportunities provide both social-emotional and cognitive advantages over large-group experiences. That said, studies of classroom practice in preschool settings have revealed that small groups are used very infrequently (e.g., Connor, Morrison, & Slominski, 2006).

Small groups allow more of the support function of teachers to enter the relationship between teacher and children. How might this happen? When there are fewer children there is opportunity for both

- more response to individual children and
- more opportunity for child input.

Thus both children and teachers are afforded more opportunity for "back and forthing" and sharing attention together. This is called *mutuality*. When children are in small groups or engaging in one-on-one conversations, less attention is given to behavior management, and routines such as distributing materials and so forth are simplified. Behavior management and lesson procedures can be distracting for the teacher and can add a negative emotional dimension to the group literacy experience. Thus teachers and children are both likely to have rich opportunities for sharing positive emotions in small-group and one-on-one contexts.

Teaching Principle 5: Use many small group and one-on-one literacy-learning opportunities, and specifically plan activities for these two contexts.

Children also have more opportunity to ask for and receive help, contributing further to their experience of adult responsiveness during learning. The opportunity for more physical contact between children and teachers that can occur during small-group and one-on-one activities may further enhance shared positive emotions when teachers and children find such contact desirable. Being physically closer to the teacher may also help children focus attention. These are the social–emotional benefits of small group (10 or less) and one-on-one in a nutshell.

Cognitive benefits of small group and one-on-one activities may include language development and children's willingness and success with challenging literacy activity. More language exchange—and in optimal conditions the kind of real exchange of meaning, expanding, and elaborating that most contributes to language development—may occur. Increased opportunity to provide individual help can help children learn better. The increased availability of adult resources during small-group and one-on-one activities may also encourage children

Educational Principle 5: Use small groups for language development, individualizing in any area (alphabet, phonological awareness, language development), and relationship-building goals.

to try challenging tasks and further task mastery. Meeting challenges is supportive of both children's learning and their motivation for literacy.

Benefits of Small Group and One-on-One Literacy Learning

- Experience positive emotion
- Ask for and receive help
- Increase language exchange
- Accommodate individual differences in competence and interests
- Increase physical closeness and contact
- Encourage challenge seeking

Apply Your Knowledge

What are some strategies that could be used to make more time for small group and one-on-one time either in your classroom or in any classroom? Hints: (1) Think of the need to plan activity for all children, (2) think of how to increase human resources in the classroom, and (3) think of how to promote self-regulation in children so you can work with smaller groups and with individual children. Organize your ideas into the three categories identified above.

INCREASING OPPORTUNITIES FOR TEACHERS' SUPPORT ROLE

There are a number of steps that can be taken to increase opportunities for teachers to enact their support function during literacy learning while still maintaining an instructional focus. Small-group and one-on-one conversations provide extensive opportunity for meaningful and responsive communication, a significant contribution to relationship building. In addition, using children's primary language can promote relationships with children by both enhancing communication and affirming the child's out-of-school familial and cultural experiences. In a study of Spanish-English bilingual preschool classrooms, more use of Spanish in the classroom was associated with closer teacher-child relationships and better social skills (Chang et al., 2007). This finding is particularly interesting because children experienced only about 17% of their teacher-child interactions in Spanish. In addition, teachers who spoke Spanish had more total interactions with children in either language than did teachers who did not speak Spanish. Spanish interactions were also more linguistically complex than those in English.

Children and teachers are also more likely to have a shared focus during literacy learning when children understand the purpose and value of the instruction they are being asked to participate in. When teachers make time for children to clarify what is expected of them and give children the help they ask for or need to be successful, children will sense that teachers care about and are resources for them. Literacy instruction and experiences where teachers demonstrate their enjoyment of their teaching and where children too are having pleasurable yet challenging learning experiences lead to the shared pleasure that contributes to warm relationships between children and teachers. When teachers follow children's lead or subtly, yet responsively, shift the child's lead to fit the goal of instruction, children sense a shared focus between themselves and the teacher, and this too contributes to strong relationships. During literacy lessons children often make personal connections or idiosyncratic responses different from responses that meet the goal of instruction. Let's revisit the example with the child's name "Fong" and an alphabet lesson on the letter *F*. Recall that the teacher is using children's names that begin with *F*. After writing Fong's name on the board, she holds up Fong's name card and places a little paper frame over the *F*. A child says, "I like Fong—he is my friend." A skillful teacher who is balancing her support and instruction function might respond, "Me too—can you name any of the letters in your friend Fong's name?" Later at the writing center she might encourage this same child to dictate a sentence telling what Fong and this child do together. Finally, when children are actively participating in instruction they are also engaging in interaction with the teacher and other children, which creates a sense of belonging and connection to others—relationships.

When the task demands of different literacy activities are differentiated to fit the skill level of individual children, relationships between teachers and children are strengthened, because again, the teacher is then demonstrating her responsiveness to the individual child and is providing assistance. Let's go back to an example from an alphabet lesson using personal names. The teacher has all children point to their names and name the first letter on their name cards. For those who are unsure, she names the letter and they repeat it. A more confident child is asked to name all the letters in her or his name, while a very advanced child is challenged to name the letters without looking. In these differentiations, children are not compared and there is no implication that those who can do more are "brighter," "more skillful," or better in any way. Teachers often value their support function more than their instructional function, yet

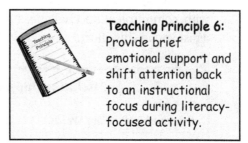

Teaching Principle 6: Provide brief emotional support and shift attention back to an instructional focus during literacy-focused activity.

Duncan et al. (2007), using several data sets that included small numbers of English learners, showed the importance for literacy learning of maintaining an instructional focus.

THE LANGUAGE OF RELATIONSHIP BUILDING

In our discussion of relationship building, it is apparent how language contributes to it. This poses a significant challenge when teachers and children are not proficient in the same language. Very often teachers of preschool English learners are proficient only in English. In the section above, the relationship between use of primary language in the classroom

Teaching Principle 7: Use primary language for responsive and warm interactions with children.

Teaching Principle 8: Teach English vocabulary and phrases that can be used to help teachers and child to meet the child's needs and thereby build relationships.

Teaching Principle 9: Add facial, gestural, and body expression to establish relationships with children.

and positive relationships and other social outcomes was reviewed (see Chapter 2 for extended discussion). An important practical implication for building teacher-child relationships during literacy learning then is to increase the use of the primary language in interactions with children. Teaching assistants and skilled family caregivers are important teacher resources to draw upon.

Another approach for addressing the link between language and relationship building would be to teach children the language of relationship building as part of the oral language and vocabulary development component of the curriculum. Teaching specific words and phrases that would be useful for English learners to use and understand to establish positive relationships could be very beneficial. Communicationof social needs, feelings, and requests for help are among some of these important functions. Some of these important words and phrases for relationship building are suggested in the box that follows. Language development specialists who work with children with communication challenges are knowledgeable resources that could assist you in this effort.

Relationship-Building Language

Relationship-Building Words:	Relationship-Building Phrases:
Help	Can you help me_____?
Share	I want _____ to share.
Like	I like_____ . What do you like?
Want	I want_____ . What do you want?
Feeling	I feel_____.
Happy	I feel happy when_____.
Sad	I feel sad when_____.
Angry	I feel angry when_____.
Afraid	I feel afraid when_____.
Lonely	I feel lonely when_____.
Excited	I feel excited when _____.
Mine	This is mine. _____took mine.
Nice	_____ is nice.

| Mean | I was mean to_____. _____ was mean to me. |
| Play | I play_____. |

Apply Your Knowledge

Get a little spiral notebook and label it "Relationship Language." Take at least five of the words and phrases from the Relationship-Building Language list and write them in your "Relationship Language" notebook. Note a few anecdotes from your teaching setting where relationship words were needed. Identify the relationship words that would have helped children in these situations.

THE BENEFITS OF EXPLICIT INSTRUCTION

In the chapters "Building and Scaffolding With Primary Language," "Second Language Development," "Befriending the Alphabet," and "Sounds in Words," you learned about teaching practices to promote children's growing literacy competence. Effective and specific strategies for helping children learn connections between letter shapes and letter names/sounds, helping children maintain attention on the sounds in words, and helping children learn new vocabulary by teaching them directly meanings of words were explained. Explicit instruction is only one aspect of a literacy-enhancing classroom. Centers, sociodramatic play, conversations, and other activities are essential in a balanced curriculum. Skilled teachers know how and when to use explicit instruction. Most often, explicit instruction lessons will last from between 10 and 20 minutes.

High-quality explicit instruction is crucial. Indicators of high quality include that the instruction is engaging, participatory, focused, and of the appropriate length and frequency to be effective (not too long, not too short). Some have equated explicit instruction with boring, repetitive, and emotionally insensitive lessons where children are required to sit still and be silent and are asked to do things that are beyond them for extended periods of time. These characteristics are not a feature of explicit instruction—they are features of poor instruction. Sometimes the term "didactic" is used to refer to these types of passive learning experiences. The type of high-quality explicit instruction that you are learning to envision and implement is quite different from the type of "didactic" instruction implemented in some interventions many years ago.

Explicit instruction also helps make sure that that all children have access to developing important literacy knowledge by providing sufficient explanation, focus, and opportunity for practice. It is the children with fewer economic resources, less background experience, and less proficiency in English for whom explicit literacy instruction is the most beneficial. Compare the results between the dotted line and the solid line in the graph below (taken from Roberts & Neal, 2004) that illustrate this point.

Educational Principle 6: Use explicit instruction for those areas of literacy learning where it is known to be effective.

When children received explicit comprehension instruction, they learned more vocabulary than children who received letter instruction. When children received explicit letter instruction, children learned more letters than children who received explicit comprehension instruction (see Figure 6.1). This pattern shows that children learn more of what they are taught, and conversely, they learn less of what is not taught.

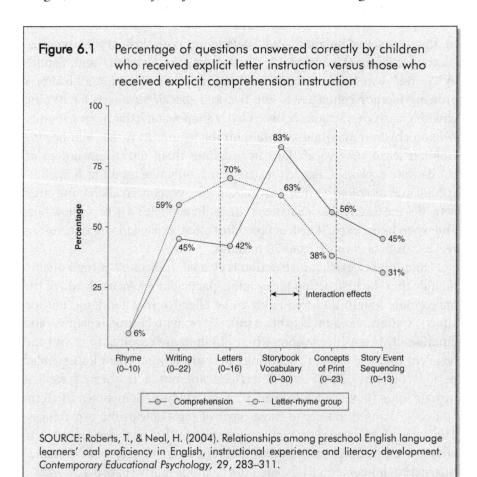

Figure 6.1   Percentage of questions answered correctly by children who received explicit letter instruction versus those who received explicit comprehension instruction

SOURCE: Roberts, T., & Neal, H. (2004). Relationships among preschool English language learners' oral proficiency in English, instructional experience and literacy development. *Contemporary Educational Psychology, 29,* 283–311.

HIGH-QUALITY TEACHING AND LEARNING

High-quality instruction improves the learning outcomes of all children. It is particularly beneficial and necessary for children who are learning English as a second language, because it will promote their ability to access the curriculum, to feel successful, and to experience positive relationships during learning.

Teaching Principle 10: Implement high-quality explicit instruction where children's participation and warm teacher-child relationships are promoted.

Teaching Principle 11: Carefully design lessons and activities to incorporate the characteristics of high-quality instruction.

The major features of high-quality instruction for English learners are summarized in the box that follows.

High-Quality Instruction

- Is goal-oriented, and its purpose and value are explained to children.
- Favors small over large group learning.
- Promotes oral language production by all children.
- Provides sufficient practice.
- Enables children to seek help when needed.
- Balances an instructional emphasis and emotional support.
- Follows the child's lead whenever possible or responsively shifts the child's lead to fit instruction.
- Establishes shared pleasure between teachers and children.
- Draws upon and includes materials representing children's diverse familial, cultural, and community experiences.
- Is "routinized" to help children know what to expect.
- Includes practices to help children understand the language of instruction and task expectations.
  - Child activities modeled/demonstrated by teacher
  - Core instructional vocabulary taught
  - Extraneous language reduced during instruction

Apply Your Knowledge

If you are a teacher, review a literacy lesson you have recently taught using the bullets in the "High-Quality Instruction" box. Think about each bullet. How many of the bullet items were present in your lesson? If all

(Continued)

(Continued)

the bullet items were there, great—if not, write how you could improve the lesson by including two additional bullet items. If you are not a teacher, write an idea for each bullet item that could help make sure it is included in all literacy lessons.

CHILD CHOICE AND LITERACY INSTRUCTION

Typical early childhood professionals equate choice with children selecting the activity they want to participate in. Yet there has been an emphasis in this book on the importance of a great deal of intentional teaching and ensuring that all children participate in teacher-designed and teacher-directed language development, alphabetic learning, and phonological awareness activities. For some, the fact that children's choice of activities is constrained within an articulated curriculum is a significant barrier for accepting the benefits of an articulated literacy curriculum. This apparent conflict can be resolved by looking more carefully and complexly at the concept of child choice.

To begin this examination, please write down all the reasons that child choice is important. On my list there are three critical dimensions of child choice that make it valuable. These dimensions are as follows:

- Choice fosters a sense of personal power, autonomy, and self-regulation.
- Choice responds to children's interests.
- Choice promotes positive emotions.

This analysis suggests that there are more practices than simply selecting an activity that can provide children with these three key dimensions of choice:

- When a child leads a conversation and the teacher follows the child's interests, the child has autonomy, is pursuing his or her own interests, and will experience positive emotions.
- When storybook reading and centers encourage children to add personalized input and select among structured alternatives, children experience autonomy and engage in self-regulation.
- When children experience positive relationships with teachers and other children during high-quality literacy activities, they experience positive emotions.

The main point is that focusing on these three benefits that are provided when children choose activities shows that experiences in addition to the traditional free choice opportunities can provide them. High-quality literacy activities can provide the sense of personal power, autonomy, and self-regulation; allow for children's inter-

Teaching Principle 12: Include the benefits of choice in literacy lessons and activities by providing experiences that include autonomy and self-regulation, response to child interests and input, and positive emotional experiences.

ests; and promote the positive emotions that are the reasons that choice is valued. High-quality literacy-related experiences that engage children in oral language, storybook reading, and center activities are particularly likely to yield the three key benefits of choice. What do you think?

USING ASSESSMENT TO BENEFIT CHILDREN

In order to ensure that children are receiving instruction and experiences that target their emerging literacy competencies, it is necessary to have an accurate understanding of what they do and do not know. Assessment is the term used to describe this finding out process. A complete curriculum will include means for assessing what children know in each of the core areas of literacy. There will be measures of oral language, alphabet knowledge, and phonological awareness at a minimum. The most important use of assessment information is to improve literacy outcomes for children. Therefore the link between collecting assessment data and using it to plan for instruction is crucial. If assessment is to result in improved outcomes for children, it must be linked to instruction. Assessment information should guide when review is given, identify children who may need more intensive instruction, and determine who would benefit from more challenging experiences. We want testing and assessment to benefit individual children. Yet, it is important to acknowledge that assessment results do not always need to be studied and reacted to at the individual level. Assessment results can be used to determine how well a curriculum is working in general or for subgroups of children such as English learners. If we know that a program works very well for English-only children and is less successful with English learners as a group, this knowledge benefits individual English learner children.

It is necessary that assessments accurately measure what children know. It is not easy to develop measures to meet this standard.

Researchers and test developers spend a great deal of time constructing assessment tools. Formal assessment tools are developed with careful planning and testing to ensure that the results they yield contain accurate information. One part of this "testing the test," among other things, is determining whether children score the same on it from one day to the next when they have not been taught anything in the intervening days that would be expected to enable them to improve their scores. These are called *formal* and sometimes *standardized* assessments, depending on how much development they have gone through. There are assessments that have gone through this careful development process for the following:

- Alphabet knowledge
- Phonemic awareness
- Spanish and English oral proficiency
- English and Spanish vocabulary

A number of these measures are discussed in Lonigan, McDowell, and Philips (2004).

Figuring Out What a Child Knows About the Alphabet

Imagine that a teacher suggests the idea of measuring a child's alphabet knowledge by determining if the child can correctly write her or his name. Alphabet letters are definitely involved in name writing. But what does it mean to know a letter of the alphabet? A child could know how to write his or her name by just learning all the correct "marks" to put down on the paper without clearly recognizing that each one is a separate letter and without knowing the name of each letter. A child could also say the names of all the letters in his or her name without knowing exactly to what that letter name refers. What does it say about alphabet knowledge if a child can name a letter when going through his or her name letter by letter and yet is unable to name the same letter in any other word? And what about all the letters that are not in a child's name? To accurately measure alphabet knowledge, we must start with the clearest definition of alphabet knowledge that we can come up with and then use a task that gets at this knowledge with as little chance of misinterpretation as possible.

Informal assessments that rely on teacher observation or what children do informally in the classroom have the advantage of being more naturalistic, can take into account observations on multiple occasions, and are performed by a teacher who knows well what the child is really capable of. These points are important. Formal individual assessment results can be examined to see if they "make sense," and if they don't, they can be complemented by additional measures. However, more-informal assessments run the risk of inaccuracy, because they are vulnerable to "seeing what you want to see" and because they may be troubled with the kind of problems illustrated in the "Figuring Out What a Child Knows About the Alphabet" text box.

Children's standing on various aspects of early literacy can change rather rapidly. In addition children may not have similar levels of competence on all aspects of early literacy. For example, a child could know a lot about the alphabet, but have limited English vocabulary. Therefore it is important to keep abreast of children's progress by regular progress monitoring of it and by assessing all of the key early literacy competencies that are truly distinguishable one from the other. Critical areas to assess include language proficiency in both L1 and L2, alphabet knowledge, and phonological awareness.

> **Educational Principle 7:** Assess children's literacy performance with accurate measures, and use the information to make instructional decisions.

TEACHERS: THE CRITICAL INGREDIENT

Teachers are the individuals who have the most interaction with children and their families and who implement the curriculum. They are crucial for securing the benefits of an articulated curriculum. There is variation in state requirements for prekindergarten teachers' training, education, and credentialing, resulting in significant variation in preschool teacher preparedness to effectively implement a curriculum (Johnson, Jaeger, Randolph, Cauce, Ward, et al., 2003). While there is some debate regarding the relative importance of formal academic preparation such as BA degrees and/or specialized training in early care and education, there is consensus that teacher quality is important for child literacy outcomes and that specialized training in early childhood curriculum and practices leads to more effective language use in early education and care settings (Burchinal, Cryer, et al., 2002; Burchinal, Howes, & Kontos, 2002; Maxwell, Field, & Clifford, 2006; National Institute of Child Health and Human Development, Early Child Care Research Network, 1999).

For these reasons, providing teachers with high-quality professional development on the core literacy areas of oral language, the alphabet, and phonological awareness is crucial. This preparation should include research-based knowledge on the nature of each of the core literacy areas and how to teach it. Professional development should also provide teachers opportunities to explore, in depth, the curriculum they are using or the opportunity to examine available curriculums and contribute to the decision about which ones to acquire in the case where an articulated curriculum is in the process of being adopted.

Evidence from five studies with school-age ELLs found that it takes up to one to three years for teachers to develop effective teaching practices for English learners. Hands-on practice, coaching, and classroom support were all found to contribute to professional development leading to high-quality classroom practice (August, Beck, Calderon, Francis, LeSaux, et al., 2008; Landry, Swank, Smith, Assel, & Gunnewig, 2006). Landry et al. (2006) found that in addition to knowledge, classroom support and dialog with colleagues, and receiving detailed assessment information on children's literacy performance and how to use it to inform instruction were elements of professional development that contributed to small gains in children's literacy achievement. Neuman, Cunningham, and Tucker (2006) reported on an innovative program where they helped preschool programs and local colleges to provide either face-to-face or online learning or a combination of both in a course for professional development to increase knowledge of child development and language and literacy for practicing preschool teachers.

The beliefs and philosophical stance of many preschool teachers are another challenge to be understood and addressed in both implementing a curriculum and providing professional development to support it. Lee and Ginsburg (2007) found that preschool teachers endorsed literacy practices where children followed their interests in a print rich environment. While teachers of low-income children strongly endorsed preschool academic education as a mean to ensure later school success, they were more reticent to endorse the full range of instructional practices (detailed in this book) that would most contribute to this success. Similarly, Hawken, Johnston, and McDonnell (2005) found that while 90% of Head Start teachers believed that literacy instruction should occur on a daily basis, fewer than 50% reported daily phonological awareness, writing, or alphabet letter activities and that a majority of the strategies teachers used did not involve explicit instruction. And there is pretty good consistency between teachers' reported beliefs and their classroom practices (Vartuli, 1999). Competence will be built when teachers see that their practice is improving as shown

> **Educational Principle 8:** Plan extended, research-based professional development that includes knowledge on the core literacy areas, how to teach them, and the curriculums that will be used.

by data collected on their own or with the help of supervisors, coaches, or peer mentors and by assessment evidence of child growth.

Apply Your Knowledge

Assess your beliefs on literacy practices using the following questions. Assign a score of 1–5 (1 = low, 5 = high) to each of the questions below. What did you learn about areas that you will be more or less open to using in this exercise?

1. How important is play in promoting literacy? __

2. How important is explicit instruction in promoting literacy? __

3. How important is the alphabet in promoting literacy? __

4. How important is an organized curriculum in promoting literacy? __

5. How important is a print rich environment in promoting literacy? __

6. How important is storybook reading in promoting literacy? __

7. How important is teacher oral English in promoting literacy? __

8. How important is knowing about the sounds in words in promoting literacy? __

9. How important is child choice in promoting literacy? __

10. How important is developmentally appropriate practice in promoting literacy? __

PROGRAM AND INSTRUCTION EVALUATIONS

PreK curriculums that specifically provide for early literacy instruction are much more readily available than they were only a few years ago. Companies that market comprehensive reading programs for K–6 often have companion literacy programs designed for prekindergarten children. The What Works Clearinghouse Web site at http://www.whatworks.ed.gov has a section that reviews and evaluates published studies that have evaluated specific preschool literacy programs or specific literacy teaching practices used in studies. Table 6.1 is a summary chart taken from the site that shows the current programs and instructional practices that have been evaluated for oral language. In the first column, labeled "Intervention," specific program are listed. Take a moment to study the key before you begin your review.

Table 6.1 Effectiveness Ratings for Early Childhood Education: Oral Language

Intervention	Improvement Index	Evidence Rating	Extent of Evidence
Phonological Awareness Training plus Letter Knowledge Training	−12	(−)	Not Rated
Doors to Discovery	−8	(0)	Small
Waterford Early Reading Level One	0	(0)	Small
Ready, Set, Leap!	0	(0)	Small
Direct Instruction	1	(0)	Small
Let's Begin With the Letter People	1	(0)	Medium to Large
Interactive Shared Book Reading	3	(+−)	Small
Shared Book Reading	3	(+−)	Not Rated
Words and Concepts	4	(0)	Not Rated
Curiosity Corner	9	(0)	Small
Literacy Express	14	(+)	Medium to Large
Dialogic Reading	19	(++)	Not Rated

Evidence Rating Key

(++) Positive Effects: strong evidence of a positive effect with no overriding contrary evidence.	(0) No Discernible Effects: no affirmative evidence of effects.
(+) Potentially Positive Effects: evidence of a positive effect with no overriding contrary evidence.	(−) Potentially Negative Effects: evidence of a negative effect with no overriding contrary evidence.
(+−) Mixed Effects: evidence of inconsistent effects.	(−−) Negative Effects: strong evidence of a negative effect with no overriding contrary evidence.

SOURCE: U.S. Department of Education, Institute of Education Sciences, What Works Clearinghouse (2004, December).

What conclusions can you draw from studying the chart? One important observation is how many programs have not demonstrated any "discernable effects" (the empty boxes or "0") on oral language. What might account for this? The programs could be weak, the implementation of the program may have been incomplete, or some element(s) important for literacy learning may not be captured in the programs.

Educational Principle 9: Seek out and use recent evidence on the effectiveness of curriculums you may be considering or already have in place.

Educational Principle 10: Examine literacy curriculums and programs to determine if high-quality instruction for English learners is consistently implemented throughout the program.

I have been examining these literacy programs as they come out and have had the opportunity to train and talk with teachers who are implementing a variety of them as well as to observe children learning from them. I will share some of my informal observations related to their suitability to English learners. The materials and content of these programs in general do address the major areas of preschool literacy and often have themes and many materials that are age appropriate and interesting to preschool children, including English learners. They also tend to incorporate stories, pictures, and photographs that show diverse children and some variety in cultural settings. They also typically have suggestions for modifications to particular lessons or activities that could be made for English learners. However, they typically do not have a conceptually based and systematic orientation to teaching practices for English learners, and they have limited emphasis on using and developing primary language.

CHALLENGES FOR MOVING FORWARD

In this chapter, there has been discussion of hot topics where the field has been engaged in significant debate. One debate has positioned social-emotional and cognitive development as competitors or adversaries. For those most stridently invested in this debate, one position seems to be "Relationship is the foundation of all learning." On the other side, the extreme argument goes something like, "Literacy is the foundation for societal success and economic well-being." Another debate centers on the value of explicit instruction for literacy learning. Related to this debate is the importance and role that play should have in early childhood. The concern is that introduction of comprehensive literacy programs and the time necessary to implement them will undermine the importance and opportunity for play. Specific to English learners, there has been significant debate on the role of primary language, when to introduce a second language, and when or if children with limited English proficiency can and should be exposed to literacy instruction in their second language. A less heated debate has been associated with the relative merits of a commercial "boxed" literacy curriculum compared to teacher-made lessons and activities. While these debates have contributed to clarification and deeper understanding of these issues in some ways, they have also consumed an awful lot of energy when pursued with strong adherence to one side or the other.

Based on the evidence reviewed in this book, I offer the following perspectives related to these debates. These perspectives are not unique to me and I believe are increasingly shared among early literacy researchers.

1. Social-emotional and cognitive outcomes are both essential for optimal development. In literacy learning, teaching that combines a focus on relationships with a focus on literacy competence promotes literacy development (e.g., Burchinal, Peisner-Fienberg, Pianta, & Howes, 2002). There still remains work to be done on this issue, as preschool teachers tend to value social-emotional outcomes over literacy outcomes (Bracken & Fischel, 2006; Lee & Ginsburg, 2007). A recent study combining data from six data sets looked at relationships between preschool social-emotional, attention, and cognitive factors and later school achievement in reading and math (Duncan et al., 2007). The researchers found that in each individual data set and in the combined one, math and reading academic skills and attention at kindergarten entry were most related to later achievement. Social-emotional variables had a minimal influence compared to the cognitive and attention variables. The same pattern was found for children from high and low socioeconomic backgrounds and for boys and girls.

2. High-quality instruction that targets specific literacy outcomes promotes preschool children's literacy learning across all the core domains (alphabet knowledge, phonological awareness, language development). There are studies specific to English learners that document this. Play contributes to children's literacy learning most clearly in the area of language development and the use of literacy materials (Morrow & Schickedanz, 2006), and more than play is needed for high levels of preschool literacy.

3. Bilingual programs and literacy experiences can promote language development in the primary language without compromising

second language learning (Roberts, 2008; Winsler, Diaz, Espinosa, & Rodriguez, 1999). Program quality and length of program matter, however (Montecel & Cortez, 2002). Preschool children at the very initial stages of second language acquisition can learn preschool literacy foundations, especially letter knowledge and vocabulary (Roberts, 2008; Roberts & Neal, 2004). Oral production during literacy learning benefits this learning.

4. Differences in preschool curriculum and instructional approach are associated with, and in some cases lead to, differences in literacy outcomes (Debaryshe & Gorecki, 2007; Fischel, Bracken, Fuchs-Eisenberg, Spira, Katz, et al., 2007; Han, Roskos, Christie, Mandzuk, & Vukelich, 2005; U.S. Department of Education, Institute of Education Sciences, What Works Clearinghouse, 2004). These studies include predominantly English-only children, although children from low socio-economic backgrounds are well represented. Small differences in instruction can make a difference in outcomes (Connor, Morrison, & Slominski, 2006).

CONCLUSION

Having a balanced and articulated literacy curriculum is necessary. It must include the core areas of language development (primary and second), the alphabet, and phonological awareness. Daily opportunities for learning in all these core areas are critical. A variety of learning contexts can promote children's achievement in each of these core areas. Conversations, centers, sociodramatic play, storybook reading, and explicit lessons are five very rich contexts for promoting high levels of literacy achievement for preschool English learners in the core areas of the alphabet, sounds in words, and language development. Learning experiences can be designed to balance emotional support and achievement of instructional goals during literacy lessons and activity. Promoting positive relationships during literacy learning is an element of instructional quality. It may also be particularly important for preschool children with limited English proficiency who may experience literacy learning as challenging. The evidence calls for early childhood educators to (1) embrace the importance of social-emotional and cognitive contributors to literacy achievement, (2) offer high-quality and challenging literacy learning opportunities to English learners, and (3) implement an intentionally selected balance of different teaching practices, activities, and contexts for children's learning. I hope you are on board.

Summary of Teaching Principles

Teaching Principle 1: Make a list of important words children will need to have to meet the goals (access the curriculum) of literacy lessons and activity.

Teaching Principle 2: Use primary language resources in teaching words of instruction.

Teaching Principle 3: Infuse all literacy lessons and activities with warm emotion and responses to children's requests, language, and emotional needs.

Teaching Principle 4: Use teaching practices that maintain the instructional purpose of literacy learning while promoting positive relationships with children.

Teaching Principle 5: Use many small-group and one-on-one literacy learning opportunities, and specifically plan activities for these two contexts.

Teaching Principle 6: Provide brief emotional support and shift attention back to instructional focus during literacy-focused activity.

Teaching Principle 7: Use primary language for responsive and warm interactions with children.

Teaching Principle 8: Teach English vocabulary and phrases that can be used to help teachers and children build relationships.

Teaching Principle 9: Add facial, gestural, and body expression to establish relationships with children.

Teaching Principle 10: Implement high-quality explicit instruction where children's participation and warm teacher-child relationships are promoted.

Teaching Principle 11: Carefully design lessons and activities to incorporate the characteristics of high-quality instruction.

Teaching Principle 12: Include the benefits of choice in literacy lessons and activities by providing experiences that include autonomy and self-regulation, response to child interests and input, and positive emotional experiences.

Summary of Educational Principles

Educational Principle 1: Select, develop, and implement a literacy curriculum that includes alphabet, phonological awareness, and oral language with special attention to vocabulary development as core content.

Educational Principle 2: Ensure that all teachers, site leadership, and family caregivers can describe this curriculum at the level appropriate for their involvement with it.

Educational Principle 3: Plan lessons and teach with a mix of in- and out-of-context teaching practices based on teaching goals and on whether children are at the point of initial learning, refinement, or personal use when designing lessons and instruction.

Educational Principle 4: Create a comprehensive plan for when and how to teach instructional words that includes a plan for frequent review of them.

Educational Principle 5: Use small groups for language development, individualizing in any area (alphabet, phonological awareness, language development) and relationship-building goals.

Educational Principle 6: Use explicit instruction for those areas of literacy learning where it is known to be effective.

Educational Principle 7: Assess children's literacy performance with accurate measures, and use the information to make instructional decisions.

Educational Principle 8: Plan and participate in extended, research-based professional development that includes knowledge on the core literacy areas, how to teach them, and the curriculums that will be used.

Educational Principle 9: Seek out and use recent evidence on the effectiveness of curriculums you may be considering or already have in place.

Educational Principle 10: Examine literacy curriculums and programs to determine if high-quality instruction for English learners is consistently implemented throughout the program.

7 Engaging Family Caregivers

★ ★ ★ ★ ★ ★ ★ ★ ★ ★ ★ ★ ★ ★ ★ ★ ★ ★

Important Research Results About Engaging Family Caregivers

- Activities, resources, and interactions in the home influence language and literacy development.

- Family caregivers of English language learners are very diverse in amount of schooling, literacy levels, beliefs about schooling, and experiences as students.

- Family caregivers of English language learners are very diverse in values and beliefs regarding authority, roles of parents, and roles of educators.

- Complex language and positive emotional interactions during language and literacy experiences in the home contribute substantially to language and literacy acquisition.

- Family caregivers are helped to support their children when they are assisted in understanding and implementing specific language and literacy practices with responsive and positive interaction.

- Family caregivers of English language learners show high support for their children's language and literacy when they are provided written materials and other resources in a language they can read.

- There is substantial variability in child language and literacy outcomes associated with efforts to engage family caregivers in support of their children's language and literacy development.

★ ★ ★ ★ ★ ★ ★ ★ ★ ★ ★ ★ ★ ★ ★ ★ ★ ★

F amily engagement is supported when caregivers feel they can contribute to their children's school success and are given opportunity to meaningfully participate in their children's education. Including and supporting primary language, even in multilingual classrooms and other nonbilingual contexts, is perhaps one of the most powerful ways to promote family caregivers' understanding that they have resources to shape their children's language and literacy. When families believe they have resources to support their children, they are empowered. Empowerment and the educational conditions that support it ensure that children and their families are rewarded by and maintain engagement with school (e.g., Au, 1998; Cummins, 1999; Delpit, 1988; Ogbu, 1992).

Characteristics of children's home life have an impact on their language and literacy development. Studies with both monolingual and English learner children illuminate these important home influences. Thus, we have some understanding of family caregiver practices that benefit children from several language backgrounds.

There are two important themes that have emerged from studies of home influences on language and literacy acquisition. The first theme is that both cognitive (thinking-related) and social-emotional characteristics of adult-child interaction in the home contribute importantly and uniquely to children's language and literacy development. Family caregivers who contribute most successfully to their preschool children's language and literacy development skillfully trigger complex thinking *and* have emotionally supportive interactions with their children. Family caregivers who engage their children in literacy-related thinking and practices contribute. Family caregivers who express positive emotions toward and respond to their children's literacy-related interests contribute.

The second important theme is that assisting family caregivers to adopt and adapt these practices to ones that work within their familial and cultural context can have positive influences on the language and literacy acquisition of both monolingual and English learner preschool children. This is the good news. However, while family engagement programs can be effective, they do not automatically or easily produce advances in language and literacy. When high-quality programs and supports to foster literacy thinking and positive caregiver-child interaction in children's homes are implemented, children's language and literacy competence grows.

Effective approaches for engaging family caregivers require carefully planned programs with components related to these two themes. Successful approaches will include components (1) to assist families in implementing specific cognitive and social-emotional practices, in both home and preschool settings, to enhance children's language and literacy competencies; and (2) will do so in a manner that is responsive to cultural characteristics and belief systems and the needs of family caregivers themselves. The organization of this chapter is shown in Figure 7.1.

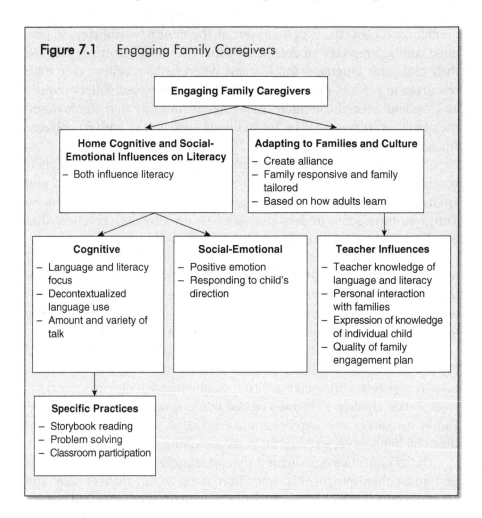

Figure 7.1   Engaging Family Caregivers

CREATE AN ALLIANCE

Two-way communication between families and teachers contributes to effective family caregiver engagement. In two-way communication, teachers and school staff see family caregivers as having knowledge, ideas, and resources that will contribute to children's language and literacy competence. Asking questions, active listening, and balanced amounts of talking between teachers and family members are indicators that two-way communication is occurring. In two-way communication families contribute their ideas to help shape language and literacy practices to benefit their children. In describing the nature of the connection between school and home, the term *alliance* has been purposefully chosen. It is hoped that this term captures a relationship quality that is deeper than family *participation* or even *collaboration*. In collaboration, individuals work together cooperatively and respectfully to achieve a shared goal. In an alliance there is a tight bond—a linking together—and a sense of shared mission.

Educational Principle 1: Plan meetings with family caregivers where the talking is shared between program staff and family caregivers.

Educational Principle 2: Plan meetings with parents that inform them of the value of home language activities, and demonstrate this by using the home languages in the meetings.

Apply Your Knowledge

Find out which language children and their family caregivers mostly use together at home. If you are not a teacher, describe ways a teacher could find this out. List two ways you could incorporate these languages in a home–school interaction such as a meeting, a field trip, a family potluck, or something else.

FOCUS ON LANGUAGE AND LITERACY

Examination of the child outcomes from various programs to engage family caregivers have been mixed (Dickinson, St. Pierre, & Pettengill, 2004). Two reasons for the uneven outcomes of programs include the degree to which child outcomes are targeted and the focus of the program. Some programs strive to increase parents' own well-being. The logic for this approach is that if parents (family caregivers) are the child's first teacher, then improvements in their well-being will make them better teachers. Programs where there is a greater focus on providing direct support to children through activities and processes they participate in with their family caregivers are more likely to enhance language and literacy outcomes. An analogy that helps make this point comes from tooth brushing. Your goal is to improve children's dental hygiene. To accomplish this you might take the view that by helping parents learn to correctly brush their own teeth and acquire the benefits that come from doing so, they will be in a better position to teach their children how to brush their teeth. Alternatively, you might say hey, if the goal is to help children correctly brush their teeth, then let's help parents learn successful techniques for directly teaching their children how to brush their teeth. In the case of language and literacy outcomes, anyway, it seems the direct focus on language and literacy is more effective.

Other family engagement programs have focused on overall effective parenting or practices to stimulate cognitive development. These programs may not be sufficiently focused on language and literacy activity to result in children's improved language and literacy. In addition, even when there is a real focus on language and literacy, the activities may not go on over a long enough period of time, may not be at the correct level, or may not be supported enough to ensure that parents will be successful in implementing them. The issues of duration, correct level of at-home activity, and amount of family caregiver support are all sensitive to the knowledge and skill of the persons planning and implementing the language and literacy family engagement program. These points highlight the amount of care and thoughtfulness required for family engagement programs to be successful. Collaboration with other professionals, particularly for those practitioners who do not feel they are experts in language and literacy development, can increase the likelihood that family engagement programs will be successful.

> **Educational Principle 3:** Make sure that your program for caregiver engagement is focused on language and literacy practices and outcomes.
>
> **Educational Principle 4:** Include suggestions for language and literacy activities that can be directly implemented with children.

Examples of Helpful Ideas and Resources to Share With Family Caregivers

- Speaking in primary language (many words, and many kinds of words)
- Being nice when talking (affirming rather than prohibiting or criticizing)
- A tape or CD of the names and sounds of alphabet letters
- Family literacy nights where family caregivers engage in interactive story-book reading
- Ideas on where to find literacy resources (information on library location and hours, library card applications and help filling them out)
- Links to primary language Web sites

Apply Your Knowledge

List two topics in language or literacy that you would like to target in a beginning family, caregiver engagement program. Vocabulary, alphabet knowledge, and writing are examples of topics. What specific child outcomes would you see if the program were effective? How will you assist family caregivers in learning how to support children's growth in these areas? Write a paragraph of what you learned about your language and literacy knowledge and child outcomes from doing this exercise.

THINKING PROCESSES AND POSITIVE RELATIONSHIPS WORKING TOGETHER

Family caregivers who engage their children in complex language and specific literacy practices contribute to language and literacy competence. Family caregivers who express positive emotions toward and respond to their children's literacy-related interests contribute to language and literacy competence (Landry & Smith, 2006). Thus, it is not just being read to or participating in literacy practices such as helping make lists for the grocery store, writing a letter to a relative, or looking at a Chinese almanac that are the active ingredients of effective family caregiver support for language and literacy. Similarly, it is not simply the expression of positive emotions and encouragement of the child that is the active ingredient of effective family caregiver support for language and literacy. Specific types of literacy-related thinking and emotionally supportive relationships between family caregivers and their children each add independently to preschool children's language and literacy competence.

Home Language and Literacy Support + Home Emotional Support = Language and Literacy Strength

Think of language and literacy as a golden crown sitting atop a complex pedestal with several legs. Each leg contributes to keeping that crown balanced on its pedestal. If you remove any of these supports, the crown may remain on the pedestal, but the crown is less secure. Certain ways of thinking and using language and certain characteristics of relationships with adults are two legs of the pedestal. Language and emotional support are mutually enhancing, and they work together to increase children's literacy competence. They are two of the developmental systems that are operating within the child.

Think about where you stand on the relative importance of cognitive and social-emotional factors on literacy. Have you typically thought one or the other leg (social-emotional or cognitive) of the pedestal was more important than the other? Have you been aware of your views about the importance of cognition compared to social-emotional relationships? Perhaps you have understood all along how they are each involved. Maybe you have never thought about this question? Maybe you feel relationship is central in some areas of preschool learning and development while cognition is central in others? As you continue with this section, bear in mind how your response to the preceding questions may influence your reactions to what you read.

HOME EMOTIONAL SUPPORT FOR LITERACY

Responsive parenting is the home emotional support that is linked to early literacy (Landry & Smith, 2006). Responsive family caregivers attend to what the child is saying, craft their response to the child's ongoing interests, and do so in a manner that makes the child feel good and important. Responsive parenting provides a support structure or *scaffold* for helping children maintain attention and self-regulate. The brain has a limited capacity for how much work it can do at any one time. When family caregivers respond to the child's current focus and help their child maintain it, the child functions at a higher cognitive and linguistic level. With this type of parent support, children can devote fewer mental resources to controlling attention and regulating their behavior, thereby freeing up more brain capacity for improving the quality of their linguistic and conceptual contribution to the ongoing language or literacy activity. When parents provide supports that help children keep their attention focused, children more easily remain engaged in the current conversation, story-reading activity, or other language and literacy related activity. This scaffolding feat is accomplished when caregivers respond to and share the child's current interests and focus (Dietrich, Assel, Swank, Smith, & Landry, 2006; Landry, Smith, & Swank, 2002).

Preschool children's attention and self-regulation are far from mature (Baumeister & Vohs, 2004). The prefrontal cortex of the brain is largely responsible for these two functions (National Research Council and Institute of Medicine, Committee on Integrating the Science of Early Childhood Development 2000). It continues to develop until early adulthood. The well known reacting without thinking and risk-taking behavior of adolescents is related to the still developing prefrontal cortex. It is no wonder that preschool children benefit from practices that help them maintain attention and thereby regulate their behavior.

This is pretty heady stuff we are considering here. One might reasonably think, "Wait a minute; I am working to understand this. How in the world could parents of English language learners get this?" This is a good question, and there are encouraging data to suggest that informational support, family caregivers' analyses of videos of their own and others' parenting, and in-home coaching can promote responsive parenting among low-income parents from several ethnic groups (Landry, Smith, & Swank, 2006). There are also studies with children learning two languages in the Netherlands that mirror some of the social circumstances of language variation in the United States; these studies show that responsive parenting influences children who are learning two languages. In the Netherlands, speaking a language other than Dutch at home is associated with low socioeconomic status and being a member of a language minority group. Cross-cultural differences were found in the amount of positive emotional support used by parents in the home. Within different cultural groups, differences in positive emotional support were related to later language and literacy outcomes (Leseman & van Tuijl, 2006). In these studies, emotional support was thought of as mother's supportive orientation, non-intrusiveness, and confidence in the child. Thus positive emotional support is an important feature of adult-child interaction that is likely to be somewhat universal across cultural groups. Explanations for why responsive parenting works focus on some basic components of the child's cognitive architecture: limited capacity, attention, language, and memory. These basic brain processes likely operate similarly across language groups. Thus there is reason to think that at least on a theoretical level, interventions to increase responsive parenting should work across many language groups.

There are some very encouraging results of recent at-home interventions to increase mothers' responsive parenting (Landry, Smith, & Swank, 2006). Shared reading and toy play were targeted in this study. Mothers participated in coaching, video analysis of other mothers and themselves, and practice supervised by trained in-home supporters. Other family members were also included in these activities. Changes in mothers' responsiveness led to related changes in children's language. The mothers increased their use of rich language as a result of the intervention. This study was a true experiment. Children in the responsive parenting group were compared to others in a comparison group whose in-home visitor focused on other things. Children were also randomly assigned to one group or the other. While the study included families from a range of ethnicities, the intervention occurred in English. What is not clear from this study is whether the same outcomes could be achieved using languages other than English and what the relative impacts were on children's first and second language.

There are characteristics of the in-home support program that should be noted. Language and literacy were specifically targeted. The intervention used a systematic and structured session format. The coaching, video analysis, and self-correction techniques took into account how adults learn. Through two-way communication and the active participation of mothers, a strong alliance was created between professionals and parents as they participated in joint problem solving to enhance mothers' responsive parenting.

A second key aspect of the social-emotional component of at-home practices that contribute to language and literacy is the degree to which the parent truly responds to the child. When parents respond to points of interest to the child, the child's sense of worth is supported, and the caregiver's investment in the child's interests is made clear. This type of responding is referred to as *contingent responding*. When caregivers respond contingently, children are willing to and interested in continuing the interaction, creating a foundation for cooperativeness. When observed in natural settings, contingent responding is associated with smiling, positive statements, physical closeness, and pacing of activity and language that matches the child's temperament. These responses contribute to the child's sense of safety, trust, and emotional equilibrium. These positive feelings support the child's continuing interest in participating more in language and literacy activities. These same parenting practices contribute to specific language outcomes as well (Tamis-LeMonda, Bornstein, & Baumwell, 2001). Responsive parenting scaffolds language acquisition. The child's ability to acquire new language is advanced, because the language input the child is receiving from family caregivers is connected to the child's interests, current knowledge, and present focus. The interplay between positive relationships with family caregivers and cognitive advancement shown in this example is illustrative of the complementary roles played by social-emotional and cognitive outcomes in language and literacy development.

HOME COGNITIVE SUPPORT FOR LITERACY

The main element of at-home cognitive influence is language. Characteristics of language input and the ebb and flow of language interaction in the home contribute to preschool children's language and literacy accomplishments. Language input that is rich, varied, and extensive plays a pivotal role in children's early language development. Hart and Risley (1995) reported two rather astonishing relationships between language in the home prior to preschool and later academic achievement. First, they found that the number and variety of words used in the home prior to age three were the two aspects of language having the greatest impact on later language and literacy abilities. Second, they reported that some preschool children received five times more verbal input than others from infancy to age three. This study was based on a small sample of English-only families. Similar influences of the home language environment have been reported for bilingual children (Leseman, 2000; Pearson & Fernandez, 1994).

Other studies that disentangle language and socioeconomic status report similar cultural differences in home language use with similar differences in child outcomes. The use of complex language, the variety of language, and the amount of language used to discuss things that were not ongoing in the immediate environment—decontextualized language—varied by cultural and language group (de Jong & Leseman, 2001; see elaborated discussion of decontextualized language on pages 27–28) The more family caregivers demonstrated each of these aspects of language, the stronger was their children's language and literacy at three, four, and six years of age. So it seems that the current evidence suggests that across a number of different language groups, there is a special relationship between language development and the amount, variety, and type of language used in their homes. More talk, more variation in the number of words used, and talk that is more like the language used in schools seems to contribute to school success.

Through our consideration of both responsive parenting and rich language input, the intimate dance between social-emotional relationships and cognition in early language and literacy is apparent. One can and should embrace both parts of the "home language and cognition support + home emotional support = language and literacy strength" equation and help families skillfully weave the connection between them. Bear in mind, though, that what has been described as effective is more than global positive climate or not being negative or valuing the use of language. What has been portrayed is a caregiver who

> **Educational Principle 5:** Include knowledge about both emotional support and cognitive support in a family engagement plan.
>
> **Educational Principle 6:** Include specific practices to promote responsive parenting and rich language input in your family caregiver engagement plan.

uses language in specific ways. And what the child does with language as a result of the caregiver's usage is at the heart and center of what makes it effective. It is the starting point.

FAMILY RESPONSIVE AND
FAMILY TAILORED APPROACHES

Crafting home language and literacy practices to the characteristics of individual families and the cultural frameworks that they are embedded in is an important aspect of a high-quality family caregiver engagement plan. We know that to be most effective as teachers of children, we must take into account children's individual differences and cultural influences on their development. Similarly, programs that will effectively engage family caregivers will be responsive to the characteristics of the individual family caregivers and their cultural frameworks. Family engagement practices need to be both child-focused *and* family caregiver–focused.

Taking into account the needs of family caregivers as adult learners will add to the effectiveness of family engagement plans. If you have teaching experience, you have probably seen many recommendations on activities to engage families in the life of the preschool classroom. Typically, these activities focus on suggestions for family caregivers to do at home with the goal of fostering some desired developmental outcome in the child. It is much less typical for these suggestions to take into account the characteristics of the family caregivers themselves. Perhaps the most obvious characteristic of parents as adult learners that need to be responded to is the language they speak. Some teachers or sites may have developed ways to reach all families in their community in a language that can be understood by the families. This is not common practice, however. I don't believe I have seen a published English curriculum, activity book, thematic unit, or other source for classroom practice that accommodates the language of family caregivers other than those who are Spanish speaking. Perhaps this statement will challenge you to prove me wrong by finding teaching resources that respond to and accommodate a variety of primary languages.

Communicating With Families (in a Language They Understand)

Some programs have bilingual family members serve as "language brokers." Bilingual family members can orally explain specific literacy activities to do at home during a 15-minute afterschool family meeting on Fridays. Another example that relies on oral language is the use of a phone tree headed by a bilingual family caregiver(s), where the tree includes all those with the same primary language. The tree is used to communicate concepts in language development to all those on the tree. For one week, the concept is, "Ask your child questions to get her or him to talk more." Another weekly concept might be to find some time each day to have a conversation about something that has recently happened in your family. Give information to your child, and also ask children to talk about the event themselves. It may help if you have these conversations at the same time each day. During meals, riding in the car, or during bath time are some possibilities, but use times that are best for you and your family to have these conversations. Calls are made to each family on the tree explaining these concepts.

An example using written language comes from a preschool where there was a Cantonese elementary bilingual program. Older children in the bilingual program wrote messages from the teacher to families in Cantonese. These messages contained suggestions for specific things to do at home that were related to classroom activity. Bilingual support staff can also help write materials for home use in languages understood by the families. Once the commitment to communicating with all families is firmly established, several successful practices will be found. As the saying goes, "Where there is a will, there is a way."

Families also differ in their cultural practices around child rearing, styles and occasions of language interaction, and family caregivers' own experiences as children. These characteristics of families will also influence the ease or challenge of engaging family caregivers. For example, consider the fact that some families use more authoritarian child-rearing practices than do others. Authoritarian parents set the standards of behavior for children independently and expect children to comply because the parent is the authority. They are very comfortable making most decisions about their children's activities. Authoritarian parents also expect compliance on the basis of their power and authority as parents. An example of how this child-rearing characteristic may impact literacy development can be seen in shared reading. When children guide conversations and interject their own personal ideas during shared reading, greater language growth occurs. More authoritarian parents may find implementing this practice challenging.

We have talked about many aspects of family caregivers that may influence the ease or challenge of engaging them in practices likely to foster language and literacy growth in their children. Wow—is there a lot to know about that would be helpful! So how is a teacher going to find this out? I refer to this finding out process as *familial-cultural study*. Possibilities for these modest familial-cultural studies that can help tailor family engagement plans to local variability are shown in the possible activities box that follows.

> ## Possible Activities for Familial-Cultural Study
>
> - Go to the park and study patterns of language interaction and grouping around age and gender among individuals from different cultures that you observe there.
> - Go to church/spiritual/social events, and study interactions between family caregivers and children in the informal parts of the activity to learn about child-rearing practices.
> - Go to an ethnic grocery; watch who is shopping and how people interact with shopkeepers. Also look for possible resources for building language and literacy in the home and in the classroom.
> - Get copies of local organization newspapers.
> - Consult with family members, school personnel such as bilingual teaching staff, parent organizations, and others about their ideas and suggestions for where you could find out more about families and their home practices.
> - Construct a questionnaire aimed to determine what language practices and literacy practices occur in children's homes.

I was once doing a training for about 50 preschool teachers in Head Start and other state-funded programs on the topic of vocabulary development. I had made the point that there is a relationship between the amount of talking in children's homes and language development for English-only children. The ensuing discussion of cultural differences in talkativeness led the group to raise questions about both the challenges and the appropriateness of informing parents of English language learners about this information or attempts to increase the amount of talking in children's homes.

That day, after the training, I was out for a run and passed a park. I noticed that there was a large group of individuals who I thought were from X cultural group—one of the very ones that we had been discussing earlier in the day. It was an opportunity for a modest cultural study right before my very eyes! I began to watch and to talk to a few people there. I first confirmed that these were indeed individuals from group X. There were several different activities going on. A group of mature men played a game with balls. The balls were wrapped in material and then spun and released with the goal of having them settle in a target circle. All the better if other balls were knocked out of the circle. The men were organized into two teams as indicated by the multiple calls of pleasure or frustration that occurred after balls were knocked away or hit the target circle. Another group of men played cards where small amounts of money were being gambled. A mixed group of teenager and young adult males and females played volleyball where both sexes took the role of hitter and setter. A fourth group consisted of women with food sitting on large blankets with mostly small children darting in and out. During this brief cultural study, I observed things related to gender, child rearing, language interaction, and a traditional cultural game I had never seen before. What I was mostly interested in, from the questions of language and literacy discussed in the vocabulary training, was the nature of observable verbal interactions. How much? Between whom? Adults compared to children?

Here is what I learned. During the ball game there was loud, positive affect–filled, and almost constant verbal interaction. In the volleyball game similarly there was much talking and laughing from both males and females. In the card game, there was quiet talk where participants looked at each other, but there was a more serious atmosphere. The women's group was the quietest, with several women seated alone or around others with less frequent interaction. When children entered the women's group, attention was immediately directed to them by at least one person—presumably their caregiver—with quiet talking and physical touching and stroking of the child.

I concluded that in this cultural group there was indeed a great deal of talking and expression of positive affect. It seemed that males were at least as talkative as females, reminding me that plans for family engagement of this group should be made with consideration of what would encourage male participation. I noted that there might be a difference in cross-gender interaction between more traditional/older and younger generations. I tucked away for later exploration the possibility of having family members teach this traditional game as a way to have families participate in the classroom with a culturally familiar and traditional activity. I would also bear in mind that each individual within the group was unique and that none of my conclusions would necessarily apply to any one individual.

> **Educational Principle 7:**
> Solve the challenge of how to communicate with parents in a language they understand.

Apply Your Knowledge

1. Identify the language resources available at your site that can be harnessed for communicating with parents. If you are not currently a teacher, identify who or what might be possible language resources. Think about teachers, caregivers of children, other children, siblings, program staff, even the Internet.

(Continued)

(Continued)

2. What are some possibilities for cultural study that exist in your preschool setting?

3. What could you actually do to learn about family caregivers, children, and their cultural frameworks in the places and activities for cultural study suggested in the box above?

TEACHER INFLUENCES ON FAMILY ENGAGEMENT

The responsiveness of teachers also contributes to successfully engaging family caregivers of English language learners in supporting language and literacy development. However, it appears that classroom literacy practices haven't fully capitalized on the potential of family caregivers to support their children's language and literacy learning. One recent study of about 90 preschool classrooms that used the Early Language and Literacy Classroom Observation (ELLCO) tool (Smith, Dickinson, Sangeorge, & Anastasopoulos, 2002) found that classroom support for parents reading to their children averaged 2.78 on a scale of 1 to 5, with a 5 indicating strong evidence of home support (Smith et al., 2002). In terms of specific practices, ELLCO ratings indicated that teachers typically provided families with some information on how to support children's literacy development and provided families with tools that could be understood and used by them. There were also some very important conditions for supporting family caregiver engagement that were missing. There was only limited evidence that teachers helped families learn about first and second language and literacy development, no evidence of building on families' social-cultural experience related to language and literacy, and no evidence that teachers helped families access community resources to support their children's language and literacy growth. Stop and think about this for a moment. What do you think are the most likely reasons for these omissions in preschool teachers' practice? Clearly, from all we have discussed about the positive impact family caregivers can have on literacy development, answers to this question and ways to remove these barriers are very important.

I suggest that one very likely reason for these omissions is that teachers' opportunities for professional development on the kinds of topics related to language and literacy development covered in this book have been limited. Hopefully, you appreciate the complexity and skill required to create high-quality professional practice and programs to foster language and literacy competence in English learners. Without deep knowledge of language and literacy development and deep knowledge of how families can participate in supporting it, teachers will be hampered in designing and implementing effective family engagement programs. While the importance of family engagement for literacy enhancement may be genuinely valued, and while the motivation to engage families may be high, the practices implemented by teachers are likely to be incomplete and not specific enough to language and literacy without this deep knowledge. You are gaining some of this important knowledge about families as you study and master the material in this chapter. So please keep on working.

Teaching Principle 1: Plan specific ways to have personal interactions with family caregivers.

Teaching Principle 2: Plan specific ways to communicate to parents that you value their individual child.

Teaching Principle 3: Tailor the home supports for language and literacy development that are suggested to families to the social/cultural characteristics of children's families.

Teaching Principle 4: Include specific language and literacy practices—such as opportunities for conversation, opportunities for using print, and opportunities for shared book reading or storytelling—in home activities.

Teaching Principle 5: Provide families the names of and contact information for community resources to support children's language and literacy development.

Parents report that personal interaction with teachers is the most important factor for encouraging family involvement (Comer & Haynes, 1991). Providing opportunities for informal and personal interaction between parents and teachers (such as potluck meals, family storybook reading events, and personal communication during classroom sign-in and sign-out), establishing a community discussion council, providing meaningful ways for caregivers to help in classrooms, and regularly providing literacy materials and activities for in-home use are examples of techniques for increasing personal contact between family caregivers and teaching staff. How do you feel about participating with parents in these informal ways? Some teachers relish these experiences, while others feel uncomfortable or uncertain how to behave in these settings. Teachers have commented that they have not learned about these practices in their teacher training. Others have commented that they feel uncertain when the teacher power role changes as they interact more personally and informally with family members.

Apply Your Knowledge

1. Divide a paper into two columns. In one column, make a list of all the barriers you can think of for why teachers may not build on families' social/cultural practices. In the other column, list all the barriers you can think of for why teachers may not help families access community resources for language and literacy growth. Underneath each of these lists of barriers, list what may be solutions for them. If you are a practicing teacher, please include those practices you currently use or could use to break down these barriers. Now take these solutions to your preschool setting, and begin to implement some of them.

2. If you are a teacher, write a list of questions that you have about engaging family caregivers to support language and literacy development of children you work with. If you are not a teacher, make a list of questions that would be important. Make sure your questions are about language and literacy. Identify one or two simple familial-cultural studies you could perform to find out about these questions.

FAMILY CAREGIVERS AND CHILDREN READING TOGETHER

Several studies with English-only children have shown that adult-child shared reading at home benefits language development (Bus, van IJzendoorn, & Pellegrini, 1995). These studies include a number that are true experiments, where children and family-caregivers who participate in shared reading are compared to other children who do not participate in shared reading. In addition, the similarity of children in both the shared reading group and the other group—which is referred to as a *control group* or *comparison group*—has been assured in the best studies by assigning children to groups on a random basis. These types of experimental studies provide the strongest evidence that some practices are better than others and that the practices themselves actually cause any significant improvement. And we have this type of evidence for shared reading.

In addition, the benefits of shared reading have been *replicated* in several studies. Replication means that similar results have been found in more than one study. When several studies point to the same finding, our confidence is increased that the practices reported in the studies are indeed effective. Happily for our focus on English language learners, there are also studies that show the effectiveness of shared reading between children and family caregivers whose primary language is a language other than English.

In one study, 80% of English language learners' families participated in shared-reading training and shared-reading events with their children; these trainings and events took place after regular program hours (Roberts, 2008). Another showed that parents learned to use interactive reading techniques after two training sessions and that children whose parents participated in these trainings fared better on language development than children whose parents did not participate. Additional studies have shown that interactive storybook reading at home promotes vocabulary learning for English language learners from several different language backgrounds (Elley, 1989; Mendelsohn et al., 2001; Raikes et al., 2006). The key ingredient of interactive reading is to encourage the child to contribute as much language as possible during the storybook reading.

When family caregivers are assisted in learning how to read storybooks in ways that draw out and expand their children's talk and thinking, language is enhanced (Bus et al., 1995). Shared reading has most consistently improved language, rather than literacy, outcomes in children. However, supporting language directly benefits literacy, since comprehending stories requires all the elements of oral language. Storybook reading also provides children with linguistic input that takes them beyond their current knowledge level and their current linguistic level. During storybook reading, children encounter more complex sentence structures, new

Teaching Principle 6: Include a family shared reading component as part of your literacy curriculum.

Teaching Principle 7: Plan a specific way to assist family caregivers in learning how to interactively read storybooks with their children.

vocabulary, and elaborated explanations and descriptions. In addition, listening comprehension and reading comprehension are highly correlated (Sticht & James, 1984). Therefore the development of oral listening skills is an important foundational literacy skill for prekindergarten children.

Apply Your Knowledge

Plan training for family caregivers on shared reading practices. Indicate specifically what will be the key points to get across.
- How will you involve families in your planning?
- How will you accommodate families with different languages?

(Continued)

(Continued)

- How will you determine when to offer the training?
- How will you handle childcare?
- How can you best ensure that families understand your suggestions?
- How can you best ensure that your suggestions will work within caregivers' family and cultural practices?

FAMILY CAREGIVERS AND CHILDREN PLAYFULLY SOLVING PROBLEMS TOGETHER

While shared book reading is quite clearly an activity related to language and literacy development, there is another type of adult-child interaction in children's homes that has a significant influence on language. What goes on between family caregivers and children during playful problem-solving experiences influences English language learner's language development.

Examples of Home Problem-Solving Activities

- Solving puzzles
- Building with blocks
- Playing with a hose
- Sorting games
- Interacting with a computer game
- Organizing a toy box

Again, we have some evidence that

- emotional aspects of the adult child relationship and
- characteristics of the language interaction

influence children's language outcomes (de Jong & Leseman, 2001; Leseman & van den Boom, 1999). Importantly, the same influences have been seen across a number of cultural and language groups. The aspects of language related to responsiveness to the child that you have already been learning about play a key role (Leseman & van Tuijl, 2006). When caregivers at home engage in these playful and goal-oriented activities with language that is positive in tone and emotional content while also providing sophisticated language that engages the child's thinking processes, language is enhanced. And when parents of children from varied socioeconomic and ethnic backgrounds are helped to learn how to do this and actually implement the practices, there is growth in children's language (Landry & Smith, 2006).

Teaching Principle 8: Plan a specific way to assist family caregivers in learning how to use emotionally positive and challenging language with their children when they are engaged in playful goal-oriented activities.

Apply Your Knowledge

Make a list of three playful, goal-oriented activities that you know children you work with participate in at home (back to the importance of familial-cultural study). List three or four specific language prompts that could be used to draw out more language and thinking on the part of the child while participating in these activities. What are three to five vocabulary words that could also be included in these discussions? For example, in some families making food is a playful experience that even preschool age children participate in. What would be some topics, questions, or responses that could be used to have children thinking more with language? What would be some specific words that parents could be encouraged to use?

ENGAGING FAMILY CAREGIVERS IN THE CLASSROOM

Engaging family caregivers in classrooms can provide many benefits to families, children, and teachers. When parents participate meaningfully in their children's classrooms, relationships between children, family caregivers, and teachers are built. In addition, when children experience either their own caregivers or those of other children, particularly those who speak the same primary language, helping in their preschool settings, it is a very concrete signal of the importance of their cultural group, the language spoken by its members, and the school's valuing of its members. In addition, relationships between community caregivers can be initiated and nourished as they share in classroom participation.

Teaching Principle 9: Draw on family caregivers' cultural and language resources in the classroom.

Teaching Principle 10: Make concrete and organized ways for family caregivers to participate in preschool settings with individual children or very small groups of children.

However, this type of meaningful engagement takes specific planning. Family caregivers come with a diverse range of skills. Careful planning of specific activities, and matching caregiver strengths to the activities, is essential for reaping the positive potential benefits. One idea is to identify key family caregivers who can serve to help organize and explain the desired classroom participation. Concrete efforts to help parents know the goals of and specific strategies for their participation are important. Activities for one-on-one interaction are likely to be easier for many family caregivers than independent management of groups of children. A huge resource that many family caregivers bring is their competence in languages other than English.

ONE MODEL FOR ENGAGING FAMILIES

In this section I will describe a program for family engagement designed to promote language development of English language learners that I implemented and evaluated in a recent study cited in this and other chapters (Roberts, 2008). The program centered on assisting family caregivers to provide interactive storybook reading in their primary language at home and providing subsequent classroom storybook reading of the same books in English. Storybook reading was selected because of the strong research base suggesting that this was a specific practice likely to provide children with vocabulary benefits and experience with decontextualized language. The at-home component of the program was also thought to build a primary language foundation that could help support subsequent English acquisition.

I also anticipated that when families and teachers were involved with activities around the same books, a bridge of familiarity and shared experience specific to language and literacy would be built between family caregivers and classrooms. When children came home with a teddy bear art project after reading the book *Corduroy* and families had also read this book, a common understanding and connection would be established. This commonality would also lend itself to richer and more elaborated opportunities for communication between family caregivers and children related to their school literacy experiences. Support your efforts with specific suggestions for family caregivers such as the following:

> Please remind your child that Corduroy, the teddy bear in the book, and Lisa were friends. Talk with your child about his or her friends. Questions you could ask are, "Who are your friends?" "What do you do together?" Listen to what your child says and respond.

Classic storybooks were translated into the primary languages (Hmong and Spanish) of children from low-income families enrolled in a state-funded preschool. Many of the storybooks had Spanish versions available, so these books were purchased. A brief familial-cultural study was begun by having bilingual family caregiver volunteers conduct family literacy surveys prior to and at the end of the project. These surveys were designed to identify the *language resources, patterns of language use, literacy skills,* and *languages* available in the children's homes. We triangulated this data with the home language survey included in the preschool registration and the teacher's knowledge and observation of family language use. Based on this survey, we determined that all families except two had a family member who could read in the primary language. For those two families, audiotapes of stories were offered with the books. We also queried families on the time(s) that would be most convenient for them and barriers to participating in family literacy sessions at school. From this we determined that the best time to offer the program was late in the afternoon and that childcare, particularly for the Hmong families who often had several young children, would be an important support to offer. These elements of the program show *family responsive* and *family tailored approaches* to family caregiver engagement.

Hmong and Spanish primary language bilingual paraprofessionals and bilingual classroom parents were recruited to assist in developing translations of classic children's storybooks. A small grant was obtained to pay parents for this work. In this process, family members had to negotiate about what was a correct or "best" translation for a particular word, statement, or phrase. Family caregivers from all three language groups were also enlisted to help in the training component of family storybook reading events.

Trainings on how to implement interactive storybook reading were created in each of the three target languages: English, Hmong, and Spanish, and training was provided in each language rather than providing the training in English with spoken translation into Spanish and Hmong. The volunteer parents explained the training content shown on colored overheads during an afterschool family engagement storybook reading event. These procedures demonstrated the school *valuing primary language, using primary language, creating an alliance*, and using *two-way communication* with family caregivers. The information given to families emphasized both specific language expansion strategies (getting the child to talk more, rereading books) and emotional support (sitting close together, having fun). These elements of the training materials show one way that the concept of *thinking processes and positive relationships working together* was implemented into the program. Bookmarks that showed pictures of each of the elements of storybook reading we were suggesting to parents were inserted into each book that was sent home each week. These bookmarks were reviews for those who attended the family literacy events and helped to make the information available to some degree to those who had not been able to attend the family literacy events.

After the family literacy training material was reviewed, family caregivers were given books and practiced the storybook reading techniques they had just learned about with their child. Cookies and punch were provided to create a relaxed, friendly, and festive atmosphere. The family trainers were available for answering questions, although this often meant asking the staff professionals how to answer the caregiver's question. It was a beautiful thing seeing all these pairs (and occasionally small groups when other siblings, grandparents, or both mother and father were included) reading storybooks together!

And in the end there were language and literacy benefits. We had an 80% parent participation in the family literacy events. Each week, children's storybook vocabulary was measured. Children learned words from both the at-home and in-class storybook reading, and they still knew most of these words a year later at the end of kindergarten. There was evidence of both English and primary language benefits.

HIGH-QUALITY FAMILY ENGAGEMENT PRACTICES

Many of the elements of high-quality family engagement techniques have been discussed in other sections of the chapter. Even so, I have included this section to draw all these points together. It is important to do so for two reasons. First, research shows the influence on language and literacy development of children's language and literacy related experiences in their homes. Second, studies on engaging families indicate that while there should be optimism for the potential benefits of family engagement, programs have not consistently shown positive influences on children's language and literacy development. A summary of important elements for a family engagement program that will successfully engage families and result in stronger language and literacy of children follows:

- Is based on the belief that all families have potential to support their children's language and literacy development
- Provides information and material in language(s) family caregivers can understand and use
- Helps families understand the reasons and potential benefits of suggested practices
- Is tailored to individual families to be served
- Is both child-focused and family caregiver–focused
- Is based on an alliance between school staff and families and has structures for ensuring two-way communication
- Specifically targets language and literacy competence
- Provides specific carefully thought-out practices for at-home implementation and the resources to accomplish the practices
- Is regular and ongoing over months to years rather than days to weeks
- Is aligned with classroom language and literacy activity
- Draws on and validates children's and family's culturally embedded beliefs and practices, including language
- Includes opportunities for engagement both at home and in classrooms

You will probably agree that this is quite a bit to ask for! Developing a comprehensive family engagement plan will take a great deal of work and need not all be accomplished at once. If you have been involved in efforts for family engagement as a professional or a parent, you may have experience with some or even most of these techniques. Which do you believe are most important? Go through the bulleted list, and assign numbers between 1 and 3 to each item, with 1 assigned to those that are most important, 2 assigned to those that are next most important, and 3 assigned to those that are least important. This exercise may help you identify how to get started or further develop your existing family engagement practices. The destination is reached by taking one step at a time—the important point is to start walking.

Apply Your Knowledge

Analyze the family engagement plan of a language and literacy curriculum or program. You could select a program you are using, a curriculum your site is considering adopting, or your own teacher-made

(Continued)

(Continued)

program. Go through each of the items on the bulleted list, and write a sentence or two about whether or not each of the bulleted elements is present. After completing this exercise, write three to four sentences stating your overall evaluation of the family engagement component according to the criteria in the bulleted list. Many family engagement programs can also be found on the Internet if you do not have one available to you. Search terms: *preschool curriculum, preschool literacy program.*

CONCLUSION

Successfully engaging family caregivers of English learners requires planning that takes into account families' individual and cultural frameworks. Substantial effort is required to address the language, resource, and practical challenges of fostering home practices that benefit children's language and literacy development. I hope that the potential powerfulness of these efforts for language and literacy outcomes portrayed in this chapter has helped convince you that the potential benefits makes it worthwhile. In order to be effective, family engagement programs should support family caregivers in implementing both (1) complex language and literacy thinking and (2) responsive and approving interactions with their children. Sensitivity to the cultural and language use issues associated with any suggestions for modification of existing home practices is necessary and should be addressed collaboratively between early care and education professionals and children's families. While language and literacy benefits are the focus of this chapter, home-school connections are also being built when family responsive and family tailored programs to engage family caregivers are implemented. Find out what you need to know about the families within your community, build with it, strengthen it, and experience the children and families blooming from your efforts.

Summary of Teaching Principles

Teaching Principle 1: Plan specific ways to have personal interactions with family caregivers.

Teaching Principle 2: Plan specific ways to communicate to parents that you value their individual child.

Teaching Principle 3: Tailor the home supports for language and literacy development that are suggested to families to the social/cultural characteristics of children's families.

Teaching Principle 4: Include specific language and literacy practices—such as opportunities for conversation, opportunities for using print, and opportunities for shared book reading or storytelling—in home activities.

Teaching Principle 5: Provide families the names of and contact information for community resources to support children's language and literacy development.

Teaching Principle 6: Include a family shared reading component as part of your literacy curriculum.

Teaching Principle 7: Plan a specific way to assist family caregivers in learning how to interactively read storybooks with their children.

Teaching Principle 8: Plan a specific way to assist family caregivers in learning how to use emotionally positive and challenging language with their children when they are engaged in playful goal-oriented activities.

Teaching Principle 9: Draw on family caregivers' cultural and language resources in the classroom.

Teaching Principle 10: Make concrete and organized ways for family caregivers to participate in preschool settings with individual children or very small groups of children.

Summary of Educational Principles

Educational Principle 1: Plan meetings with family caregivers where the talking is shared between program staff and family caregivers.

Educational Principle 2: Plan meetings with parents that inform them of the value of home language activities, and demonstrate this by using the primary language in the meetings.

(Continued)

(Continued)

Educational Principle 3: Make sure that your program for caregiver engagement is focused on language and literacy practices and outcomes.

Educational Principle 4: Include suggestions for language and literacy activities that can be directly implemented with children.

Educational Principle 5: Include knowledge about both emotional support and cognitive support in a family engagement plan.

Educational Principle 6: Include specific practices to promote responsive parenting and rich language input in your family caregiver engagement plan.

Educational Principle 7: Solve the challenge of how to communicate with parents in a language they understand.

Motivation for Literacy 8

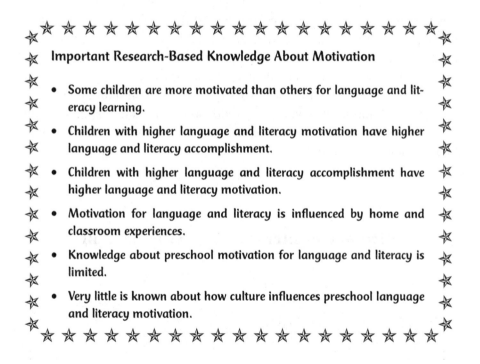

★★★★★★★★★★★★★★★★★★★★★★★★★★

Important Research-Based Knowledge About Motivation

- Some children are more motivated than others for language and literacy learning.

- Children with higher language and literacy motivation have higher language and literacy accomplishment.

- Children with higher language and literacy accomplishment have higher language and literacy motivation.

- Motivation for language and literacy is influenced by home and classroom experiences.

- Knowledge about preschool motivation for language and literacy is limited.

- Very little is known about how culture influences preschool language and literacy motivation.

★★★★★★★★★★★★★★★★★★★★★★★★★★

Think of a child you would consider motivated for some activity. The activity could be art, bike riding, interacting with others, or even reading. What does the motivated child you have thought about do that is different from what an unmotivated child would do? Your answer to this question provides a definition of motivation. In the scientific study of motivation, motivation is seen as *an intent to act*. Motivation initiates, focuses, maintains, and regulates the ebb and flow of behavior. It would be fair to say that motivation even terminates behavior, because when motivation is absent, a behavior will stop. Motivation is purposeful and directed toward accomplishing some goal. Other terms that may be used in other sources to refer to the meaning of *motivation* as it is used in this chapter include *engagement, approaches to learning,* and *interest.* Figure 8.1 shows the cyclical process between an "intent to act" that signals the activation of motivation to reach a goal and how a child will respond when the goal is attained or not yet reached.

Motivation exerts a powerful influence on what children do during literacy experiences. What they do may be different from what they are capable of doing (McInerney & Etten, 2004). For example, a four-year-old English learner who is in his or her second year of preschool may have the English oral language competence to construct a few short sentences while using story props to retell events from the *The Napping House* storybook that has been read in class a few times. However, if that child is not motivated to participate in storybook discussion, he or she may say nothing and even engage in off-task behavior such as scooting over to the block area to play at the time the storybook retelling activity is being offered.

There is research, based on a variety of ways of thinking about and measuring children's motivation, that documents a relationship between literacy motivation and literacy competence. Motivation contributes to literacy learning, and literacy skill contributes to motivation. The relationship is *reciprocal:*

Motivation for literacy ⟺ Literacy skill

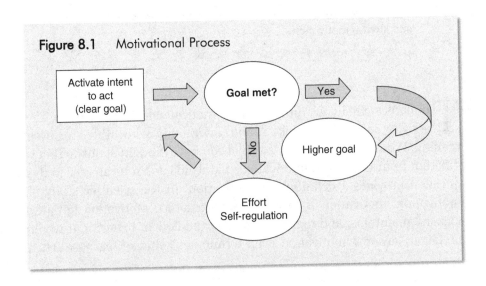

Figure 8.1   Motivational Process

Unfortunately, there has been less study of motivation and literacy relationships in preschool children than in older children, and again, even less research on literacy and motivation relationships within the English learner population. However, there is some research on motivation and literacy relationships in preschool age children, and there are some fairly good reasons to think these research results can contribute to our understanding of motivation for literacy in English language learners.

One important understanding that has emerged from the existing studies with preschool children is that they are relatively optimistic about their abilities (Stipek, Roberts, & Sanborn, 1984) and that this optimism supports their willingness and ability to engage with literacy. Yet individual differences in thinking, emotions, and behaviors that influence motivation do begin to emerge in preschool. The existing research also suggests that making sure preschool children experience the types of activities, instruction, environments, and interactions that lead to an eagerness for language and literacy learning and the ability to sustain engagement in language and literacy activity is very important. The significance of classroom experience in shaping motivation has been well documented with older children. Not surprisingly, parents and home experiences both before and during preschool also influence motivation for literacy.

In this chapter, only a few of the possible ways of thinking about motivation will be featured. One way of looking at motivation is this: It is an inborn predisposition to be competent. Becoming competent is necessary for adaptation to the environment and ultimately survival. This view of motivation is called competence or *effectance motivation.* One category of the theories and models of motivation that I have selected explains motivation as being a result of children's thoughts about a particular domain of learning (reading, math, science) in combination with certain emotional feelings about that domain of learning. More specifically, children's expectations for success in literacy coupled with the degree to which they value literacy will significantly determine their motivation for literacy. This view of motivation is called an *expectancy x value theory.* Cognitive (thinking) and emotional factors together influence motivation. The field of early childhood has deeply rooted commitment to ensuring that preschool experience balances cognitive and social-emotional development. Therefore, this expectancy x value approach to motivation for literacy aligns well with early childhood professionals' view of child development and the early care and education experiences designed to advance it. Another reason for selecting an expectancy x value view of motivation is that this theory has served as the theoretical foundation of some of the most important studies on preschool motivation. *Mastery and performance theory* builds on expectancy x value theory by linking children's thoughts and feelings to specific patterns of behavior that play out in classrooms.

The final view of motivation featured in this chapter focuses on three needs of children that, when met, lead to motivation by affirming and adding to and their perception of themselves as worthy persons who can influence their environment. This theory is called *self-determination theory*. A basic understanding of these four theories of motivation provides a rich foundation for understanding how to promote preschool children's motivation for literacy. And there is some evidence suggesting that the understandings about motivation based on these theories may apply to English learners. I begin by painting a picture of a preschool child that will help you envision what a motivated preschool child does. Figure 8.2 shows the four theories that will be covered in this chapter.

Figure 8.2   Four Theories of Motivation

1. **EFFECTANCE MOTIVATION:**

   Need for competence, biological base,   = Motivation
   exploration, pleasure, sense of efficacy

2. **EXPECTANCY   X   VALUE:**

   Thoughts (expectancy)   Emotion (value)   = Motivation
   (How successful will I be?)   (How much do I
                                 care about this?)

3. **MASTERY AND PERFORMANCE:**

   Oriented to growth or oriented to looking smart   = Motivation

4. **SELF-DETERMINATION:**

   Competence + Autonomy + Relatedness   = Motivation

CHARACTERISTICS OF MOTIVATED CHILDREN

How can you tell that one child is more motivated for literacy than another?

In the study of motivation, scientists have looked at behaviors that show motivation. They have also looked at children's thoughts and beliefs that influence these same behaviors. We will look at both the behaviors and thinking patterns that differentiate children with higher levels of literacy motivation during a literacy activity from those with lower levels of motivation for literacy during that same activity. After this brief introduction to child behaviors and thinking/feeling processes, we will turn to theories and models of motivation that will account for these differences and ultimately lead to an understanding of how you can influence those behaviors in work with preschool children.

Let's return to that motivated child you imagined at the beginning of this chapter. Imagine that this child is in a classroom setting where there are a variety of literacy activities available related to a book about the adventures of a farm animal. There is a flannel board area where there are character pieces from the storybook and papers and marking pens for story retelling or new story writing. There is a play area with a barn, farmhouse, farm animals, farm machinery, and small blocks for building corrals, pastures, or additional farm structures. There is a table with a variety of fruits and vegetables that children can count, sort, and weigh. There is an area for free painting that is not related to the storybook.

What does the child that is highly motivated for literacy learning do that would provide clues to her or his high level of motivation for literacy? Stay with this question until you can think of two different things. The highly motivated child will be more likely to choose one of the literacy-related centers. The child who is highly motivated will stick with the center longer than will other children. The child who is more highly motivated will be more focused than less motivated children. The highly motivated child will look for ways to make the task more challenging compared to less motivated children. A very important characteristic of the highly motivated child is revealed if the child experiences significant difficulty or even a sense of failure. In this case, the highly motivated child will try harder or seek assistance while maintaining optimism for eventual improvement or success. The next vignette provides an example.

Highly Motivated Kao Lee Sticks With It

Three-year-old Kao Lee is in the play center. She is highly motivated for storybook reading. Her primary language is Hmong. She has decided that she wants to build a tall silo to store farm grain from the small blocks at the center. The word *silo* was part of the rich content and language of the farm storybook that was read to the class and that Kao Lee "read" several times during choice time. She can't get her structure to stand higher that five or six rows of blocks, and it tumbles over whenever she attempts this. Kao Lee continues to try and uses a few different strategies but still has no success. She then goes to the Hmong-speaking parent working with children at the center and asks, "Can you help me make this stay taller?" The parent makes a suggestion to which Kao Lee responds, "I will try that. I hope it works. I will also look at the picture in the book to see if that helps me."

Which of the characteristics of motivated children shown in the following box did Kao Lee demonstrate in the vignette?

> **Characteristic Behaviors of Children Who Are Highly Motivated for Literacy**
>
> - Freely choose literacy experiences
> - Persist at literacy activities
> - Focus attention during literacy activities
> - Choose and create moderately challenging literacy activities
> - Seek help and maintain optimism in the face of difficulty with literacy activities

ARE ALL PRESCHOOL CHILDREN HIGHLY MOTIVATED FOR LITERACY?

Preschool children are quite optimistic about their future academic performance in literacy and other areas (Stipek et al., 1984). They have not as yet developed stable understandings about the nature of achievement, ability, and what may cause differences in them. Nor have they typically had a great deal of experience with academic tasks in comparison to other children that would lead them to develop stable conceptualizations of how good they are at specific literacy activities.

Early childhood professionals also typically have great optimism for children's capacity to learn and to be engaged with learning. Indeed, optimism for the positive possibilities for English language learners is an important attitude for early childhood educators to have. This optimism toward children creates an inclination to believe that all preschool children are motivated for literacy. The National Research Council noted in its influential book *From Neurons to Neighborhoods* (2001) that there was little variation in achievement motivation in young children. Stipek and Ryan (1997) also found little difference in the motivation for school learning between children from families of low socioeconomic status and those of higher socioeconomic status, with children from both groups showing an eagerness to learn. This is all good news, showing that overall children from both advantaged and disadvantaged families (the latter being the type of families from which a disproportionate number of English language learners come) bring positive motivational orientations to learning in general.

However, studies specific to language and literacy suggest that there are differences in children's levels of motivation for literacy emerging in the preschool years. Not all children even enjoy storybook reading!

Children have shown differences in their requests and preferences for storybook reading, their attention to book pages, how much language they spontaneously produce, and how much they engage with books on their own at home (Chang & Burns, 2005; Chapman & Tunmer, 1997). Different levels of engagement during storybook reading and during other types of structured and less structured literacy activities in classrooms during toddlerhood, preschool, and early elementary school relate to both later motivation for literacy and literacy achievement (e.g., Wells, 1985). For example, Smiley and Dweck (1994) found that there were differences among middle-class preschool children in how likely they were to choose a challenging puzzle task.

Apply Your Knowledge

Write the names of 10 of the children in your classroom on the following form if you are a teacher. For each of these children, go through the checklist that shows indicators of motivation for literacy of each of these children. If you can't complete the checklist, plan how you could find out what you don't know.

NAME	Asks to have books read	Chooses book or writing center	Asks questions and talks during book reading	Seems happy and excited during literacy activities
1.				
2.				
3.				
4.				
5.				
6.				
7.				
8.				
9.				
10.				

LINKAGES BETWEEN PRESCHOOL
MOTIVATION AND LATER READING

The relationship between motivation and literacy competence is reciprocal:

Motivation for literacy ⟺ Literacy skill

What this means is that the level of motivation influences literacy competence and that how competent a child is at literacy will also influence the child's level of motivation for literacy. Another important question is, "Does motivation in the early years relate to later reading?" The answer to this question is, "Yes it does, based on the limited evidence we have." Chapman, Tunmer, and Prochnow (2000) found that children who entered school with low knowledge of sounds in words and low letter knowledge already had negative motivational beliefs related to literacy. Similarly, in another study, children who turned out to be poor readers after three to four years of school had shown lower levels of task-oriented behavior with literacy before they began formal schooling (Hagtvet, 2000). Finnish monolingual children (average age about age five-and-a-half) with low prereading skills showed lower word reading and lower motivation scores at age eight (Lepola, 2004; Lepola, Poskiparta, Laakkonen, & Niemi, 2005). As children began having difficulties with learning to read and write, they became less task oriented. Low motivation meant children were less focused on literacy tasks, were more dependent on adults, and used more defensive or "trying to cover-up" behavior. Similarly Dally (2006) found that inattentive behaviors and phonological processing influenced each other.

The reciprocal nature of motivation and reading and the fact that differences in both motivation and literacy competence can be seen in preschool children has important implications for classroom practice. Literacy programs that implement the best practices for literacy competence and the best practices for motivation for literacy will produce better outcomes that those that emphasize either alone. We cannot assume that all preschool age children are motivated for literacy activity. Classrooms that are designed to effectively increase literacy achievement and that also build on existing motivation will contribute to preschool children's motivation for literacy. Achievement promotes children's engagement and the quality of that engagement influences literacy learning.

Hopefully, this knowledge has made you curious about and eager to learn more about how to foster preschool English learners' motivation for literacy. So on we go! You will learn about four theories of motivation that will lead to a deep understanding of how motivation works and the preschool practices that will promote motivation for literacy. Put on your thinking caps and settle into a comfortable spot where you can focus, as there will be a fair amount of complexity and new vocabulary needed to build a deep understanding of motivation.

THE NEED FOR COMPETENCE AND MASTERY—INSIDE EVERY CHILD

In 1959, Robert White presented a theory of motivation emphasizing that children are born with a need for competence. He described this inborn need as the foundation for effectance motivation. According to White, children have a biologically based predisposition to experiment with, to achieve an understanding of, and to exercise some control over themselves and their surroundings. Thus, according to White, children have a natural curiosity to explore and master their environment. The purpose of this curiosity and resulting exploration is to ensure adaptation to the environment, which is necessary for survival. This predisposition and need to master the environment does not have to be learned over time. This point is particularly relevant to preschool English language learners. If effectance motivation is biologically based, or inborn, then it will be present in children from all cultural or linguistic backgrounds, although it may not be activated in all situations.

When effectance motivation is exercised and leads to increased competence, children experience pleasure and a *feeling of efficacy*. When children have a feeling of efficacy, they believe that they are capable of accomplishing things. When children's effectance motivation is activated during literacy experiences, their accomplishments will result in a pleasurable feeling of efficacy. Similarly, when children have a feeling of efficacy for literacy, they will feel that they can master tasks such as dictating stories, hearing the sounds in words, writing a grocery list in the playhouse center, finding letters in their names, or contributing to discussion during storybook reading. Notice that when children increase their competence in areas *they* see as beneficial to their adaptation to the environment, they experience pleasure (e.g., Kagan, 1971; Piaget, 1951). This pleasure that comes with increasing competence serves as a built-in reward for engaging in the activity (Harter, 1974; Harter, Shultz, & Blum, 1971). Thus when effectance motivation is active and children increase their competence, the activity itself is rewarding. This discussion may have led you to connect White's ideas to the notion of intrinsic motivation that is familiar to many adults who work with children in early childhood. Indeed the foundations for the idea that young children are intrinsically motivated can be traced way back to White's 1959 paper. Look back at Figure 8.2 on page 204, which summarizes the major ideas of effectance motivation.

Hopefully, you are curious and want to explore how the theory of effectance motivation applies to preschool settings. One important implication of the theory is that effectance motivation is triggered by those experiences that children *perceive* as advancing their adaptation to the environment. More is needed than the teacher's or family's belief that literacy is important. It must be seen as useful by the child. This concept within effectance motivation theory provides a motivation explanation for why literacy experiences that are mean-ingful to the child are important. One reason meaningful experiences are important is that they are more likely to result in motivation for literacy.

Educational Principle 1: View all children as being motivated to increase their competence.

Educational Principle 2: Help children understand and believe that literacy is useful and adaptive for them personally.

A second implication of effectance motivation theory is that children should have literacy experiences that are moderately challenging. Because children are motivated to increase their competence, activation of their inborn effectance motivation is enhanced when they encounter tasks that are moderately difficult for them, because they will learn new things from these tasks. Moderately difficult tasks mean that the tasks will be challenging—but not too much so—and there is the possibility of success. A moderately challenging task is not accomplished with ease and requires some effort.

Teaching Principle 1: Provide children with activities that are slightly more difficult than those they can currently do but that are achievable with effort.

Teaching Principle 2: Provide literacy experiences that children see as meaningful.

Teaching Principle 3: Promote curiosity about words, letters, and language.

Let's stop here for a moment and think about this idea. Why might moderately challenging tasks be especially effective for activating effectance motivation? One answer to this question is that moderately challenging tasks are those that offer the most oppor-tunity for increasing competence. Easy tasks do not increase competence, because little is learned when the child does them. Very difficult tasks also do not increase competence, because the child is not likely to succeed on them. One of the most robust findings in scientific studies of motivation is that moderately challenging tasks increase motivation more than do either easy or very difficult ones (e.g., Cole & Cole, 1993; Danner & Lonky, 1981). See an example of a study showing children's preference for moderately challenging activities in the "Research Highlight" box.

Research Highlight

Children were presented a range of Piagetian tasks such as categorizing and ordering objects. Some tasks were more difficult than others. They were then given opportunities to choose amongst similar tasks that varied in how difficult they were. Their choices of difficulty level and subsequent engagement with the tasks were observed. Indeed, these preschool children tended to select tasks that were slightly hard for them. Increased motivation (the amount of time they spent working on the tasks) and higher levels of interest in the task were also associated with selection of moderately difficult tasks.

—Danner and Lonky (1981)

The box below shows the nature of effectance motivation and the child behaviors that show it.

Effectance Motivation

Nature of Effectance Motivation

- Biologically given
- Need to be competent
- Within every child
- Directed toward perceived adaptation
- Expressed as curiosity
- Exercised through exploration
- Increasing competence results in pleasure and a feeling of efficacy

Characteristic Behaviors

- Show curiosity
- Select moderately difficult tasks
- Seek novelty
- Desire manipulation
- Actively explore
- Enact causality
- Select perceived meaningful (adaptive) tasks

Apply Your Knowledge

1. Imagine that you have been hired as a "motivation consultant" for a preschool program The preschool staff has identified to you a child that is unmotivated for literacy and wants your expert consultation to help in planning some steps that could be taken to activate the child's effectance motivation. Using the column of characteristic behaviors associated with effectance in the "Effectance Motivation" box, list one thing for each behavior that you would suggest to get that effectance motivation going. If you are a teacher, you can actually select a real child from your classroom for this exercise.

2. Present a set of puzzles of different levels of challenge (number of pieces, complexity of puzzle shapes) at one of the tables in your classroom or to a preschool child you know. Tell children that some of the puzzles are more difficult than others, but they can choose to work on any puzzle they like. Observe to see which puzzles different children select, and ask children why they choose the puzzle they did. What did you learn about challenge seeking?

EFFECTANCE MOTIVATION THEORY MOVES FORWARD

White's 1959 seminal work on motivation changed how motivation was viewed among motivation researchers. Prior to White's work, motivation was believed to be a characteristic of children that was formed by the rewards and punishments that children experienced. Motivation was learned. In the case of literacy, it would have been believed that children would be motivated to read and write if they had experienced success with it and if they were rewarded for their engagement. Prizes, food, and certain kinds of teacher praise are examples of the rewards that could be used. Conversely, it was believed children would become unmotivated for literacy when they experienced challenge and failure. They would also be unmotivated for literacy if they received criticism, negative consequences, or experienced displeasure during literacy activity, as these would all be punishments. Effectance motivation theory shifted the lens to look more closely at how children's natural, internal predisposition to become competent operated. As the motivation lens became more focused on the individual child, interest grew in understanding how children's motivation would be activated or suppressed by children's thoughts, feelings, and literacy experiences (Harter, 1978). Subsequent research on motivation has detailed how both children's thinking and children's emotions influence their motivation.

The focus on children's thoughts and feelings led to understanding how children develop *adaptive* motivational patterns that lead to mastery motivation for literacy and further learning or conversely develop *maladaptive* motivational patterns that decrease motivation and learning. This maladaptive pattern is called *performance motivation*. In addition, White's assertion that children have an internal *need* for competence that sets motivation into action led scientists to identify other important needs. The need for autonomy and the need for relatedness are two other important needs influencing motivation that have been identified in self-determination theory. We now turn to examining the following three areas:

- How thinking and emotion together influence children's motivation for literacy
- How mastery and performance patterns of motivation develop and influence children's motivation for literacy
- How children's needs for competence, autonomy, and relatedness influence children's motivation for literacy

THE MOTIVATIONAL LINK
BETWEEN THINKING AND EMOTION

How children think about experiences such as storybook reading, writing, and the alphabet and how children feel about the value of literacy (or art, math, or physical education, for that matter) influence their motivation for literacy learning. Children's thoughts about how good they are at a task and their resulting expectation for success at a particular task will influence their motivation toward it. If a child thinks she or he is pretty good at learning about alphabet letters, then the child is likely to approach alphabet-learning opportunities with an expectation for success. This expectation for success will encourage the child to engage with the alphabet learning tasks and to persist at them. (Remember how these behaviors were identified as ones that show motivation in an earlier section of this chapter.) But expectation for success alone is not enough to account for how motivated a child will be. An important affective characteristic (*affective* means "emotional") that will also influence a child's motivation is how much the child values the task. A child's answers to the following questions would indicate how much she or he might value literacy:

Does learning how to read matter to me?

Do I feel this is something important to do?

Do I really want to learn to read?

Do I like reading?

A combination of a child's level of expectation for success in literacy activity and the child's valuing of literacy activity will determine the child's level of motivation for literacy. Thus this view of motivation is called *expectancy x value theory.* This theory draws attention to how children's assessment of their own competence will influence motivation. It also draws attention to caring about how much children value literacy activity, because that too will influence their motivation for literacy.

Teaching Principle 4: Ensure that children are mostly successful with literacy activities.

Teaching Principle 5: Help children to see and believe in the value of literacy.

Apply Your Knowledge

Rewrite two of the four questions above in a way that you can ask them to preschool children. Write two more questions to help you understand a child's level of expectation for success. You might show the child his or her name and say, "Can you write you name just like it is on this name card? Are you sure, kind of sure, or not sure at all that you can write your name just like it is on this name card?" Ask three children these questions. What did you learn about their valuing of literacy and their expectation for success?

MASTERY AND PERFORMANCE ORIENTATIONS

The *mastery* and *performance* motivation patterns explained by Dweck (1986) are an extension of effectance motivation. Some children have a predominant mastery motivation pattern while others have a predominant performance orientation to literacy learning. The mastery orientation is adaptive, while the performance orientation is considered maladaptive. Table 8.1 summarizes the primary characteristics of mastery- and performance-oriented children. There are some pretty striking differences.

Table 8.1   Mastery and Performance Behaviors

Mastery Orientation	Performance Orientation
Prefer challenging tasks	Avoid challenge
Persist on hard tasks	Give up on hard tasks
Believe they can change their ability	Believe their ability cannot change
Focus on growth	Focus on "looking smart"
Optimistic about achievement	Doubtful or fearful about achievement

Children with the mastery profile seek out challenging tasks, persist in the face of difficulty, view their ability as changeable with effort, focus on their progress and growth, and are generally optimistic in achievement situations. On the other hand, performance-oriented children avoid challenge, give up when faced with difficult tasks, view their ability as fixed, focus on appearing smart in learning situations more than on improvement, and approach achievement situations with less optimism.

While the source of these differences reflects complex processes, classroom practices contribute to their development. Mastery orientations are promoted in classrooms

- where children are consistently presented with high expectation and academic challenges where they will sometimes struggle but are given opportunities to correct their mistakes and do better with more effort,
- that emphasize the importance of effort over ability and ensure that effort leads to positive outcomes,
- that minimize social comparison and competition resulting from practices such as posting stars and awards, and
- that emphasize growth and improvement rather than attainment of uniform goals and expectations.

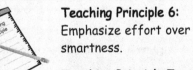

Teaching Principle 6: Emphasize effort over smartness.

Teaching Principle 7: Avoid practices that allow children to compare themselves to others.

Teaching Principle 8: Provide challenge, and support children through it.

Teaching Principle 9: Help children to concretely see evidence of their growth.

Children, including those from low socioeconomic status families, have begun to show mastery or performance profiles in preschool, and practices in preschool settings and parenting practices contribute to them (Smiley & Dweck, 1994; Turner & Johnson, 2003).

THREE MOTIVATIONAL NEEDS (COMPETENCE, AUTONOMY, RELATEDNESS)

The self-determination theory of motivation focuses on three needs that children have, that when met, will lead to motivation for literacy. *Competence, autonomy,* and *relatedness* are these three needs. You have already learned about children's need for competence in White's effectance motivation theory. Recall that children have an internal and inborn need for competence. In self-determination theory, the need for autonomy and the need for relatedness are two other needs children have that must be nourished if they are to maintain high motivation for literacy (Reeve, Deci, & Ryan, 2004). Because the need for competence was treated in the section on effectance motivation, autonomy and relatedness are the needs that will be explained more fully in this section. When children's need for autonomy is nourished, they feel that their literacy behavior is initiated from within or at least that they have an inner endorsement of the significance and value of the literacy activity. They have personally bought in to the importance of literacy. When children have autonomy, they control their own behavior, or self-regulate (Baumeister & Vohs, 2004). The need for relatedness is expressed by a desire to establish warm and positive connections with others during literacy activity (see Figure 8.3).

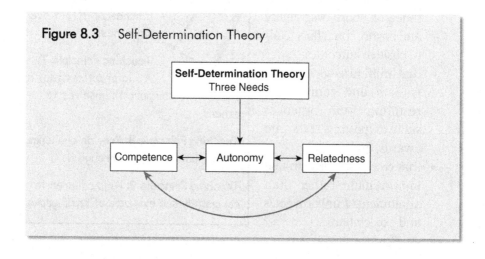

Figure 8.3   Self-Determination Theory

When these three inner needs of children are supported during literacy lessons and other literacy experiences, children will be more motivated for literacy learning. When a child's needs for competence, autonomy, and relatedness are activated and met, the child comes to see himself or herself as an integrated, important, and powerful being. The child feels, "I have the power" to accomplish great literacy things. While there have been few studies applying self-determination theory to early childhood motivation and none that I am aware of that test these ideas specifically with preschool English learners, there is an easy fit between the three needs emphasized in self-determination theory and the social-emotional conditions in early childhood education and care settings that are associated with a range of positive social, behavioral, and cognitive outcomes. Self-determination theory helps us see the motivational benefits that result from these similar social-emotional characteristics and the conditions that support them.

According to self-determination theory, classrooms and other settings such as the home will influence children's motivation by the degree to which these settings recognize, provide for, and nourish these three needs. Classrooms and other settings that ensure children's increasing competence, that foster children's sense of autonomy, and that provide interaction in relationships that are warm with a quality of mutual connection between participants will support children's motivation for literacy. Like what you learned with effectance motivation, children do not need to learn to be motivated through practices such as rewards and recognition charts. Rather, children want to express their inner needs and resources and have them valued. They will be motivated for literacy when this occurs. Think about the types of literacy experiences that would be responsive to each of these three needs. What experiences will make children more competent? What experiences will support children's autonomy? What experiences will create opportunities for relatedness?

Teaching Principle 10: Provide literacy experiences that lead to competence, allow for autonomy, and promote collaboration and interaction with adults and other children.

Apply Your Knowledge

Identify which need(s) might be influenced by each of the literacy practices in the following box. In the additional columns, indicate whether

(Continued)

(Continued)

you think the need is supported or thwarted by the practice or whether the practice's effect is unclear (the column under the question mark). Add additional literacy practices from your own classroom, and perform the same analysis. What did you learn related to the three needs? Hopefully one thing that you learned was that you can't completely tell just by the nature of the activity—it would depend on how it is implemented. Another thing that I hoped you learned was that different activities might relate to different needs.

Practice	Need(s)	Supported	Thwarted	?
1. Teacher-led lesson on alphabet letter *T*				
2. Child dictating story				
3. Practice on singing nursery rhymes				
4. Retelling a previously read story using a flannel board				
5. Practice name in writing				
6. Dramatic play with props				
7. Counting the number of syllables in a word				
8. Teacher-led instruction on the meaning of words that will be used in a center				
9. Coloring paper pictures of characters from a recently viewed children's movie				
10. Pretend reading with an assigned partner				
11. Pretend reading with a friend				
12. Extended conversation with a teacher on a topic of interest to the child				

THE COMPATIBILITY OF AUTONOMY AND STRUCTURE

At first blush, thinking about the importance of autonomy might lead you to logically conclude that only unstructured literacy experiences will satisfy the need for autonomy and thereby promote motivation for literacy. Yet in other chapters in this book there is evidence that children's literacy benefits from participation in teacher-led, explicit, and structured literacy experiences. An important concept within self-determination theory is that structure can be very supportive of autonomy. How can that be? Well, recall that motivation is always directed toward some goal. Structure affords teachers and children the opportunity to know the goals toward which intent to act may be directed. Experiences that help

Teaching Principle 11: Establish goals, provide structure that leads to goal attainment, and allow for autonomy, choice, and self-regulation within the structure.

children clarify, value, and understand how to meet goals will actually help them feel more autonomous. The difference between an autonomy-supporting environment and a controlling environment is that in the autonomy-supporting condition, there is a balance of structure and "choice, voice and initiative within that structure, whereas controlling environments provide students with little freedom within that structure" (Reeve et al., 2004, p. 50). When teachers organize literacy activity, provide students information about the reasons for and value of literacy goals, include ideas on procedures for achieving literacy goals, help in selection of goals, and give information and assistance, the need for autonomy can flourish.

THE SPECIAL WORRY OF FAILURE

You have learned that challenge is important in promoting motivation for literacy. Challenging experiences provide children the opportunity to increase their competence and help children learn the usefulness of effort and therefore to be more willing to apply it. Children must see that their efforts lead to greater competence and experience the pleasure associated with goal achievement a significant part of the time.

You have also learned that children's thinking influences their motivation for literacy in powerful ways. The way children think about their nonsuccesses is very important. When children believe that they are not capable of being successful and do not have that sense of efficacy toward literacy activity, they may give up. A child who thinks, "I am not good at writing," or "Finding sounds in words is too hard for me" is unlikely to feel inspired to work hard on these tasks. In addition, the more unsuccessful experiences children have, the more likely they are to come to develop low expectations for success. Imagine a child who begins enthusiastically to write her or his name. The child struggles with making the letters and observes that others can do this much more quickly and more completely. After several weeks, the child begins to avoid attempting to write his or her name and comments, "I can never finish all the letters." If children do not particularly value literacy experiences, the possible motivational effects of nonsuccess and failure will be even greater (expectancy × value motivation, page 203). When children are not able to learn some aspect of literacy, they will also be denied the opportunity to feel the pleasure that you have learned comes from experiences creating a sense of increasing competence (effectance motivation, page 203).

Children at Risk for Motivation for Literacy

- Experience repeated nonsuccess
- Do not see that effort leads to achievement
- Believe they are not very good at literacy skills
- See little value in literacy activity
- Experience learning environments that are controlling (remember the distinction between structure and control)
- Have little opportunity for participating in emotionally satisfying interactions with teachers and peers

---

Yet simply assuring that children have success and receive positive reinforcement on literacy tasks is not likely to solve the issue. In another oldie but goodie study, Dweck (1975) tested the idea that success-only learning would fix motivational profiles of children who had very low levels of motivation for math. One group of children worked on problems where their success was ensured, and they were told how good they were at math; they received positive reinforcement continuously. Another group of children worked on challenging tasks and were taught to tell themselves that with effort they could be more successful. After training that lasted only 25 days, the children's motivation behavior (persistence, challenge-seeking) was measured. And the children who actually continued to experience some nonsuccess, but whose thinking was changed, showed more persistence than those with the success-only and positive reinforcement experiences!

The effects of success and nonsuccess on preschool English language learners have not as yet been studied, let alone understood. However, preschool English learners are more likely than English-only or socio-economically advantaged children to enter school at risk for difficulty in literacy achievement due to their lower initial second language and literacy abilities. This fact implies that in preschool settings, English learner children may be at risk for experiencing more nonsuccesses than other children due to their lower second language abilities. This may be particularly so in those settings where English learners and English-only children are in the same classrooms, which is the classroom constellation experienced by most English learners. It may also be particularly so on those tasks that require the most second language proficiency for success. Which preschool literacy experiences that you use or know about require the most oral language proficiency? Such experiences could then contribute to lower motivation for literacy for children who were not having sufficient success.

One response to this possibility would be to reduce the demands of the language and literacy curriculum or to delay exposure to it in order to ensure a significant amount of success. However, this approach would result in having comparatively lower expectations and restricted access to learning opportunities for English learner children than for other children. It is also the case that more at-risk children benefit most from earlier, more intensive, and more explicit literacy experiences. And if concerns about children's differences in preparation to be successful with preschool literacy expectations due to English oral proficiency lead in preschool to avoiding areas like literacy because of worries about it being too challenging, addressing the issue is just delayed until kindergarten.

Another factor related to worries about possible motivational vulnerability in preschool English learners is the recent trend toward introduction of more structured curriculums and early literacy standards (e.g., Elkind, 1987). These trends might also lead to children being more aware of their own performance compared to the performance of others. This could occur because children are participating in group instruction where there are specific goals and there is also interest in how all children are faring in meeting a common set of literacy expectations. For example, a child participating in a lesson where the goal is to identify sounds of letters in children's first names may become aware of how many letters other children know, may hear the teacher respond positively to demonstrations of such knowledge, and may begin to experience his or her own performance as nonsuccess if he or she is able to

Teaching Principle 12: Monitor the level of success children are having in your setting, paying particular attention to challenging literacy experiences and those that require more language skill for success.

Teaching Principle 13: For children having less success, provide more experience/practice with literacy activities they are good at.

Teaching Principle 14: Break down literacy tasks that children are having limited success on into smaller parts or subgoals where they can be successful.

Teaching Principle 15: Ensure that children have extra time or opportunity to change, improve, or correct literacy activities that are very difficult for them.

Teaching Principle 16: Draw children's attention to their successes.

do less. Comparing of self to others, or social comparison, is believed to be one of the processes used by children that leads to the more realistic or decreased optimism for school achievement that is observable in children from about age five onward (Wigfield, Tonks, & Eccles, 2004).

So the important question really becomes how to provide preschool children the motivational (and literacy learning) benefits of challenge while protecting them from the significant problems that can develop from repeated nonsuccess. Any thoughts on how to accomplish this balance? Jot down some ideas. The knowledge about motivation that you are acquiring in this chapter can offer some good ideas. Add your ideas to the following teaching principles that give some of my ideas.

Apply Your Knowledge

Identify a child, preferably an English learner, that you believe may be experiencing more nonsuccess in literacy activities than other children. Make a plan of specific practices that could be used during literacy activity for each of principles 14 through 18 to help this child be more successful.

DOES EXPLICIT INSTRUCTION
UNDERMINE MOTIVATION?

The conditions for learning in classrooms definitely influence motivation for literacy. We have discussed the recent trend toward increasing levels of explicit literacy instruction for preschool children and the reasons for it. Concerns about the motivation outcomes of explicit instruction have been raised in the past. I frequently field questions on the motivational consequences of explicit, teacher-led, and/or structured classroom literacy practices. Early childhood professionals are concerned that this type of literacy activity interferes with or decreases curiosity, autonomy, intrinsic interest, opportunity for relatedness, meaningfulness, and other important factors that you have learned influence motivation for literacy. On the other hand, proponents of explicit teaching would argue that the increasing literacy competence that will occur from explicit teaching will benefit motivation for literacy. Similarly, proponents of explicit teaching might also say that explicit, teacher-led, instruction provides the goal identification, structure, and support needed as an impetus for an "intent to act". They might also argue that it is the degree to which explicit instruction includes opportunities for choice, connections to child interests, moderate challenge, and relatedness with the teacher and other children that will determine how it influences motivation for literacy. This is a hot topic for the field right now. There are a few relevant studies examining this issue. I expect and hope that more will follow.

Researchers have reported declines in motivation and a negative social climate in classrooms where teachers chose on their own to use explicit (didactic) teaching, whereas child-centered classrooms were associated with a positive social-emotional climate and positive child control practices (Stipek, Feiler, Daniels, & Millburn, 1995; Stipek, Feiler, & Gauzes, 1992; Stipek et al., 1998). Stipek et al. (1995) reported that children in didactic programs had higher achievement on one letter/reading measure but not on a math measure. Motivation was lower in these same classes. Children showed lower self-perceptions of ability and expectancies for success, less pride in their accomplishments, and more dependency on adults. This study is of particular interest because 28% of the children were described as "Latino" children whose primary language was Spanish, but results for these children were not given separately. The Stipek et al. 1998 study included classroom observations of motivation and found essentially the same results.

However, there are a number of features of these studies that render the results inconclusive. Teachers had selected and implemented their own type of preschool program. Perhaps teachers who chose the didactic programs were different from those in the child-centered programs, and it was in fact these differences that led to the differences in children. In the 1995 study, there were differences between the children in the two groups, with more at-risk children in the didactic programs. Another important consideration is that there was no determination of the quality of the literacy teaching, curriculum, and learning experiences within the didactic programs.

Carol Sadler and I have recently completed a study with English-only preschool children designed to look more specifically at how high-quality explicit literacy instruction influenced children's motivation for literacy (Roberts & Sadler, 2007). In one group, children participated in explicit alphabet letter-sound instruction that implemented several of the factors you have learned activate and support children's motivation. Letters were introduced with characters that were interesting and imaginative and added an element of meaningfulness to the letters. Children made choices and had opportunities for personal input during lessons and in follow-up activities. Pretests and posttests of children's literacy skills and motivational orientations were given. There was no evidence of any decrease in motivation for literacy. Children experienced greater cognitive growth and enhanced motivation for literacy when they participated in explicit instruction designed to be highly motivating. Explicit instruction on alphabet letters with motivating characteristics was also associated with increasing perceptions of ability and desire for literacy.

CULTURE, LANGUAGE, AND MOTIVATION FOR LITERACY

The scientific evidence is quite beautiful in the picture it paints of the importance of the child's sense of personal power for optimal motivation for literacy. The child comes into the world eager to learn and indeed with a need to be powerful, effective and growing, and connected to others. In the four theories of motivation that you have learned about (try to name them), the characteristics of the individual child are paramount in understanding motivation for literacy. Yet many of you and particularly those of you who work with and study English learners have also learned how culture shapes a child's values, beliefs, behaviors, emotions, thinking, and language use. There is cross-cultural variation in how much the individual, or the group is emphasized. In general, European-based cultures are more likely to have a greater emphasis on the individual, or on an independent worldview, while non-European and more traditional cultures are more likely to emphasize the group and to have an interdependent worldview. A reasonable and important question to ask is, "To what extent is the picture of the motivated child presented in the effectance, expectancy × value, mastery-performance, and self-determination theories of motivation accurate across differing cultures?" Fortunately there is research that has looked at this question. Unfortunately most of it has been conducted with older children, adolescents, and adults and has not included groups with the most recent immigration to the United States.

A general conclusion from this research is that across all cultural groups that have been studied, individual thought and emotions influence motivation. Studies have shown that autonomy is indeed valued cross culturally. For example, college students from an independent (United States) and from a strongly interdependent (South Korea) culture ranked the importance of 10 different needs. For both groups, the need for autonomy, relatedness, and competence emerged at the top of the list. In some cultural groups relatedness may be more satisfying than autonomy, and motivation may be less disrupted by controlling environments than it is for individuals from European backgrounds. Children can experience autonomy even as they are influenced by social goals such as making their family proud of their literacy achievements. If a child truly values making his or her family proud, she or he may still experience this motivation as autonomy supporting. Autonomy implies that one has come to value and endorse one's actions and beliefs and has not been pressured, forced, or induced with negative emotion to achieve a goal. Autonomy is not synonymous with isolationism, intense individualism, or separateness (Reeve et al., 2004).

Children across different cultures also show the same pattern of declining expectations for literacy success that have been found in United States studies. There is also evidence that in several cultures, how capable children believe they are in literacy activity (expectancy for success) and how much they value achievement (value) in areas such as literacy is related to levels of motivation (Guthrie & Wigfield, 2000). An important point, though, about this picture of motivation from cross-cultural studies is that the studies do not exactly mirror the cultural context of most English language learners in the United States. In the United States, English learner children are experiencing cultural influences related to competence, autonomy, relatedness, mastery, challenge, and academic learning from both the home culture *and* the English dominant culture in which it is embedded. Even preschool children encounter the effects of media, computers, and cross-cultural interactions. Their preschool classroom experiences present them with varied cultural values and practices related to motivation. So keep asking the questions, probing the answers, observing the children, and talking to the families to learn more about cultural influences on motivation.

Let's take these points from cross-cultural studies on motivation to think more specifically about preschool English learners in preschool classrooms in the United States. Challenges to autonomy may be tolerated better by groups with a relatively greater emphasis on relatedness. This might explain the reported ease with which some English learners appear to be able to comply with limits in the controlling environments that characterize many school classrooms where the teacher is not informed by the science of motivation. In these types of classrooms, teachers believe that the way to motivate children for literacy learning is through ongoing reward and incentive programs, which are controlling practices. For children from cultural groups that may value relatedness more than autonomy, group/partner learning, a sense of cohesive classroom community, and a greater sensitivity to preventing negative social comparison may be important practices to promote motivation for literacy when they are balanced with a need for autonomy within those structures.

THE LANGUAGE OF MOTIVATION

The role of language in promoting motivation for literacy has not been systematically examined in research. You have learned how emotionally positive language and gentle guidance orients children to enjoy literacy activity and be willing to participate in it. You have learned that what teachers and others say to children can help them value effort over ability, which in turn helps them persist at literacy tasks, particularly in the face of challenge.

> **Teaching Principle 17:** Teach the English vocabulary necessary for building motivation for literacy (e.g., *goal, effort, purpose, choice, sharing, enjoyment, etc.*).

You have learned how language that helps children see the personal value of literacy can promote and sustain motivation for literacy. You have learned how language that helps children gain meaning during storybook reading ensures continued and growing motivation for achievement. You have learned how differences in teachers' verbal responses to children's literacy activity can maintain or interfere with the children's motivation for literacy. You have learned how relatedness with others occurs through the use of language.

> **Educational Principle 3:** Identify and use primary language resources such as teaching staff, materials, and families to provide language resources that promote motivation for literacy.

Language, language, language! The availability of primary language resources and second language strategies to provide the assistance, verbal feedback, positive emotion, and valuing needed for optimal motivation is clearly important. How this can be achieved with children who are just learning English is an area where there is a great need for more knowledge.

Language Influences on Motivation

1. Helps children appreciate the personal value of literacy

2. Helps children enjoy and engage with literacy activity

3. Helps children gain meaning during storybook reading, which leads to interest and sustaining attention

4. Helps children see their competence, experience autonomy, and establish relatedness with others

---

Apply Your Knowledge

1. On a sheet of paper, list the four language influences on motivation from the box above, spaced to fill up the whole page. Make a column labeled "Primary Language" and another labeled "English." List language resources (people and materials) and language practices that could be used to provide for each of these language influences on motivation. Let me provide an example to get you started.

2. For Item 1 in the box, it could be helpful to have a primary language support person to regularly but briefly (one or two minutes) explain to children how literacy is all around them and used by them and their families; this person could show them familiar materials from their home lives such as food containers, calendars, almanacs, banners, birthday cards, letters, magazines, children's books, and so forth. Another idea would be to send a note home in primary language suggesting that family caregivers play a game with their child where the child is a "reading and writing detective." Suggest that the family caregiver could encourage the children to "find evidence" of reading and writing. Suggest that the family caregiver respond with a smile or statement about how the child is learning to see reading and writing rather than with any kind of point system, treats, or money.

3. If you are a teacher, think of ideas that could actually be used in your preschool setting. Make a specific plan to implement a few of your ideas.

HOME INFLUENCES ON LANGUAGE
AND LITERACY MOTIVATION

Not surprisingly there are also home influences on motivation for literacy. Cognitive experiences at home and children's relationships with their caregivers influence children's motivation. Experiences during infancy, toddlerhood, and the preschool years influence later motivation either directly or by how they shape early language and literacy competence. Closeness between parent and child predicted later mastery motivation in socioeconomically at-risk preschoolers in one study (Harris, Robinson, Chang, & Burns, 2007).

In an important study conducted in the Netherlands, where cultural differences were isolated by matching children on socioeconomic status, researchers found cultural background differences in home practices between Dutch, Turkish-Dutch, and Surinamese-Dutch families. In the Netherlands, Turkish-Dutch and Surinamese-Dutch children are both linguistic and cultural minorities whose linguistic and socioeconomic status is similar to that of many Latina/o, Southeast Asian, Eastern European, and Russian families in the United States. Differences in how much parents helped children understand and extend language beyond the storybook were found. Differences in the amount of emotional support provided during storybook reading were also found (Leseman & de Jong, 2001; Leseman & van den Boom, 1999). Children whose parents provided the most instructional and emotional support obtained higher ratings of literacy motivation. These findings show that culture can influence motivation for literacy.

Another study found that providing first-grade children rereading experiences at home where stories on audiotape was provided was especially beneficial for the motivation of English learner children. A study with first graders, of whom 105 out of 162 were ELLs (46 spoke Spanish at home, 23 spoke Vietnamese, and the remaining children each spoke 1 of 15 other languages), showed that rereading classroom books at home increased reading motivation, parental involvement, and reading achievement (on one of three measures; Koskinen et al., 2000). It seems that helping children and their families share books—where family caregivers give help as

Teaching Principle 18: Help family caregivers read storybooks with children in ways that gently help children understand and extend story meaning.

Teaching Principle 19: Help family caregivers read storybooks with children where the experience is pleasurable and creates warm connections between caregiver and child.

needed or where the school provides a resource (audiotapes)—so that children can both experience meaning during storybook reading and have pleasurable emotions during it can promote motivation for literacy. Another study found that the parent-child relationship in general (communication, closeness, and encouragement of autonomy) between African American four-year-old children and their parents predicted their level of overall (not reading specific) mastery motivation, which was in turn related to a combined test of literacy and math achievement (Turner & Johnson, 2003). Together these studies show a commonality in the practices in homes that are supportive of motivation for literacy across cultural groups on page 204.

Apply Your Knowledge

Write a short letter (not more than one page) informing family caregivers about the value of

- helping their child acquire meaning during storybook reading and
- making the shared book reading enjoyable and positive.

Divide your letter into two sections with the two items above as the headings for each section.

CONCLUSION

Preschool English learners have an inborn need to become competent in their environment. Their efforts to affect their environment will be guided by their perceptions of personally meaningful and personally valued activity. Preschool children think complexly about the questions, "Will I be successful?" and "Does this activity matter to me?" How they answer these questions will influence their motivation for literacy. A delicate tapestry weaving together challenge, opportunity for effort, success and nonsuccess, and positive emotion must be created.

The research base on motivation for literacy provides guidance on specific classroom practices and language use that can support children's natural inclination to be competent, to develop a strong sense of autonomous personhood, and to connect with others. You can be optimistic that these practices will work across cultures and for children who are learning English, based on the available evidence. However, the evidence specific to the various cultural groups that comprise preschool English learners in the United States is limited. The importance of language processes in building and sustaining motivation for literacy is clear. Providing the kinds of language interactions that help children's motivation be activated and flourish is likely to be a significant challenge for ensuring motivation for literacy in English language learners. Efforts to help family caregivers provide instructional and emotional support in home literacy experiences are also important. The four theoretical frameworks that were used in reaching these research-based conclusions are summarized in Figure 8.2 on page 204.

Summary of Teaching Principles

Teaching Principle 1: Provide children with activities that are slightly more difficult than those they can currently do but that are achievable with effort.

Teaching Principle 2: Provide literacy experiences that children see as meaningful.

Teaching Principle 3: Promote curiosity about words, letters, and language.

Teaching Principle 4: Ensure that children are mostly successful with literacy activities.

Teaching Principle 5: Help children to see and believe in the value of literacy.

Teaching Principle 6: Emphasize effort over smartness.

Teaching Principle 7: Avoid practices that allow children to compare themselves to others.

Teaching Principle 8: Provide challenge, and support children through it.

Teaching Principle 9: Help children to concretely see evidence of their growth.

Teaching Principle 10: Provide literacy experiences that lead to competence, allow for autonomy, and promote collaboration and interaction with adults and other children.

Teaching Principle 11: Establish goals and provide structure that leads to goal attainment, and allow for autonomy, choice, and self-regulation within the structure.

Teaching Principle 12: Monitor the level of success children are having in your setting, paying particular attention to challenging literacy experiences and those that require more language skill for success.

Teaching Principle 13: For children having less success, provide more experience/practice with literacy activities they are good at.

Teaching Principle 14: Break down literacy tasks that children are having limited success on into smaller parts or subgoals where they can be successful.

Teaching Principle 15: Ensure that children have extra time or opportunity to change, improve, or correct literacy skills that are very difficult for them.

Teaching Principle 16: Draw children's attention to their successes.

Teaching Principle 17: Teach the English vocabulary necessary for building motivation for literacy (e.g., *goal, effort, purpose, choice, sharing, enjoyment,* etc.).

Teaching Principle 18: Help family caregivers read storybooks with children in ways that help children understand and extend story meaning.

Teaching Principle 19: Help family caregivers read storybooks with children where the experience is pleasurable and creates warm connections between caregiver and child.

Summary of Educational Principles

Educational Principle 1: View all children as being motivated to increase their competence.

Educational Principle 2: Help children understand and believe that literacy is useful and adaptive for them personally.

Educational Principle 3: Identify and use primary language resources such as teaching staff, materials, and families to provide primary language that promotes motivation for literacy.

References

Adams, M. (1990). *Beginning to read: Thinking and learning about print.* Cambridge, MA: MIT Press.

Administration on Children, Youth, and Families. (2003). *Head start FACES 2000: A whole-child perspective on program performance. Fourth progress report.* Washington, DC: U. S. Department of Health and Human Services.

Anthony, J. L., Williams, J. M., McDonald, R., Corbitt-Shindler, D., Carlson, C. D., & Francis, D. J. (2006). Phonological processing and emergent literacy in Spanish-speaking preschool children. *Annals of Dyslexia, 56,* 239–270.

Au, K. (1998). Social constructivism and the school literacy of students of diverse backgrounds. *Journal of Literacy Research, 30*(2), 297–319.

Au, K. & Mason, J. M. (1981). Social organizational factors in learning to read: The balance of rights hypothesis. *Reading Research Quarterly, 17*(1), 115–152.

August, D., Beck, I. L., Calderon, M., Francis, D. J., LeSaux, N. K., Shanahan, T., et al. (2008). Instruction and professional development. In D. August & T. Shanahan (Eds.), *Developing reading and writing in second-language learners* (pp. 131–250). New York: Routledge.

August, D., & Hakuta, K. (Eds.). (1997). *Improving schooling for language-minority children: A research agenda.* Washington, DC: National Academy Press.

August, D., & Shanahan, T. (2008). Introduction and methodology. In *Developing reading and writing in second language learners* (pp. 1–17). New York: Routledge.

Barnett, S. W., Yarosz, D. J., Thomas, J., Jung, K., & Blanco, D. (2007). Two-way and monolingual immersion in preschool education: An experimental comparison. *Early Childhood Research Quarterly, 22,* 277–293.

Baumeister, R., & Vohs, K. (Eds.). (2004). *Handbook of self-regulation.* New York: Guilford Press.

Bernhard, J. K., Cummins, J., Campoy, F. I., Ada, A. F., Winsler, A., & Bleiker, C. (2006). Identity texts and literacy development among preschool English language learners: Enhancing opportunities for children at risk of learning disabilities. *Teacher's College Record, 108,* 2380–2405.

Best, C. T. (1994). The emergence of native-language phonological influences in infants: A perceptual assimilation model. In J. C. Goodman & H. C. Nussbaum (Eds.), *The development of speech perception* (pp. 167–224). Cambridge, MA: MIT Press.

Bialystok, E. (2001). *Bilingualism in development: Language, literacy and cognition.* New York: Cambridge University Press.

Bialystok, E. (2006). Second-language acquisition and bilingualism at an early age and the impact on early cognitive development. In R. E. Tremblay, R. G. Barr, & R. D. Peters (Eds.), *Encyclopedia on Early Childhood Development* [Electronic version]. Montreal, QC, Canada: Centre of Excellence for Early Childhood Development. Retrieved February 14, 2008, from http://www.child-encyclo pedia.com/documents/BialystokANGxp.pdf.

Bialystok, E., & Hakuta, K. (1999). Confounded age: Linguistic and cognitive factors in age differences for second language acquisition. In D. Birdsong (Ed.), *Second language acquisition and the critical period hypothesis* (pp. 161–181). Mahwah, NJ: Erlbaum.

Biemiller, A. J., & Boote, C. (2006). An effective method for building meaning vocabulary in the primary grades. *Journal of Educational Psychology, 98,* 44–62.

Bloodgood, J. (1999). What's in a name? Children's name writing and name acquisition. *Reading Research Quarterly, 34,* 342–367.

Bloom, P. (2000). *How children learn the meanings of words.* Cambridge, MA: MIT Press.

Brabham, E. G., & Lynch-Brown, C. (2002). Effects of teachers' reading-aloud styles on vocabulary acquisition and comprehension of students in the early elementary grades. *Journal of Educational Psychology, 94,* 465–473.

Bracken, S. S., & Fischel, J. E. (2006). Assessment of preschool classroom practices: Application of Q-sort methodology. *Early Childhood Research Quarterly, 21,* 417–430.

Browman, C. P., & Goldstein, L. (1986). Towards an articulatory phonology. *Phonology Yearbook, 3,* 219–252.

Brown, C. (1998). The role of the L1 grammar in the L2 acquisition of segmental structure. *Second Language Research, 14,* 136–193.

Bryant, P. E., MacLean, M., Bradley, L. L., & Crossland, J. (1990). Rhyme and alliteration, phoneme detection and learning to read. *Developmental Psychology, 26,* 429–438.

Burchinal, M. R., Cryer, D., Clifford, R. M., & Howes, C. (2002). Caregiver training and classroom quality in child care centers. *Applied Developmental Science, 6*(1), 2–11.

Burchinal, M., Howes, C., & Kontos, S. (2002). Structural predictors of child care quality in child care homes. *Early Childhood Quarterly, 17*(1), 87–106.

Burchinal, M., Peisner-Fienberg, E., Pianta, R., & Howes, C. (2002). Development of academic skills from preschool through second grade: Family and classroom predictors of developmental trajectories. *Journal of School Psychology, 40*(5), 415–436.

Burgess, S. R. (2002). The influence of speech perception, oral language ability, the home literacy environment, and pre-reading knowledge on the growth of phonological sensitivity: A one-year longitudinal investigation. *Reading and Writing: An Interdisciplinary Journal, 15,* 709–737.

Burgess, S. R., & Lonigan, C. J. (1998). Bidirectional relations of phonological sensitivity and prereading abilities: Evidence from a preschool sample. *Journal of Experimental Child Psychology, 70,* 117–141.

Bus, A., & van IJzendoorn, M. (1999). Phonological awareness and early reading: A meta-analysis of experimental training studies. *Journal of Educational Psychology, 91,* 403–414.

Bus, A. G., Belsky, J., van IJzendoorn, M. H., & Crnic, K. (1997). Attachment and book reading patterns: A study of mothers, fathers and toddlers. *Early Childhood Research Quarterly, 12,* 81–98.

Bus, A. G., van IJzendoorn, M. H., & Pellegrini, A. D. (1995). Joint storybook reading makes for success in learning to read: A meta-analysis on intergenerational transmission of literacy. *Review of Educational Research, 65,* 1–21.

Byrne, B., & Fielding-Barnsley, R. (1991). Evaluation of a program to teach phonemic awareness to young children. *Journal of Educational Psychology, 83,* 451–455.

Byrne, B., & Fielding-Barnsley, R. (1993). Evaluation of a program to teach phonemic awareness to young children: A 1-year follow-up. *Journal of Educational Psychology, 85,* 104–111.

Byrne, B., & Fielding-Barnsley, R. (1995). Evaluation of a program to teach phonemic awareness to young children: A 2- and 3-year follow-up and a new preschool trial. *Journal of Educational Psychology, 87,* 488–503.

California Department of Education. (2007). *Preschool English learners: Principles and practices to promote language, literacy, and learning.* Sacramento, CA: Author.

Campbell, R., & Sais, E. (1995). Accelerated metalinguistic awareness in bilingual children. *British Journal of Developmental Psychology, 13,* 61–68.

Campos, S. J. (1995). The Carpinteria preschool program: A long term effects study. In E. Garcia & B. McLaughlin (Eds.), *Meeting the challenge of linguistic and cultural diversity in early childhood education* (pp. 23–45). New York: Teachers College Press.

Caplan, N., Chou, M. H., & Whitmore, J. K. (1991). *Children of the boat people: A study of educational success.* Ann Arbor: University of Michigan Press.

Capps, R., Fix, M., Ost, J., Reardon-Anderson, J., & Passel, J. (2004). *The health and well-being of young children of immigrants.* Washington, DC: The Urban Institute.

Carey, S. (1978). The child as a word learner. In M. Halle, J. Bresnan, & G. A. Miller (Eds.), *Linguistic theory and psychological reality* (pp. 101–122). Cambridge, MA: MIT Press.

Castiglioni-Spalten, M., & Ehri, L. (2003). Phonemic awareness instruction: Contribution of articulatory segmentation to novice beginners' reading and spelling. *Scientific Studies of Reading, 7,* 25–52.

Castle, J. M., Riach, J., & Nicholson, T. (1994). Getting off to a better start in reading and spelling: The effects of phonemic awareness instruction within a whole language program. *Journal of Educational Psychology, 86,* 350–359.

Chang, F., & Burns, B. M. (2005). Attention in preschoolers: Association with effortful control and motivation. *Child Development, 76*, 247–263.

Chang, F., Crawford, G., Early, D., Bryant, D., Howes, C., Burchinal, M., et al. (2007). Spanish-speaking children's social and language development in pre-kindergarten classrooms. *Early Education and Development, 18(2)*, 243–269.

Chapman, J. W., & Tunmer, W. E. (1997). Development of young children's reading self-concepts: An examination of emerging subcomponents and their relationship with reading achievement. *Journal of Educational Psychology, 87*, 154–167.

Chapman, J. W., Tunmer, W. E., & Prochnow, J. E. (2000). Early reading-related skills and performance, reading self-concept, and the development of academic self-concept: A longitudinal study. *Journal of Educational Psychology, 92*, 703–708.

Chesterfield, R. A., Chesterfield, K. B., Hayes-Latimer, K., & Chavez, R. (1983). The influence of peers and teachers on second language acquisition in preschool programs. *TESOL Quarterly, 17*(3), 401–419.

Cheung, A., & Slavin, R. (2005). Effective reading programs for English language learners and other language-minority students. *Bilingual Research Journal, 29*(2), 241–267.

Cirino, P. T., Pollard-Durodola, S. D., Foorman, B. R., Carlson, C. D., & Francis, D. J. (2007). Teacher characteristics, classroom instruction and student literacy and language outcomes in bilingual kindergarteners. *Elementary School Journal, 107*(4), 341–361.

Cole, M., & Cole, S. R. (1993). *The development of children* (2nd ed.). New York: Scientific American.

Comer, J. P., & Haynes, N. M. (1991). Parent involvement in schools: An ecological approach. *The Elementary School Journal, 91*(3), 271–277.

Connor, C. M., Morrison, F. J., & Slominski, L. (2006). Preschool instruction and children's emergent literacy. *Journal of Educational Psychology, 98*, 665–689.

Crosnoe, R. (2004). Double disadvantage or signs of resilience? The elementary school contexts of children from Mexican immigrant families. *American Educational Research Journal, 42*, 269–303.

Cummins, J. (1999). Beyond adversarial discourse: Searching for common ground in the education of bilingual students. In C. J. Ovando & P. McLaren (Eds.), *The politics of multiculturalism and bilingual education: Students and teachers caught in the cross fire* (pp. 126–147). Boston: McGraw Hill.

Cummins, J. (2000). *Language, power, and pedagogy: Bilingual children in the cross-fire.* Clevedon, UK: Multilingual Matters.

Cunningham, T. H., & Graham, C. R. (2000). Increasing native English vocabulary recognition through Spanish immersion: Cognate transfer from foreign to first language. *Journal of Educational Psychology, 92*(1), 37–49.

Dally, K. (2006). The influence of phonological processing and inattentive behavior on reading acquisition. *Journal of Educational Psychology, 98*(2), 420–437.

Danner, F. W., & Lonky, E. (1981). A cognitive-developmental approach to the effects of rewards on intrinsic motivation. *Child Development, 52*, 1043–1052.

Davine, M., Tucker, G. R., & Lambert, W. E. (1971). The perception of phoneme sequences by monolingual and bilingual elementary school children. *Canadian Journal of Behavioral Science, 3*(1), 72–77.

Debaryshe, B. D., & Gorecki, D. M. (2007). An experimental validation of a preschool emergent literacy curriculum. *Early Education and Development, 18*(1), 93–110.

de Jong, P. F., & Leseman, P. P. M. (2001). Lasting effects of home literacy on reading achievement in school. *Journal of School Psychology, 39*(5), 389–414.

Delpit, L. D. (1988). The silenced dialog: Power and pedagogy in educating other people's children. *Harvard Educational Review, 58,* 280–298.

DeTemple, J. M. (2001). Parents and children reading books together. In D. K. Dickinson & P. O. Tabors (Eds.), *Beginning literacy with language: Young children learning at home and school* (pp. 31–51). Baltimore, MD: Brookes.

Diaz, R. (1985). Bilingual cognitive development: Addressing three gaps in current research. *Child Development, 56,* 1376–1388.

Dickinson, D. K., McCabe, A., & Clark-Chiarelli, N. (2004). Preschool-based prevention of reading disability: Realities vs. possibilities. In C. A. Stone, E. R. Silliman, B. J. Ehren, & K. Apel (Eds.), *Handbook of language and literacy: Development and disorders* (pp. 209–227). Hillsdale, NJ: Erlbaum.

Dickinson, D. K., & Smith, M. W. (1994). Long-term effects of preschool teachers' book readings on low-income children's vocabulary and story comprehension. *Reading Research Quarterly, 29*(2), 105–122.

Dickinson, D. K., & Snow, C. E. (1987). Interrelationships among prereading and oral language skills in kindergartners from two social classes. *Early Childhood Research Quarterly, 2,* 1–25.

Dickinson, D. K., St. Pierre, R. G., & Pettengill, J. (2004). High quality classrooms: A key ingredient to family literacy programs' support of children's literacy. In B. H. Wasik (Ed.), *Handbook of family literacy* (pp. 137–154). Mahwah, NJ: Erlbaum.

Dickinson, D. K., & Tabors, P. O. (2001). *Beginning literacy with language: Young children learning at home and school.* Baltimore, MD: Brookes.

Dietrich, S. E., Assel, M. A., Swank, P., Smith, K. E., & Landry, S. H. (2006). The impact of early maternal verbal scaffolding and child language abilities on later decoding and reading comprehension skills. *Journal of School Psychology, 43*(6), 484–494.

Dulay, H., & Burt, M. (1974). Natural sequences in child second language acquisition. *Language Learning, 24,* 37–53.

Duncan, G. J., Claessens, A., Huston, A. C. , Pagani, L. S., Engel. M., Sexton, H., et al. (2007). School readiness and later achievement. *Developmental Psychology, 43,* 1428–1446.

Durgunoglu, A. Y., Nagy, W., & Hancin-Bhatt, B. J. (1993). Cross-language transfer of phonological awareness. *Journal of Educational Psychology, 85*(3), 453–465.

Dweck, C. S. (1975). The role of expectations and attributions in the alleviation of learned helplessness. *Journal of Personality and Social Psychology, 31*(4), 674–685.

Dweck, C. S. (1986). Motivational processes affecting learning. *American Psychologist, 41*(10),1040–1048.

Ehri, L. C. (1987). Learning to read and spell words. *Journal of Reading Behavior, 19,* 5–31.

Ehri, L. C. (1998). Grapheme-phoneme knowledge is essential for learning to read words in English. In J. L. Metsala & L. C. Ehri (Eds.), *Word recognition in beginning literacy* (pp. 3–40). Mahwah, NJ: Erlbaum.

Ehri, L. C., & Roberts, T. A. (2006). The roots of learning to read and write. In D. Dickinson & S. Newman (Eds.), *Handbook of early literacy research* (Vol. II, pp. 113–131). New York: Guilford Press.

Ehri, L. C., & Wilce, L. S. (1985). Movement into reading: Is the first stage of printed word learning visual of phonetic? *Reading Research Quarterly, 20*(2), 163–179.

Elkind, D. (1987). *Miseducation: Preschoolers at risk.* New York: Knopf.

Eller, R. G., Pappas, C. C., & Brown, E. (1988). The lexical development of kindergarteners: Learning from written context. *Journal of Reading Behavior, 20,* 5–24.

Elley, W. B. (1989). Vocabulary acquisition from listening to stories. *Reading Research Quarterly, 24,* 174–187.

Erickson, M. F., Stroufe, L. A., & Egeland, B. (1985). The relationship between quality of attachment and behaviors problems in preschool in a high-risk sample. *Monographs of the Society for Research in Child Development, 50,* 1–2, Serial No. 209.

Espinosa, L. M. (2006). Social, cultural, and linguistic features of school readiness in young Latino children. In B. Bowman & E. Moore (Eds.), *School readiness and social-emotional development* (pp. 33–47). Washington, DC: National Black Child Development Institute.

Fischel, J. E., Bracken, S. S., Fuchs-Eisenberg, A., Spira, E. G., Katz, S., & Shaller, D. (2007). Evaluation of curricular approaches to enhance preschool literacy growth. *Journal of Literacy Research, 39*(4), 471–501.

Fisher, E. P. (1992). The impact of play on development: A meta-analysis. *Play and Culture, 5*(2), 159–181.

Fitzgerald, J. (1995). English-as-a-second-language learner's cognitive reading processes: A review of research in the United States. *Review of Educational Research, 65*(2), 145–190.

Foster, M., Lewis, J., & Onafowora, L. (2003). Anthropology, culture and research on teaching and learning: Applying what we have learned to improve practice. *Teacher's College Record, 105*(2), 201–227.

Fox, B., & Routh, D. (1976). Phonemic analysis and synthesis as word-attack skills. *Journal of Educational Psychology, 68,* 70–74.

Garcia, G. E. (1991). Factors influencing the English reading test performance of Spanish-speaking Hispanic children. *Reading Research Quarterly, 26*(4), 371–392.

Garcia, G. E. (2000). Bilingual children's reading. In M. Kamil, P. D. Pearson, & R. Barr (Eds.), *Handbook of reading research* (pp. 813–834). Mahwah, NJ: Erlbaum.

Gass, S. M., & Selinker, L. (2001). *Second language acquisition: An introductory course.* Mahwah, NJ: Erlbaum.

Gee, J. P. (1989). Literacy, discourse, and linguistics: Introduction. *Journal of Education, 171*, 5–17.

Genesee, F., Lindholm-Leary, K., Saunders, W., & Christian, D. (2006). *Educating English language learners: A synthesis of research evidence.* Cambridge, UK: Cambridge University Press.

Geva, E., Wade-Woolley, L., & Shany, M. (1997). Development of reading efficiency in first and second language. *Scientific Studies of Reading, 1,* 119–144.

Geva E., & Zadeh, Z. Y. (2006). Reading efficiency in native English-speaking and English-as-a-second-language children: The role of oral proficiency and underlying cognitive-linguistic processes. *Scientific Studies of Reading , 10*(1), 31–57.

Gonz, L., & Kodzopeljic, J. (1991). Exposure to two languages in the preschool period: Metalinguistic development and the acquisition of reading. *Journal of Multilingual and Multicultural Development, 12*(3), 137–163.

Graue, E., Clements, M. A., Reynolds, A. J., & Niles, M. D. (2004). More than teacher directed or child initiated: Preschool curriculum type, parent involvement, and children's outcomes in the child-parent centers. *Education Policy Analysis Archives, 12*(72). [Electronic version]. Retrieved May 14, 2008, from http://epaa.asu.edu/epaa/v12n72/.

Guthrie, J. T., & Wigfield, A. (2000). Engagement and motivation in reading. In M. Kamil, P. D. Pearson, & R. Barr (Eds.), *Handbook of reading research* (Vol. III, pp. 503- 524). Mahwah, NJ: Erlbaum.

Haddock, M. (1976). Effects of an auditory and an auditory-visual method of blending instruction on the ability of prereaders to decode synthetic words. *Journal of Educational Psychology, 68,* 825–831.

Hagtvet, B. E. (2000). Prevention and prediction of reading problems. In N. A. Badian (Ed.), *Prediction and prevention of reading failure* (pp. 105–132). Baltimore, MD: York.

Hammer, C. S., Lawrence, F. R., & Miccio, A. W. (2007). Bilingual children's language abilities and early reading outcomes in Head Start and kindergarten. *Language, Speech, and Hearing Services in Schools, 38,* 237–248.

Han, M., Roskos, K., Christie, J., Mandzuk, S., & Vukelich, C. (2005). Learning words: Large group time as a vocabulary development opportunity. *Journal of Research in Childhood Education, 19*(4), 333–346.

Harris, R. C., Robinson, J. B., Chang, F., & Burns, B. M. (2006). Characterizing preschool children's attention regulation in parent-child interaction: The roles of effortful control and motivation. *Applied Developmental Psychology, 28,* 25–39.

Hart, B., & Risley, T. R. (1995). *Meaningful differences in the everyday experience of young American children.* Baltimore, MD: Brookes.

Harter, S. (1974). Pleasure derived by children from cognitive challenge and mastery. *Child Development, 45,* 661–669.

Harter, S. (1978). Effectance motivation reconsidered. Toward a developmental model. *Human Development, 21*(1), 34–64.

Harter, S., Shultz, T. R., & Blum, B. (1971). The assessment of effectance motivation in normal and retarded children. *Developmental Psychology, 12,* 396–404.

Hawken, L. S., Johnston, S. S., & McDonnell, A. P. (2005). Emerging literacy views and practices: Results from a national survey of Head Start preschool teachers. *Topics in Early Childhood Special Education, 25*(4), 232–242.

Heath, S. B. (1983). *Ways with words: Language, life and work in communities and classrooms.* Cambridge, UK: Cambridge University Press.

Helburn, S., & Bergmann, B. (2002). *America's childcare problem: The way out.* Hampshire, UK: Palgrave Macmillan.

Iversen, S., & Tunmer, W. E. (1993). Phonological processing skills and the reading recovery program. *Journal of Educational Psychology, 85,* 112–120.

Johnson, D. J., Jaeger, E., Randolph, S. M., Cauce, A. M., Ward, J., & the NICHD Early Child Care Research Network. (2003). Studying the effects of early child care experiences on the development of children of color in the United States: Towards a more inclusive research agenda. *Child Development,* 1227–1244.

Kagan, J. (1971). *Changes in continuity in infancy.* New York: Wiley.

Kan, P. F., & Kohnert, K. (2005). Preschoolers learning Hmong and English: Lexical-semantic skills in L1 and L2 (first language and second language). *Journal of Speech, Language, and Hearing Research, 48,* 372–383.

Karoly, L. A., Ghosh-Dastidar, B., Zellman, G. L., Perlman, M., & Fernyhough, L. (2008). *Prepared to learn: The nature and quality of early care and education for preschool-age children in California.* Rand technical report. Retrieved August 5, 2008, from http://www.rand.org/pubs/technical_reports/TR539/.

Kohnert, K., Yim, D., Nett, K., Kan P. F., & Duran, L. (2005). Intervention with diverse preschool children: A focus on developing home language(s). *Language, Speech, and Hearing Services in Schools, 36,* 251–263.

Koskinen, P. S., Blum, I. H., Bisson, S. A., Phillips, S. M., Creamer, T. S., & Baker, T. K. (2000). Book access, shared reading, and audio models: The effects of supporting the literacy learning of linguistically divers students in school and home. *Journal of Educational Psychology, 92,* 23–36.

Lanauze, M., & Snow, C. E. (1989). The relation between first- and second-language writing skills: Evidence for Puerto Rican elementary school children in bilingual programs. *Linguistics and Education, 1(4),* 323–339.

Landry, S. H., & Smith, K. E. (2006). The influence of parenting on emergent literacy skills. In D. K. Dickinson & S. B. Neuman (Eds.), *Handbook of early literacy research* (Vol. 2, pp. 135–148). New York: Guilford Press.

Landry, S. L., Smith, K. E., & Swank, P. R. (2006). Responsive parenting: Establishing early foundations for social, communication, and independent problem-solving skills. *Developmental Psychology, 42*(4), 627–642.

Landry, S. H., Swank, P. R., Smith, K. E., Assel, M. A., & Gunnewig, S. B. (2006, July). *Scaling up effective comprehensive professional development programs for teachers of at-risk preschoolers.* Paper presented at the annual meeting of the Society for the Scientific Study of Reading, Vancouver, BC, Canada.

Langer, J. A., Barolome, L., & Vasquez, O. (1990). Meaning construction in school literacy tasks: A study of bilingual students. *American Educational Research Journal, 27*(3), 427–471.

La Paro, K. M., Pianta, R. C., & Stuhlman, M. (2004). Classroom Assessment Scoring System (CLASS): Findings from the pre-K year. *Elementary School Journal 104*(5), 409–426.

Lee, J. S., & Ginsburg, H. P. (2007). Preschool teachers' beliefs about appropriate early literacy and mathematics education for low- and middle-socioeconomic status children. *Early Education and Development, 18*(1), 111–143.

Lepola, J. (2004). The role of gender and reading competence in the development of motivational orientations from kindergarten to grade 1. *Early Education and Development, 15*, 215–240.

Lepola, J., Poskiparta, E., Laakkonen, E., & Niemi, P. (2005). Development of and relationship between phonological and motivational processes and naming speed in predicating word recognition in grade 1. *Scientific Studies of Reading, 9*, 367–399.

Leseman, P. M. (2000). Bilingual development of Turkish preschoolers in The Netherlands. *Journal of Multicultural Development, 21*, 93–112.

Leseman, P. P. M., & de Jong, P. F. (2001). How important is home literacy for acquiring literacy in school? In L. Verhoeven & C. E. Snow (Eds.), *Literacy and motivation: Reading engagement in individuals and groups* (pp. 71–93). Hillsdale, NJ: Erlbaum.

Leseman, P. P. M., & van den Boom, D. C. (1999). Effects of quantity and quality of home proximal processes on Dutch, Surinamese-Dutch, and Turkish-Dutch preschoolers' cognitive development. *Infant and Child Development, 8*, 19–38.

Leseman, P. P. M., & Van Tuijl, C. (2006). Cultural diversity in early literacy: Findings in Dutch studies. In D. K. Dickinson & S. B. Neuman (Eds.), *Handbook of early literacy research* (Vol. 2, pp. 211–228). New York: Guilford Press.

Leung, C. B., & Pikulski, J. J. (1990). Incidental learning of word meanings by kindergarten and first-grade children through repeated read aloud events. In J. Outsell & S. McCormick (Eds.), *Literacy theory and research: Analyses from multiple paradigms* (pp. 231–241). Chicago: National Reading Conference.

Liberman, A. M. (1999). The reading researcher and the reading teacher need the right theory of speech. *Scientific Studies of Reading, 3*, 95–111.

Lindholm, K., & Aclan, Z. (1991). Bilingual proficiency as a bridge to academic achievement: Results from bilingual/immersion programs. *Journal of Education, 173*(2), 99–113.

Lindholm-Leary, K. (2001). *Dual language education.* Avon, UK: Multilingual Matters.

Llagas, C., & Snyder, T. (2003). *Status and trends in the education of Hispanics.* Report No. 2003-008. Washington, DC: National Center for Education Statistics.

LoCasale-Crouch, J., Konold, T., Pianta, R., Howes, C. Burchinal, C., Bryant, D., et al. (2007). Observed classroom quality profiles in state-funded pre-kindergarten programs and associations with teacher, program and classroom characteristics. *Early Childhood Research Quarterly, 22*, 3–17.

Lonigan, C. J., McDowell, K. D., & Phillips, B. M. (2004). Standardized assessments for children's emergent literacy skills. In B. H. Wasik (Ed.), *Handbook of family literacy* (pp. 525–550). Mahwah, NJ: Erlbaum.

López, L. M., & Greenfield, D. B. (2004). The cross-language transfer of phonological skills of Hispanic head start children. *Bilingual Research Journal, 28,* 1–18.

Mages, W. K. (2008). Does creative drama promote language development in early childhood? A review of the methods and measures employed in the empirical literature. *Review of Educational Research, 78*(1), 124–152.

Mann, V. A., & Foy, J. G. (2007). Speech development patterns and phonological awareness in preschool children. *Annals of Dyslexia, 57,* 51–74.

Martin, M., & Byrne, B. (2002). Teaching children to recognize rhyme does not directly promote phonemic awareness. *British Journal of Educational Psychology, 72,* 561–572.

Mashburn, A. J., Pianta, R. C., Hamre, B. K., Downer, J. T., Barbarin, O. A., Bryant, D., et al. (2008). Measures of classroom quality in prekindergarten and children's development of academic, language and social skills. *Child Development, 79,* 732–749.

Mather, N. (1992). Whole language instruction for students with learning disabilities: Caught in the crossfire. *Learning Disabilities Research & Practice, 7,* 87–95.

Mattingly, I. G. (1984). Reading, linguistic awareness, and language acquisition. In J. Downing & R. Valtin (Eds.), *Language awareness and learning to read* (pp. 9–25). New York: Springer-Verlag.

Maxwell, K., Field, C., & Clifford, R. (2006). Defining and measuring professional development in early childhood research. In M. Zaslow & I. Martinez-Beck (Eds.), *Critical issues in early childhood professional development* (pp. 21–48). Baltimore, MD: Brookes.

McCabe, A. (1995). *Chameleon readers: Some problems that cultural differences in narrative structure pose for multicultural literacy programs.* New York: McGraw Hill.

McCabe, A., & Rollins, P. R. (1994). Assessment of preschool narrative skills. *American Journal of Speech-Language Pathology, 3*(1), 45–56.

McGill-Franzen, A., Lanford, C., & Adams, E. (2002). Learning to be literate: A comparison of five urban early childhood programs. *Journal of Educational Psychology, 94,* 443–464.

McInerney, D. M., & Etten, S. V. (Eds.). (2004). *Big theories revisited.* Greenwich, CT: Information Age.

McLoyd, V. C. (February, 1998). Socioeconomic disadvantage and child development. *American Psychologist,* 185–204.

Mendelsohn, A., Mogliner, L., Dreyer, B. P., Forman, J. A., Weinstein, S. C., Broderick, M., et al. (2001). The impact of a clinic-based literacy intervention on language development in inner-city preschool children. *Pediatrics, 107,* 130–134.

Metsala, J. L., & Walley, A. C. (1998). Spoken vocabulary growth and the segmental restructuring of lexical representations: Precursors to phonemic awareness and early reading ability. In J. L. Metsala & L. Ehri (Eds.), *Word recognition in beginning literacy* (pp. 89–120). Hillsdale, NJ: Erlbaum.

Moll, L. C., Amanti, C., Neff, D., & Gonzalez, N. (1992). Funds of knowledge for teaching: Using a qualitative approach to connect homes and classrooms. *Theory Into Practice, 31*(1), 132–141.

Montecel, M. R., & Cortez, J. D. (2002). Successful bilingual education programs: Development and the dissemination of criteria to identify promising and exemplary practices in bilingual education as the national level. *Bilingual Research Journal, 26*(1), 1–21.

Morris, D., Bloodgood, J., & Perney, J. (2003). Kindergarten predictors of first- and second-grade reading achievement. *Elementary School Journal, 104*(2), 93–110.

Morrow, L. M. (1990). Preparing the classroom environment to promote literacy during play. *Early Childhood Research Quarterly, 5,* 537–554.

Morrow, L. M., & Schickedanz, J. A. (2006). The relationships between sociodramatic play and literacy development. In D. Dickinson & S. Neuman (Eds.), *Handbook of early literacy research* (Vol. II, pp. 269–280). New York: Guilford Press.

Murray, B. A., Stahl, S. A., & Ivey, M. G. (1996). Developing phoneme awareness through alphabet books. *Reading and Writing, 8,* 307–322.

Muter, V., Hulme, C., Snowling, M. J., & Stevenson, J. (2004). Phonemes, rimes, vocabulary, and grammatical skills as foundations of early reading development: Evidence form a longitudinal study. *Developmental Psychology, 40,* 665–681.

National Institute of Child Health and Human Development. (2000). *Teaching children to read: An evidence-based assessment of the scientific research on reading and its implications for reading instruction.* Report of the National Reading Panel. NIH publication No. 00-4769. Washington, DC: National Institutes of Health.

National Institute of Child Health and Human Development Early Child Care Research Network. (2005). Pathways to reading: The role of oral language in the transition to reading. *Developmental Psychology, 25*(4), 428–442.

National Institute of Child Health and Human Development Early Child Care Research Network. (1999). Child outcomes when child care center classes meet recommended standards for quality. *American Journal of Public Health, 89,* 1072–1077.

National Research Council and Institute of Medicine, Committee on Integrating the Science of Early Childhood Development. (2000). *From neurons to neighborhoods: The science of early childhood development.* J. Shonkoff & D. Philips, (Eds.). Washington, DC: National Academy Press.

Neuman, S. B., Cunningham, L., & Tucker, S. A. (2006, April). *Imagine/align: Improving access to professional development for early childhood educators.* Paper presented at the annual meeting of the American Educational Research Association: San Francisco, CA.

Neuman, S., & Roskos, K. (1997). Literacy knowledge in practice: Contexts of participation for young writers and readers. *Reading Research Quarterly, 32*(1), 10–32.

Ngo, B., & Lee, S. J. (2007). Complicating the image of model minority success: A review of Southeast Asian American education. *Review of Educational Research, 77*(4), 415–453.

NICHD Early Child Care Research Network. (2005). Pathways to reading: The role of oral language in the transition to reading. *Developmental Psychology, 25*(4), 428–442.

Nittrouer, S., Studdert-Kennedy, M., & McGowan, R. S. (1989). The emergence of phonic segments: Evidence from the spectral structure of fricative-vowel syllables spoken by children and adults. *Journal of Speech and Hearing Research, 30,* 319–329.

Ogbu, J. U. (1992). Understanding cultural diversity and learning. *Educational Researcher, 21*(8), 5–14.

Olson, D. R. (1977). From utterance to text: The bias of language in speech and writing. *Harvard Educational Review, 47,* 257–281.

Ordoñez, C. L., Carlo, M. S., Snow, C. E., & McLaughlin, B. (2002). Depth and breadth of vocabulary in two languages: Which vocabulary skills transfer. *Journal of Educational Psychology, 94*(4), 719–728.

Paradis, J., & Nicoladis, E, (2007). The influence of dominance and sociolinguistic context on bilingual preschoolers' language choice. *International Journal of Bilingual Education & Bilingualism, 10*(3), 277–297.

Pearson, B. Z., & Fernandez, S. C. (1994). Patterns of interaction in the lexical growth in two languages of bilingual infants and toddlers. *Language Learning, 44*(4), 617–653.

Pemberton, E. F., & Watkins, R. V. (1987). Language facilitation through stories: Recasting and modeling. *First Language, 7,* 79–89.

Penno, J. F., Wilkinson, I. E., & Moore, D. W. (2002). Vocabulary acquisition from teacher explanation and repeated listening to stories: Do they overcome the Matthew effect? *Journal of Educational Psychology, 94,* 23–33.

Phillips, S. U. (1972). Participation structures and communication competence: Warm Springs children in community and classroom. In C. Cazden, D. Hymes, & W. Johns (Eds.), *Functions of language in the* classroom (pp. 370–394). New York: Teachers College Press.

Piaget, J. (1951). *Play, dreams, and imitation in childhood.* New York: Norton.

Pianta, R. C. (2006). Teacher-child relationships and early literacy. In D. Dickinson & S. Neuman (Eds.), *Handbook of early literacy research* (Vol. II, pp. 149–162). New York: Guilford Press.

Pianta, R. C., Hamre, B., & Stuhlman, M. (2003). Relationships between teacher and children. In W. Reynolds & G. Miller (Eds.), *Comprehensive handbook of psychology: Vol. 7. Educational psychology* (pp. 199–234). Hoboken, NJ: Wiley.

Pinker, S. (1994). *The language instinct.* New York: Morrow.

Porter, R. P. (1998). The case against bilingual education. *Atlantic Monthly, 281*(5), 28–39.

Portes, A., & Hao, L. (2002). The price of uniformity: Language, family, and personality adjustment in the immigrant second generation. *Ethnic and Racial Studies, 25,* 889–912.

Preschool Curriculum Evaluation Research Consortium. (2008). *Effects of preschool curriculum programs on school readiness.* Report from the Preschool Curriculum Evaluation Research Initiative. NCER 2008-2009. Washington, DC: National Center for Education Research, Institute of Education Sciences, US Department of Education.

Pressley, M., & Rankin, J. (1994). More about whole language methods of reading instruction for students at risk for early reading failure. *Learning Disabilities Research & Practice, 9*(3), 157–168.

Purcell-Gates, V. (2004). Family literacy as the site for emerging knowledge of written language. In B. Wasik (Ed.), *Handbook of family literacy* (pp. 101–114). Mahwah, NJ: Erlbaum.

Raikes, H., Luze, G., Brooks-Gunn, J., Raikes, H. A., Pan, A., Tamis-LeMonda, C. S., et al. (2006). Mother-child bookreading in low-income families: Correlates and outcomes during the first three years of life. *Child Development 77*(4), 924–953.

Ramey, C. T., Yeats, K. O., & Short, E. J. (1984). The plasticity of intellectual development: Insights from prevention interventions. *Child Development, 55*, 1913–1925.

Raz, I. S., & Bryant, P. (1990). Social background, phonological background and children's reading. *British Journal of British Psychology, 8*, 209–225.

Reese, L., Garnier, H., Gallimore, R., & Goldenberg, C. (2000). Longitudinal analysis of the antecedents of emergent Spanish literacy and middle-school English reading achievement of Spanish-speaking students. *American Educational Research Journal, 37*(3), 633–662.

Reeve, J. R., Deci, E. L., & Ryan, R. M. (2004). Self-determination theory: A dialectical framework for understanding sociocultural influences on student motivation. In D. M. McInerney & S. V. Etten (Eds.), *Big theories revisited* (pp. 31–60). Greenwich, CT: Information Age.

Riches, C., & Genesee, F. (2006). Literacy: Crosslinguistic and crossmodal issues. In F. Genesee, K. Lindholm-Leary, W. Saunders, & D. Christian (Eds.), *Educating English language learners: A synthesis of research evidence* (pp. 64–108). Cambridge, UK: Cambridge University Press.

Robbins, C., & Ehri, L. C. (1994). Reading stories to kindergartners helps them learn new vocabulary words. *Journal of Educational Psychology, 86*, 54–64.

Roberts, T. A. (2003). Effects of alphabet letter instruction on young children's word recognition. *Journal of Educational Psychology, 95*, 41–51.

Roberts, T. A. (2005). Articulation accuracy and vocabulary size contributions to phonemic awareness and word reading in English language learners. *Journal of Educational Psychology, 97*, 601–616.

Roberts, T. A. (2008). Home storybook reading in primary or second language with preschool children: Evidence of equal effectiveness for second-language vocabulary acquisition. *Reading Research Quarterly, 43*(2), 103–130.

Roberts, T. A., & Corbett, C. (1997). *Efficacy of explicit English instruction in phonemic awareness and the alphabetic principle for English learners and English proficient kindergarten children in relationship to oral language proficiency, primary language and verbal memory.* ERIC Document Reproduction Service No. ED 417 403.

Roberts, T., & Neal, H. (2004). Relationships among preschool English language learners' oral proficiency in English, instructional experience and literacy development. *Contemporary Educational Psychology, 29*, 283–311.

Roberts, T. A., & Sadler, C. (2007, December). *The interplay between type of letter-sound instruction, motivation and literacy competence.* Paper presented at the meeting of the National Reading Conference, Austin, TX.

Rodríguez, J. L., Díaz, R. M., Duran, D., & Espinosa, L. (1995). The impact of bilingual preschool education on the language development of Spanish-speaking children. *Early Childhood Research Quarterly, 10*, 475–490.

Rogoff, B., & Waddell, K. J. (1982). Memory for information in a scene by children from two cultures. *Child Development, 53*, 1224–1228.

Rolstad, K., Mahoney, K., & Glass, G. V. (2005). The big picture: A meta-analysis of program effectiveness research on English language learners. *Educational Policy, 19*, 572–594.

Rubin, H., & Turner, A. (1989). Linguistic awareness skills in grade 1 children in a French immersion setting. *Reading and Writing: An International Journal, 1*, 73–86.

Saville-Troike, M. (1988). Private speech: Evidence for second language learning strategies during the "silent period." *Journal of Child Language, 15*, 567–590.

Scarborough, H. S. (2001). Connecting early language and literacy to later reading (dis)abilities: Evidence, theory, and practice. In S. B. Neuman & D. K. Dickinson (Eds.), *Handbook of early literacy research* (pp. 97–110). New York: Guilford.

Scarborough, H. S., & Dobrich, W. (1994). On the efficacy of reading to preschoolers. *Developmental Review, 14*, 245–302.

Schaerlaekens, A., Zink, I., & Verheyden, L. (1995). Comparative vocabulary development in kindergarten classes with a mixed population of monolinguals, simultaneous and successive bilinguals. *Journal of Multilingual and Multicultural Development, 16*, 477–495.

Schiefflin, B. B., & Ochs, E. (1986). *Language socialization across cultures.* Cambridge, UK: Cambridge University Press.

Sénéchal, M. (1997). The differential effect of storybook reading on preschoolers' acquisition of expressive and receptive vocabulary. *Journal of Child Language, 24*, 123–138.

Sénéchal, M., & Cornell, E. H. (1993). Vocabulary acquisition through shared reading experience. *Reading Research Quarterly, 28*, 360–375.

Sénéchal, M., Thomas, E. H., & Monker, J. A. (1995). Individual differences in 4-year-old children's acquisition of vocabulary during storybook reading. *Journal of Educational Psychology, 87*, 218–229.

Share, D. (2004). Knowing letter names and learning letter sounds: A causal connection. *Journal of Experimental Child Psychology, 88*, 213–233.

Smiley, P. A., & Dweck, C. S. (1994). Individual differences in achievement goals among young children. *Child Development, 65*, 1723–1743.

Smith, M. W., Dickinson, D. K., Sangeorge, A., & Anastasopoulos, L. (2002). *The Early Language and Literacy Classroom Observation (ELLCO).* Baltimore, MD: Brookes.

Snow, C. E. (1977). Mother's speech to children learning language. *Child Development, 43*, 549–565.

Snow, C. E. (1983). Literacy and language: Relationships during the preschool years. *Harvard Educational Review, 53*, 165–189.

Snow, C. E. (1991). The theoretical basis for relationships between language and literacy in development. *Journal of Research in Childhood Education, 6*, 5–10.

Snow, C. E. (2008). Cross-cutting themes and future research directions. In D. August & T. Shanahan (Eds.), *Developing reading and writing in second-language learners* (pp. 275–300). New York: Routledge.

Snow, C. E., Burns, S., & Griffin, P. (Eds.). (1998). *Preventing reading difficulties in young children.* Washington, DC: National Academy of Sciences.

Solity, J. (1996). Phonological awareness: Learning disabilities revisited? *Educational and Child Psychology, 13*, 103–113.

Stanovich, K. (1986). Matthew effects in reading: Some consequences of individual differences in reading. *Reading Research Quarterly, 21*, 360–407.

Sticht, T. G., & James, J. H. (1984). Listening and reading. In P. D. Pearson (Ed.), *Handbook of reading research* (pp. 293–317). White Plains, NY: Longman.

Stipek, D. J., Feiler, R., Byler, P., Ryan, R., Milburn, S., & Salmon, J. (1998). Good beginnings: What difference does the program make in preparing young children for school? *Journal of Applied Developmental Psychology, 19*, 41–66.

Stipek, D., Feiler, R., Daniels, D., & Millburn, S. (1995). Effects of different instructional approaches on young children's achievement and motivation. *Child Development, 66*, 209–233.

Stipek, D., Feiler, R., Galuzzo, D., & Millburn, S. (1992). Characterizing early literacy programs for poor and middle-class children. *Early Childhood Research Quarterly, 7*, 1–19.

Stipek, D. T., Roberts, T. A., & Sanborn, M. E. (1984). Pre-school age children's performance expectations for themselves and another child as a function of the incentive value of success and the salience of past performance. *Child Development, 55*, 1983–1989.

Stipek, D. J., & Ryan, R. H. (1997). Economically disadvantaged preschoolers: Ready to learn but further to go. *Developmental Psychology, 33*, 711–723.

Storch, S. A., & Whitehurst, G. J. (2002). Oral language and code-related precursors of reading: Evidence from a longitudinal structural model. *Developmental Psychology, 38*, 934–945.

Storkel, H. L., & Rogers, M. A. (2000). The effect of probabilistic phonotactics on lexical acquisition. *Clinical Linguistics and Phonetics, 14*, 407–425.

Stroufe, L. A. (1996). *Emotional development: The organization of emotional life in the early years.* New York: Cambridge University Press.

Stuart, M., Masterson, J., & Dixon, M. (2000). Spongelike acquisition of sight vocabulary in beginning readers. *Journal of Research in Reading, 23,*12–27.

Tabors, P. O. (1997). *One child, two languages: A guide for preschool educators of children learning English as a second language.* Baltimore, MD: Brookes.

Tamis-LeMonda, C. S., Bornstein, M. H., & Baumwell, L. (2001). Maternal responsiveness and children's achievement of language milestones. *Child Development, 72*, 748–767.

Terrell, T., & Krashen, S. (1983). *The natural approach: Language acquisition in the classroom.* San Francisco, CA: Alemany Press.

Thao, Y. (2003). Empowering Mong students: Home and school factors. *The Urban Review, 35*(1), 25–42.

Tharp, R. (February, 1989). Psychocultural variables and constants: Effects on teaching and learning in the schools. *American Psychologist,* 349–394.

Treiman, R., & Baron, J. (1983). Phonemic-analysis training helps children benefit from spelling sound rules. *Memory and Cognition, 11,* 382–389.

Treiman, R., & Broderick, V. (1998). What's in a name: Children's knowledge about the letters in their own names. *Journal of Experimental Child Psychology, 70,* 97–116.

Treiman, R., Cohen, J., Mulqueeny, K., Kessler, B., & Schechtman, S. (2007). Young children's knowledge about printed names. *Child Development, 78*(5), 1458–1471.

Treiman, R., & Kessler, B. (2003). The role of letter names in the acquisition of literacy. In R. Kail (Ed.), *Advances in child development and behavior* (Vol. 31, pp. 105–135), San Diego, CA: Academic Press.

Treiman, R., & Rodriguez, L. (1999). Young children use letter names in learning to read words. *Psychological Science, 10*(4), 334–339.

Treiman, R., Tincoff, R., & Richmond-Welty, E. D. (1996). Letter names help children to connect print and speech. *Developmental Psychology, 32*(3), 505–514.

Treiman, R., Tincoff, R., Rodriguez, K., Mouzaki, A., & Francis, D. (1998). The foundations of literacy: Learning the sounds of letters. *Child Development, 69*(6), 1524–1540.

Treiman, R., Weatherston, S., & Berch, D. (1994). The role of letter names in children's learning of phoneme-grapheme relations. *Applied Psycholinguistics, 15,* 97–122.

Turner, L. A., & Johnson, B. (2003). A model of mastery motivation for at-risk preschoolers. *Journal of Educational Psychology, 95*(3), 495–505.

Umbel, V. M., Pearson, B. Z., Fernandez, M. C., & Oller, D. K. (1992). Measuring bilingual children's receptive vocabularies. *Child Development, 63,* 1012–1030.

U.S. Department of Education, Institute of Education Sciences, What Works Clearinghouse. (2004, December). *Topic report: Early Childhood Education.* Retrieved March 15, 2008, from http://ies.ed.gov/ncee/wwc/reports/topic.aspx?tid=13.

U.S. Department of Health and Human Services. (2003). *Headstart FACES 2000: A whole child perspective on program performance.* Washington, DC: Author.

Vartuli, S. (1999). How early childhood teacher beliefs vary across grade level. *Early Childhood Research Quarterly, 14*(4), 489–514.

Verhoeven, L. T. (1990). Acquisition of reading in a second language. *Reading Research Quarterly, 25*(2), 90–111.

Walton, P. D. (1995). Rhyming ability, phoneme identity, letter-sound knowledge, and the use of orthographic analogy by prereaders. *Journal of Educational Psychology, 87*(4), 587–597.

Wells, G. (1985). Preschool literacy-related events and success in school. In D. Olson, N. Torrance, & A. Hillyard (Eds.), *Literacy, language, and learning: The nature and consequences of reading and writing* (pp. 229–255). Cambridge, UK: Cambridge University Press.

White, R. W. (1959). Motivation reconsidered: The concept of competence. *Psychological Review, 66,* 297–333.

Whitehurst, G. J., Epstein, J. N., Angel, A. L., Payne, A. C., Crone, D. A., & Fischel, J. E. (1994). Outcomes of an emergent literacy intervention in Head Start. *Journal of Educational Psychology, 86*(4), 542–555.

Whitehurst, G. J., Falco, F. L., Lonigan, C. J., Fischel, J. E., Debaryshe, B. D., Valdez-Menchaca, M. C., et al. (1988). Accelerating language development through picture book reading. *Developmental Psychology, 24,* 552–559.

Whitehurst, G., J., & Massetti, M. (2004). How well does Head Start prepare children to learn to read? In E. Zigler & S. J. Styfco (Eds.), *The Headstart debates (friendly and otherwise)* (pp. 251–262). New Haven, CT: Brooks.

Wigfield, A., Tonks, S., & Eccles, J. S. (2004). Expectancy value theory in cross-cultural perspective. In D. M. McInerney & S. V. Etten (Eds.), *Big theories revisited* (pp. 165–198). Greenwich, CT: Information Age.

Winsler, A., Díaz, R. M., Espinosa, L., & Rodríguez, J. L. (1999). When learning a second language does not mean losing the first: Bilingual language development in low-income, Spanish-speaking children attending bilingual preschool. *Child Development, 70,* 349–362.

Wirt, J., Choy, S., Rooney, P., Provasnik, S., Sen, A., & Tobin, R. (2004). *The condition of education 2004.* Report No. 2004-077. Washington, DC: National Center for Education Statistics.

Wong-Fillmore, L. (1991). When learning a second language means losing the first. *Early Childhood Research Quarterly, 63*(3), 323–346.

Wood, C., & Terrell, C. (1998). Pre-school phonological awareness and subsequent literacy development. *Educational Psychology, 18*(3), 253–274.

Worden, P. E., & Boettcher, W. (1990). Young children's acquisition of alphabet knowledge. *Journal of Reading Behavior, 22,* 227–295.

Yaden, D., Smolkin, L., & Conlon, A. (1989). Preschoolers' questions about pictures, print conventions, and story text during reading aloud at home. *Reading Research Quarterly, 24,* 188–214.

Yaden, D., Smolkin, L., & MacGillivray, L. (1993). A psychogenetic perspective on children's understanding about letter associations during alphabet book readings. *Journal of Reading Behavior, 25*(1), 43–68.

Yelland, G. W., Pollard, J., & Mercuri, A. (1993). The metalinguistic benefits of limited contact with a second language. *Applied Psycholinguistics, 14,* 423–444.

Zhou, M., & Bankston, C. L. (2006). *Growing up American: How Vietnamese children adapt to life in the United States.* New York: Russell Sage.

Index

CORWIN

A SAGE Company

The Corwin logo—a raven striding across an open book—represents the union of courage and learning. Corwin is committed to improving education for all learners by publishing books and other professional development resources for those serving the field of PreK–12 education. By providing practical, hands-on materials, Corwin continues to carry out the promise of its motto: **"Helping Educators Do Their Work Better."**

CPSIA information can be obtained
at www.ICGtesting.com
Printed in the USA
FSOW04n0810060617
35063FS

9 781412 965644